# THE PHILOSOPHY OF FREEDOM

## Ideological Origins of the Bill of Rights

Edited by

### Samuel B. Rudolph
Chabot College

UNIVERSITY
PRESS OF
AMERICA

Lanham • New York • London

Copyright © 1993 by
**University Press of America®, Inc.**
4720 Boston Way
Lanham, Maryland 20706

3 Henrietta Street
London WC2E 8LU England

**Library of Congress Cataloging-in-Publication Data**

The Philosophy of freedom : ideological origins of the Bill of Rights /
edited by Samuel B. Rudolph.
p.    cm.
Includes bibliographical references.
1. Civil rights—United States—History—Sources.
I. Rudolph, Samuel B.
JC599.U5P47    1993    323'.0973—dc20    92–44281 CIP

ISBN 0–8191–9029–2 (cloth : alk. paper)
ISBN 0–8191–9030–6 (pbk. : alk. paper)

*To my mother, and in memory of my*
*beloved sister, Fran,*
*whose length of days ended*
*in the flower of her youth*

# TABLE OF CONTENTS

## PART THREE

## PART FOUR

## POSTSCRIPT

## APPENDIX

James Gillray. The Rights of Man
Print Collection, Miriam & Ira D. Wallach Division
The New York Public Library
Astor, Lenox and Tilden Foundations

"Give me your tired, your poor,
Your huddled masses, yearning to breathe free,
The wretched refuse of your teeming shore.
Send these, the homeless, tempest-tost to me,
I lift my hand beside the golden door!"

*from Emma Lazarus,*
***The New Colossus***

# PREFACE

It is my purpose in this project to present in a single volume a selection of original writings that will elucidate the ideological origins of our fundamental rights. It has been my guiding principle throughout to unearth and bring to light those often neglected, forgotten and, perhaps, lost philosophical roots of our basic freedoms. The unique heritage of freedom that lies behind our Bill of Rights is itself a deep and a rich one. It is indeed one often lost sight of amid the clamor and controversy of litigation , of popular movements and much debate and discussion about our civil rights and liberties today.

We Americans are perhaps the most freedom-conscious of peoples in the world today, and have probably held that status throughout our national history. Liberty has for us been a vital and an enduring theme throughout our history. This country was born and conceived in freedom. The theme of liberty has for this author been a continuing and ennobling source of inspiration throughout the execution of this work. He is aware of the high degree of sensibility and the gravity with which we Americans take our fundamental rights under the Constitution.

This work is itself a labor of love from conception to completion. It is indeed my hope and trust that the ennobling and refreshing words of these original pieces will find their audience among all thoughtful and concerned readers who care about their basic, but fragile, freedoms and the rich heritage that brought them forth on our shores. This work is thus addressed to all who are sensible of our great freedoms under the Constitution and Bill of Rights, who appreciate not merely their civil and political rights, and who exercise those rights, but who also appreciate the depth of history, of heritage and struggle that lie behind them.

This anthology is thus built of the substance, the written words, of our founders, framers and their English and French forerunners. Philosophers in their own right, our framers were also an immensely practical group of thinkers. They were sensible both of ideas and principles, on the one hand, and the difficult complexities of human nature, on the other. It is the conviction of this author that any attempt to glean the likes of an "original intent" from the clauses of our Constitution and Bill of Rights must ultimately derive from a careful reading of their written words and works.

It is appropriate here to acknowledge some debt to several scholars who have offered useful ideas, suggestions and simple encouragements along the way. These include Professors Gerald Gunther and Jack Rakove of Stanford University for useful suggestions. Also of encouraging assistance in reviewing the proposed outline of this work was Professor John Phillip Reid of New York University School of Law. My gratitude goes to Bernard Bailyn, Adams University Professor of History at Harvard University, for useful source references relevant to original meanings of the American concept of liberty. My appreciation goes also to the Doe Library of the University of California at Berkeley for the availability of their collections to alumni, and to Professor Robert C. Post of Boalt Hall.

Finally, my gratitude goes to the publisher and staff of the University Press of America for providing the opportunity and assistance in the publication of this work under their imprint.

# INTRODUCTION

Our tradition of liberty as a check upon the encroaching powers of government is one of the most vital and enduringly noble themes in American history. Viewed as the freedom from arbitrary coercion or intrusion by the state, our concept of constitutional liberty has a long and varied story throughout the Anglo-American experience. Traceable back to the glorious Magna Carta of 1215 and the ancient common laws of England even before that, the struggle for the cherished rights of man continues still. Our quest for individual liberty, as against the coercive authority of the state, has remained a continuing theme of vital public concern since the first settlements and town meetings on our shores nearly 400 years ago.

For English speaking peoples on both sides of the Atlantic and for a growing number of peoples elsewhere who cherish freedom, the idea of civil liberty is a vital measure of the law and the validity of constitutions themselves. Civil and political liberties are, without doubt, regarded as fundamental rights of all Americans today. They are explicitly set forth in both the Bill of Rights and the body of the Constitution itself.

The theme of constitutional freedom has pervaded the social, the economic and political life-blood of this country since our national birth now over two centuries ago. The cry and struggle for civil rights, for civil and political liberties, have been heard everywhere in this land, and it continues as loud and as actively as ever. It continues as a cause of popular action in the form of social reform and political movements. It is manifest in the laws, through legislation and in issues of continuing litigation in the courts. It echoes through our statehouses and in the halls of Congress. Nearly every important piece of social or economic legislation, bearing at all upon rights and freedoms of individuals, bespeaks our preoccupation with those freedoms we hold to be our birthright.

What we consider to be our fundamental rights have met with endless controversy and reinterpretation in our state and federal courts. In over two centuries of jurisprudence, we have added, detracted, refined and otherwise clarified matters relating to our basic freedoms. We have found about every type of right conceivable, from the right to privacy to the right to life itself, implicit in the words of our Constitution and Bill of Rights. Our litigation of freedom in the courts is further mirrored in our society at large, from the local town meeting to state legislatures and the halls of Congress.

If such a deep sensibility to issues of liberty does not already pervade every corner of American life, we see also an ever increasing recognition of basic limits to government at all levels. Within the second half of this century alone, our Bill of Rights has undergone a literal metamorphosis, as one fundamental right after another is applied against the government at every level of our federal system. Our basic freedoms are today nationalized as never before, the exceptions being in the minority. What we have seen and lived through is, in legal terms, the "incorporation" of most of our express constitutional rights through the Due Process Clause of the Fourteenth Amendment. We thus see both a clarification and a rapid expansion of our fundamental rights in an historically short period of time.

It is the purpose of this project to contribute in a timely way to a wider understanding of our heritage of freedom under law. It is a rich and a deep heritage, one worthy indeed of our attention. The selected writings that follow focus upon those intellectual and ideological origins of our liberties, the great freedoms we have long taken for granted. This anthology of writings is focused upon the philosophical origins of those great freedoms in the Anglo-American tradition and struggle for the rights of man. The work proceeds from the conviction that principles of liberty are what bind us together as a free people, as a nation singular in its devotion to the rights of mankind. Principles of freedom are indeed part of our identity and definition, our roots that have made us what we are. It is thus my intent to present a series of intellectually relevant writings that shed light upon **original** meanings, to wit the meaning of liberty common to early Americans and their

European precursors. They speak here in their own words. Their ideas, fears and motivations regarding liberty are manifest throughout these writings. We should indeed see what drove them to forge a new order in a new world, one to be established upon principles grounded in ideas of individual human freedom.

The language and content of these pieces thus reflect directly the tenor of thought and speech current at the founding of our republic. Our framers speak for themselves and for liberty, before two centuries and more of jurisprudence in the courts of the nation they founded. They represent the original meanings, the understanding and concerns of a people newly liberated from the tyranny of colonial power. We can see in their words a principled and deeply passionate concern for the rights of man in a world where right and liberty were scarce indeed.

This work Further proceeds on the conviction that liberty is a somewhat fragile but enduring thing. Its thread of continuity has been broken at many points, its strength challenged and overcome in the centuries of long struggle for survival. It is a traceable thread, however, and one that weaves together a common heritage of English-speaking peoples throughout the world. Indeed, in the words of our former Supreme Court Justice Benjamin Cardozo over fifty years ago, our fundamental rights are shared on "a principle of justice so rooted in the traditions and conscience of our people as to be ranked as fundamental".* That there is such a reality of "ordered liberty", rooted in the American conscience and experience as a free people, has been a guiding principle in the selection of the pieces that follow.

This work finds further motivation in current debates surrounding the question of "original intent", original understandings and the like regarding the meanings our framers attached to their hallowed words. This editor is not entirely convinced of any such fixed notions of meaning held by the framers or, if so fixed at the time, that they were intended to be so forever henceforth. This would seem to be especially so in the domain of our fundamental rights and liberties. If, however, such fixed, original understandings were in fact prevalent among the framers, we do well to turn to their writings, the record of their thoughts and deliberations on the subject. Some vagueness notwithstanding, they set forth their ideas of freedom in a forceful and eloquent way,

---

*Palko v. Connecticut, 302 US 319 [1937] Justice Cardozo further stated that a right must be founded on the "Fundamental principles of liberty and justice which lie at the base of all our civil and political institutions," and that a violation must be "so acute and shocking that our polity will not endure it."

focused around issues widely debated and discussed to the most urgent degree of the day. Must not any such quest for an "original intent" go at last to those whose written words bear the sense and meaning of that intent? To those whose political and philosophical expression stood at the very source of our Constitution and Bill of Rights?

Our tradition of liberty under law is, of course, something more than a simple, uninterrupted story. It is a story not without its chapters of struggle, of bloody and oppressive authority, of the loss of untold millions of innocent lives in this century alone. A sober recognition of this fact, however, should lend even further support in evidence of our strength as a free people. Early Americans of the Revolutionary era were themselves driven by the same sense of destiny and purpose with respect to their freedoms that we share and inherit from them today. It was, specifically, the sense of duty to carry forth, into a new world and a new order of things, a threatened heritage of freedom, of liberty and right under law.

That threatened heritage, however, was already an aged and cherished one at our founding. Indeed, as John Adams wrote in a letter to Thomas Jefferson in 1815, "The Revolution was in the minds and hearts of the people — before a drop of blood was ever shed at Lexington". If such an animating heritage of liberty and its principles were in place nearly a century before the American Revolution began, then again we are well advised to go to the original sources of our great charters, i.e. the writings of the framers themselves. Should we not then glean the clauses of their written words for those standards and principles that guided and inspired their work as authors of the great charters of our freedoms?*

The pieces that follow are thus meant to bring to light the rich and varied thoughts of our framers, where they drew them from, what they meant and intended in the way of liberty. These include both British and French political philosophers of the Enlightenment in Europe. The likes of Locke, Hume, Burke, Montesquieu and others were among those European antecedents, the intellectual forerunners who deeply influenced our founding fathers and framers. It was in part from them that we inherit the philosophical bearings of a newborn nation with a written Constitution and Bill of Rights. Their influence is clearly reflected in these pamphlets, the papers and even popular tabloids of

---

*For a magnificent collection of writings from pamphlets of the colonial era, see Bernard Bailyn's work, *The Ideological Origins of the American Revolution,* Harvard, 1968.

the day. They formed much of the context in which early Americans discussed and exchanged their viewpoints regarding freedom, rights and self-government. It is their intellectual influence too, which is seen in the earliest of our state charters and written constitutions. These were largely coincident with the Revolution itself and they stood as precedents to the later federal constitution and Bill of Rights that were to follow within fifteen years of our independence.

Several practical considerations have served to narrow somewhat the scope of this project. Faced with an immensity of writings relevant to the subject of liberty in the eighteenth century alone, I've necessarily had to be quite selective from among a great many worthy candidates for inclusion. This has meant the necessity of a working standard of selection on the basis of clarity of expression and relevance to the root concept of liberty in early America. I've sought to select those writings most reflective of the uniquely philosophical and ideological basis of Anglo-American liberty, i.e. the original meanings and conceptions of liberty. There is indeed a great variety of political or polemical essays published in eighteenth century Britain and America, each with some merit in its own right. From among these many early publications, however, I've attempted to cull out those with the most apparent potential for elucidating the concept of liberty, its original meanings and relevance to contemporary American, other English speaking readers. With such a focus upon the ideological, I've necessarily had to exclude those pieces of a more narrow political legal or economic focus geared to the issues of the day.

The task of selection has, however, been a labor of love. The sheer majesty of the subject of liberty, its vital relevance as a topic of continuing public concern, has itself served as a guiding light in the work of this project. The manifest relevance of liberty to freedom of expression, to freedom of religion, to the constitutional rights of the criminally accused and others is readily evident. The work of research, of selection and writing has indeed kept me quite close to the historical and the vital philosophical roots of our fundamental rights.

I note finally some of the temporal limits that have kept this project within bounds. With a focus on the ideological **roots** of our rights and liberties, I've stopped with the close of the eighteenth century. The writings to follow thus present the original thought behind those fundamental rights that specifically found their way into our Constitution and Bill of Rights. As a result, later developments, such as the application of specific rights as against state governments (the nationalization or legal "incorporation" of the Bill of Rights in our own time) are therefore not reached and dealt with here. The tremendously historical and significant "incorporation" of our rights, through the Due Process clause of the Fourteenth Amendment [in the twentieth century for the most part] is thus not reflected in these writings.

It is indeed my hope that this selection of writings will contribute to a greater understanding and appreciation of our fundamental rights, their original meanings and specific applications for early Americans. It was they who set the blueprints, who authored our written Constitution and forged the charter of our great freedoms. It is my hope and trust that this book will provide some insight and context for further discussion regarding the heritage behind those freedoms.

Samuel B. Rudolph
Hayward California, 1992

# PART ONE

*"And though all the winds of doctrine were let loose to play upon the earth, so Truth be in the Field, we do injuriously by licensing and prohibiting, to misdoubt her strength. Let her and Falsehood grapple; who ever knew Truth put to the worst, in a free and open encounter?"*

John Milton
in *Areopagitica*

# EUROPEAN PRECEDENTS OF THE AMERICAN CONCEPT OF LIBERTY

A study of the origins of our concept of liberty is, in great measure, a study of the history of England. The framers of our Bill of Rights themselves lived in the aftermath and afterglow of a great revolution, the Glorious Revolution that led to an English Bill of Rights in 1688. Those vital and fundamental rights our framers sought to protect were indeed viewed as the inherent rights of all Englishmen on both sides of the Atlantic.

The often vague but impassioned arguments in behalf of liberty in the eighteenth century spoke to the rights to life, liberty and property. These were to our early American ancestors the topics of impassioned debate no less than of reasoned and principled discussion. The record of their written words remains extant and available to us today. These are the words of political philosophers, of jurists, of radical reformers and journalists in England and France. The thought ran wide and deep that all English subjects of the King had inherited their liberties as birthrights, enforceable against Parliament and against the King. It was but the authority and sanctity of tradition itself, embodied in the common laws of England, that afforded such great and fundamental rights. Their claim to liberty needed only the best of tradition and the force of the common law itself. The precedents were already set.

The pieces that follow are selected with a view to elucidate those ideas of liberty, engendered to our framers by their English and French forerunners. Most of these authors are British, Englishmen who found themselves in an England of growing discontent with the powers of Parliament, the King and a corrupt body of officials in government. It is important to note that literally all of these authors were deeply concerned about the rights and liberties of Englishmen, *all* Englishmen on both sides of the Atlantic. While our own Revolution was uniquely American in origin and motivation, the whole of the Anglo-American struggle for liberty was, in its fundamental sense, fought on both sides of the Atlantic. The issues were the same, the controversy embroiled all within its wake, both in England and in the new world. The relevant question here is thus not which people, but rather which issue, which ideology and philosophical view served to galvanize the forces of liberty in *both* England and America in the later part of the eighteenth century.

It was John Locke who, in the aftermath of the English Revolution of 1688, expounded the natural law basis of fundamental rights and liberties: rights to life, liberty itself, and to property. It was the essential purpose of government, for Locke, to safeguard, to protect and defend the natural rights of each as against the ravages and onslaughts of the other. Government is thus serving its vital function when protecting the security of individual rights and liberties. Its central role is just the protection of such natural civil and political rights, the adjudication of disputes regarding those rights, and the securing of a general respect for the natural rights of the individual.

John Trenchard and Thomas Gordon argue the cause of liberty with the greatest force of eloquence in *Cato's Letters*. Playing upon the contrast between freedom and slavery in its many subtle dimensions, these radical English journalists wrote with lucid force about liberty in its many effects and manifestations. The freedom of speech and expression, the right to property in the fruits of one's labor, the active life of the intellect and imagination are only a few among the many positive manifestations of liberty in society. These are among the most vital possessions of any free people. They are likewise, however, the bane of tyrants, who will forever oppose themselves to any attempt, however enlightened, to check the encroachments of their arbitrary and capricious power. The benefits of liberty are many and varied. The effects of slavery are, however, debasing of the very idea of freedom, of learning and progress in the arts and sciences, of the human spirit itself. Finally for these journalists, liberty is itself the father of fairness and just laws, of virtue and of active civic duty. It is indeed the "inalienable" birthright of all mankind, the trust of every proper government to preserve, protect and defend.

Sir David Hume writes on matters of free speech and of the press, such as these were in eighteenth century England. It is the beacon of a free press that serves the purpose of alerting, of informing and thus protecting against the abuses of government. This is true of all government that would seek to oppress. This vital role, however, faces the deadly prospect of censorship by a government that will not permit a critical light cast upon its actions from any source of publication. An act of censorship, on the political content of speech of any kind, is indeed the first act of tyranny.

Hume attributes the relatively free press of his day to the fact of a mixed government in England. It is the combination of kings, lords and commons within a strong republican democracy that prevailed and that insured the freedom of press. While Hume does sound emphatic in speaking of a free press as a right most peculiar to England, we should note that the free speech we enjoy today under our First Amendment is more uniquely an American than an English creation.

Baron Montesquieu speaks to the need for laws that protect against the arbitrary deprivation of life, liberty and property. In particular, Montesquieu addresses the need for criminal punishment in a form appropriate to the crime. We are familiar with the principle that the penalty must be *proportionate* to the offense, that this is as much the right of the convicted criminal defendant as it is a measure of society's right and of social justice. Montesquieu's admonishment against cruel and unusual punishment rings loud with constitutional echoes in our Eighth Amendment. Similar thoughts on the proportionality of punishment to fit the crime echo in the writings of Jefferson.

William Blackstone further marks out, with lucid clarity, those liberties considered to be among the natural rights of Englishmen at common law. He speaks of the very same fundamental rights to life, liberty and property as does Locke, with the added detail and support of the common laws of England. Tracing the lineage of English liberty back to the Magna Carta of 1215 and earlier, Blackstone delineates the essential rights and liberties that find support in the precedents of the common law, formal declarations of rights and other sources within Englands unwritten constitution. These include the right to bear arms in defense of one's life and property, upon default by the state's obligation to do the same. It is indeed the duty of government to protect against danger to life and limb resulting from the private aggression of its own subjects and citizens, according to Blackstone. In thus expounding on the common laws of eighteenth century England, Blackstone lends both support and confirmation Locke's theory of natural rights and, indirectly, our own understanding of fundamental rights.

Edmund Burke's piece is chiefly a statement on the character and spirit of the early American quest for liberty. Their pursuit of freedom is derived from their very character as a free people by tradition and practice. They indeed viewed themselves as the inheritors of a tradition of liberty under the law, of civic duty and of town meetings providing a free forum for every responsible voice in the community. They developed early on a growing tolerance and sense of freedom for religious worship in all persuasions of faith. They recognized the need for public education both in itself and as a means to further inform themselves of their fundamental civil and political rights. It was, finally, the geographical separation from Europe and the old world of tyranny and oppression that provided fertile ground for a new and a freer people on new continent.

Richard Price addresses liberty in many dimensions important to eighteenth century thinkers and to us today. True liberty must consist of a freedom to choose and to command one's own conduct in the quiet enjoyment of one's life and property. A people and its nation are free when it is so constituted that its government will afford just such a liberty to its citizens. The rulers must allow the ruled a reasonable and intelligent control over their own lives. Such a self-determination is as fundamental among societies and nations as it is among individuals. Finally, for Price, true liberty in any civil society is afforded only through consensual laws and a popular constitution of government. This all entails mutual rights and duties of each to the other, much as a contract between two parties spells out all essential rights and obligations between the parties.

The foregoing pieces thus reflect the ideological origins, in part, of our fundamental rights. Several of these are explicit in the Bill of Rights and the body of our Constitution itself. It must be noted, however, that much of eighteenth century thinking on the subject of rights -took a *broadly principled* view of the matter, sometimes general and vague but always passionate and principled. We should be mindful, too, of the fact that the early Americans were driven by a powerful motive toward independence and sovereignty. This meant a sometimes overbearing desire to free themselves from what they perceived as absolute power, as tyranny and oppression. It was the oppression of an arbitrary and capricious king and of an irresponsible and unrepresentative parliament in England. The refinements of our civil and political rights, such as we know them today after two centuries of jurisprudence in the courts, were hardly yet felt or conceivable by the early pioneers of American liberties. The revolutionary generations were all the more urgently concerned with the corruptions and the oppressions of government on a soil other than their own. It is, therefore, not surprising that the details of liberty, the safeguards and protections such as we know them today, would have to await the establishment of a new constitution and its interpretation in the courts of our land. Our American colonial ancestors deeply considered their rights to be inherited, much as a family heirloom passed down is as valuable personal property, from one generation to the next. Indeed, they spoke often of specific liberties as their birthright, their "inalienable rights" in the words of Jefferson, and the inheritance of all freeborn Englishmen on both sides of the Atlantic. Their common law right to a jury trial, to private property and the security of their persons and possessions, to due process of law, were in every case thought to be the birthright of all British subjects. They were considered by American colonists to be both inheritable and inviolable from one generation to the next. Neither king nor parliament their could take back these hallowed and ancient rights, already enshrined in the likes of the Magna Carta, the English Bill of Rights (Petition of Right) and the common laws of England itself.

Yet several other theories were abundant, by which our colonial forbearers sought to claim their rights and liberties under the crown and from parliament. First and foremost, perhaps, was the concept of inheritance itself, discussed above. Those who came to the new world and to our shores carried with them all the rights of Englishmen. Repeated references to birthright, to the authority of their free charters granting liberty, to the common law and tradition itself, all attest to their conviction of inheritance as the basis of their most fundamental rights and liberties in America.

Still other concepts of liberty in currency at the time included those of contract and purchase. The thought was widespread that earliest immigrants to these shores took their liberties as grants of right, in exchange for their labor of taming a wild and uncultivated land for the benefit of king and empire. In so doing, they felt themselves the lawful recipients of liberty in the bargain. The concept of purchase is itself illustrated in the presence of indentured servants, whose motivation to come to America was to literally buy back their freedom as debtors from their masters.

Still another source of authority for their liberties was, as noted already, the common law itself. The cherished right to a trial by a jury of one's peers, the right to a trial itself and of due process, the right against compelled self-incrimination we know today as our Fifth Amendment, all found their lineage through the ancient common law of England. Such rights were formally declared as such and reaffirmed in major documents of liberty, including the Magna Carta and the Petition of Right [see Appendix] as well as several of of the early charters of settlement.

Finally and, perhaps, most ideological of all, is the fact that early Americans saw the origin of their rights as grounded in natural law, the laws of God and Nature itself. "Fundamental rights" were viewed as natural rights, the eternal and unalterable rights of all mankind everywhere. As such, these rights find their origin in the "higher law" of God and Nature. No man and no political body of whatever authority could divest them of such God-given rights and liberties.

Granted by God and nature's law to all of mankind, such rights were indeed thought to be "inalienable", permanent and unchangeable by the will of any human authority.

The reader should thus be alert in the perception of emerging patterns of thought among eighteenth century thinkers as to the origins of our fundamental rights. The pieces that follow represent those precedent concepts and principles of liberty then current in England and America. They are presented here with the view that they could not have seen the light of day, without having major implications for the framers of our Constitution and Bill of Rights.

# JOHN LOCKE

# ON THE EXTENT
# OF LEGISLATIVE POWER

*Of the Ends of Political Society*
*And Government*

123. IF MAN in the state of nature be so free, as has been said, if he be absolute lord of his own person and possessions, equal to the greatest, and subject to nobody, why will he part with his freedom, why will he give up his empire and subject himself to the dominion and control of any other power? To which it is obvious to answer that though in the state of nature he has such a right, yet the enjoyment of it is very uncertain and constantly exposed to the invasion of others; for all being kings as much as he, every man his equal, and the greater part no strict observers of equity and justice, the enjoyment of the property he has in this state is very unsafe, very unsecure. This makes him willing to quit a condition which, however free, is full of fears and continual dangers; and it is not without reason that he seeks out and is willing to join in society with others who are already united, or have a mind to unite, for the mutual preservation of their lives, liberties, and estates, which I call by the general name 'property.'

124. The great and chief end, therefore, of men's uniting into commonwealths and putting themselves under government is the preservation of their property. To which in the state of nature there are many things wanting:

First, there Wants an established, settled, known law, received and allowed by common consent to be the standard of right and wrong and

From John Locke, *Second Treatise of Government* (originally published in 1690)

the common measure to decide all controversies between them; for though the law of nature be plain and intelligible to all rational creatures, yet men, being biased by their interest as well as ignorant for want of studying it, are not apt to allow of it as a law binding to them in the application of it to their particular cases.

125. Secondly, in the state of nature there wants a known and indifferent judge with authority to determine all differences according to the established law; for every one in that state being both judge and executioner of the law of nature, men being partial to themselves, passion and revenge is very apt to carry them too far and with too much heat in their own cases, as well as negligence and unconcernedness to make them too remiss in other men's.

131. But though men when they enter into society give up the equality, liberty, and executive power they had in the state of nature into the hands of the society, to be so far disposed of by the legislative as the good of the society shall require, yet it being only with an intention in every one the better to preserve himself, his liberty and property—for no rational creature can be supposed to change his condition with an intention to be worse—the power of the society, or legislative constituted by them, can never be supposed to extend farther than the common good, but is obliged to secure every one's property by providing against those three defects above-mentioned that made the state of nature so unsafe and uneasy. And so whoever has the legislative or supreme power of any commonwealth is bound to govern by established standing laws, promulgated and known to the people, and not by extemporary decrees; by indifferent and upright judges who are to decide controversies by those laws; and to employ the force of the community at home only in the execution of such laws, or abroad to prevent or redress foreign injuries, and secure the community from inroads and invasion. And all this to be directed to no other end but the peace, safety, and public good of the people.

*Of the State of Nature*

4. To UNDERSTAND political power right and derive it from its original, we must consider what state all men are naturally in, and that is a state of perfect freedom to order their actions and dispose of their possessions and persons as they think fit, within the bounds of the law

of nature, without asking leave or depending upon the will of any other man.

A state also of equality, wherein all the power and jurisdiction is reciprocal, no one having more than another; there being nothing more evident than that creatures of the same species and rank, promiscuously born to all the same advantages of nature and the use of the same faculties, should also be equal one amongst another without subordination or subjection; unless the lord and master of them all should, by any manifest declaration of his will, set one above another, and confer on him by an evident and clear appointment an undoubted right to dominion and sovereignty.

5. This equality of men by nature the judicious Hooker* looks upon as so evident in itself and beyond all question that he makes it the foundation of that obligation to mutual love amongst men on which he builds the duties we owe one another, and from whence he derives the great maxims of justice and charity. His words are:

The like natural inducement hath brought men to know that it is no less their duty to love others than themselves; for seeing those things which are equal must needs all have one measure; if I cannot but wish to receive good, even as much at every man's hands as any man can wish unto his own soul, how should I look to have any part of my desire herein satisfied unless myself be careful to satisfy the like desire, which is undoubtedly in other men, being of one and the same nature? To have anything offered them repugnant to this desire must needs in all respects grieve them as much as me; so that, if I do harm, I must look to suffer, there being no reason that others should show greater measure of love to me than they have by me showed unto them; my desire therefore to be loved of my equals in nature, as much as possibly may be, imposeth upon me a natural duty of bearing to them-ward fully the like affection; from which relation of equality between ourselves and them that are as ourselves, what several rules and canons natural reason hath drawn, for direction of life, no man is ignorant. *(Eccl. Pol.* lib. i.).

138. Thirdly, the supreme power cannot take from any man part of his property without his own consent; for the preservation of property being the end of government and that for which men enter into society,

---

*[Richard Hooker (1554?–1600): Author of *The Laws of Ecclesiastical Policy*, which was one of the most influential works in the development of political theory from medieval thought to the natural rights concept. It had a profound influence on Locke, as can be seen from his many quotations from Hooker. The work consists of eight books; Books I-IV were published in 1594, Book V in 1597, and Books VI-VIII posthumously in 1648.]

it necessarily supposes and requires that the people should have property; without which they must be supposed to lose that, by entering into society, which was the end for which they entered into it—too gross an absurdity for any man to own. Men, therefore, in society having property, they have such right to the goods which by the law of the community are theirs, that nobody has a right to take their substance or any part of it from them without their own consent; without this, they have no property at all, for I have truly no property in that which another can by right take from me when he pleases, against my consent. Hence it is a mistake to think that the supreme or legislative power of any commonwealth can do what it will and dispose of the estates of the subject arbitrarily, or take any part of them at pleasure. This is not much to be feared in governments where the legislative consists, wholly or in part, in assemblies which are variable, whose members, upon the dissolution of the assembly, are subjects under the common laws of their country, equally with the rest. But in governments where the legislative is in one lasting assembly, always in being, or in one man, as in absolute monarchies, there is danger still that they will think themselves to have a distinct interest from the rest of the community, and so will be apt to increase their own riches and power by taking what they think fit from the people; for a man's property is not at all secure, though there be good and equitable laws to set the bounds of it between him and his fellow subjects, if he who commands those subjects have power to take from any private man what part he pleases of his property and use and dispose of it as he thinks good.

139. But government, into whatsoever hands it is put, being, as I have before shown, entrusted with this condition, and for this end, that men might have and secure their properties, the prince, or senate, however it may have power to make laws for the regulating of property between the subjects one amongst another, yet can never have a power to take to themselves the whole or any part of the subject's property without their own consent; for this would be in effect to leave them no property at all. And to let us see that even absolute power, where it is necessary, is not arbitrary by being absolute, but is still limited by that reason and confined to those ends which required it in some cases to be absolute, we need look no farther than the common practice of martial discipline; for the preservation of the army, and in it of the whole commonwealth, requires an absolute obedience to the command of every superior officer, and it is justly death to disobey or dispute the

most dangerous or unreasonable of them; but yet we see that neither the sergeant, that could command a soldier to march up to the mouth of a cannon or stand in a breach where he is almost sure to perish, can command that soldier to give him one penny of his money; nor the general, that can condemn him to death for deserting his post or for not obeying the most desperate orders, can yet, with all his absolute power of life and death, dispose of one farthing of that soldier's estate or seize one jot of his goods, whom yet he can command anything, and hang for the least disobedience. Because such a blind obedience is necessary to that end for which the commander has his power, viz., the preservation of the rest; but the disposing of his goods has nothing to do with it.

140. It is true, governments cannot be supported without great charge, and it is fit every one who enjoys his share of the protection should pay out of his estate his proportion for the maintenance of it. But still it must be with his own consent — i.e., the consent of the majority, giving it either by themselves or their representatives chosen by them. For if any one shall claim a power to lay and levy taxes on the people, by his own authority and without such consent of the people, he thereby invades the fundamental law of property and subverts the end of government; for what property have I in that which another may by right take, when he pleases, to himself?

# TRENCHARD AND GORDON

# LETTERS OF CATO

**Saturday, June 17, 1721.**

*Cautions against the natural Encroachments of Power.*

SIR,

Considering what sort of a Creature Man is, it is scarce possible to put him under too many Restraints, when he is possessed of great Power: He may possibly use it well; but they act most prudently, who, supposing that he would use it ill, inclose him within certain Bounds, and make it terrible to him to exceed them.[1]

Men that are above all Fear, soon grow above all Shame. *Rupto pudore & metu, suo tantum ingenio utebatur*, says Tacitus of Tiberius.[2] Even *Nero* had lived a great while inoffensively, and reigned virtuously: But finding at last that he might do what he would, he let loose his Appetite for Blood, and committed such mighty, such monstrous, such unnatural Slaughters and Outrages, as none but a Heart bent on the Study of Cruelty could have devised. The good Counsels of Seneca and Burrhus were, for some Time, Checks upon his wolfish Nature; and doubtless he apprehended, that if he made direct and downright War upon his People, they would use Resistance and make Reprisals: But discovering, by degrees, that they would bear any thing, and his Soldiers would execute everything, he grew into an open Defiance with Mankind, and daily and wantonly wallowed in their Blood. Having no

---

[1]From *Cato's Letters* and *The Independent Whig*

[2]This is another variant from Tacitus, Annals VI. 51: "... Postremo in scelera simul ac dedecora rorupit, postquam remoto pudore et metu suo tantum ingenio utebatur." ". . . Finally, when the restraints of shame and fear were gone, and nothing remained but to follow his own bent, he plunged impartially into crime and into ignominy."

other Rival, he seemed to rival himself, and every Day's Wick[ed]ness was blacker than another.

Yet *Nero* was not the worst of all Men: There have been Thousands as bad as he, and only wanted the same Opportunity to shew it. And there actually have been many Princes in the World who have shed more Blood, and done more Mischief to Mankind, than Nero did. I could instance in a late One, who destroyed more Lives than ever Nero destroyed, perhaps an Hundred to One. It makes no Difference, that Nero committed Butcheries out of Cruelty, and the other only for his Glory: However the World may be deceived by the Change of Names into an Abhorrence of the One, and an Admiration of the Other; it is all one to a Nation, when they are to be slaughtered, whether they be slaughtered by the Hangman or by Dragoons, in Prison or in the Field; nor is Ambition better than Cruelty, when it begets Mischief as great.

It is nothing strange, that Men, who think themselves unaccountable, should act unaccountably, and that all Men would be unaccountable if they could: Even those who have done nothing to displease, do not know but some time or other they may; and no Man cares to be at the entire Mercy of another. Hence it is, that if every Man had his Will, all Men would exercise Dominion, and no Man would suffer it. It is therefore owing more to the Necessities of Men, than to their Inclinations, that they have put themselves under the Restraint of Laws, and appointed certain Persons, called Magistrates, to execute them; otherwise they would never be executed, scarce any Man having such a Degree of Virtue as willingly to execute the Laws upon himself; but, on the contrary, most Men thinking them a Grievance, when they come to meddle with themselves and their Property. *Suarum legum auctor & eversor*, was the Character of Pompey: He made Laws when they suited his Occasions, and broke them when they thwarted his Will.[1] And it is the Character of almost every Man possessed of Pompey's Power: They intend them for a Security to themselves, and for a Terror to others. This shews the Distrust that Men have of Men; and this made a great Philosopher[2] call the State of Nature, a State of War; which Definition is true in a restrained Sense, since human Societies and human Laws are the Effect of Necessity and Experience: Whereas were

[1]Gnaeus Pompeius (106-48 B.C.) was, of course, the successful general and violent politician who joined Caesar and Crassus in the First Triumvirate. For Trenchard and Gordon, he stands again as a symbol of the dangers of unlimited military power, of standing armies, of personal and whimsical violations of constitutional provisions. *"Suarem legem auctor & eversor"* may be translated, "Author and violator of his own laws."

[2]Thomas Hobbes (1588-1679) argued, most notably in the thirteenth chapter of his *Leviathan*, that "Out of Civil States, there is always Warre of every one against every one."

all Men left to the boundless Liberty which they claim from Nature, every Man would be interfering and quarrelling with another; every Man would be plundering the Acquisitions of another; the Labour of one Man would be the Property of another; Weakness would be the Prey of Force; and one Man's Industry would be the Cause of another Man's Idleness.

Hence grew the Necessity of Government; which was the mutual Contract of a Number of Men, agreeing upon certain Terms of Union and Society, and putting themselves under Penalties, if they violated these Terms, which were called Laws, and put into the Hands of one or more Men to execute. And thus Men quitted Part of their Natural Liberty to acquire Civil Security. But frequently the Remedy proved worse than the Disease; and human Society had often no Enemies so great as their own Magistrates; who, where-ever they were trusted with too much Power, always abused it, and grew mischievous to those who made them what they were. Rome, while she was free (that is, while she kept her Magistrates within due Bounds) could defend herself against all the World, and conquer it: But being enslaved (that is, her Magistrates having broke their Bounds) she could not defend herself against her own single Tyrants, nor could they defend her against her foreign Foes and Invaders; for by their Madness and Cruelties they had destroyed her Virtue and Spirit, and exhausted her Strength. This shews that those Magistrates that are at absolute Defiance with a Nation, either cannot subsist long, or will not suffer the Nation to subsist long; and that mighty Traytors, rather than fall themselves, will pull down their Country.

What a dreadful Spirit must that Man possess, who can put a private Appetite in balance against the universal Good of his Country, and of Mankind! Alexander and Caesar were that Sort of Men; they would set the World on fire, and spill its Blood, rather than not govern it. Caligula knew that he was hated, and deserved to be hated; but it did not mend him. *Oderint dum metuant*, was his By-word: All that the Monster aimed at, was to be great and terrible. Most of these Tyrants died as became them; and, as they had reigned, by Violence: But that did not mend their Successors, who generally earned the Fate of those that went before them, before they were warm in their Place. "If unfortunate Villainy thus finds Rivals, what shall we say, when it exalts its Head and prospers?"

There is no Evil under the Sun but what is to be dreaded from Men, who may do what they please with Impunity: They seldom or never stop at certain Degrees of Mischief when they have Power to go farther; but hurry on from Wickedness to Wickedness, as far and as fast as human Malice can prompt human Power. So that when we see any great Mischief committed with Safety, we may justly apprehend Mischiefs still greater.

The World is governed by Men, and Men by their Passions; which, being boundless and insatiable, are always terrible when they are not controlled. Who was ever satiated with Riches, or surfeited with Power, or tired with Honours? There is a Tradition concerning Alexander, that having penetrated to the Eastern Ocean, and ravaged as much of this World as he knew, he wept that there was never another World for him to conquer. This, whether true or no, shews the Spirit of the Man, and indeed of human Nature, whose Appetites are infinite.

People are ruined by their Ignorance of human Nature; which Ignorance leads them to Credulity, and too great a Confidence in particular Men. They fondly imagine that he, who, possessing a great deal of their Favour, owes them great Gratitude, and all good Offices, will therefore return their Kindness: But, alas! how often are they mistaken in their Favourites and Trustees; who, the more they have given them, are often the more incited to take All, and to return Destruction for generous Usage. The common People generally think that great Men have great Minds, and scorn base Actions; which Judgment is so false, that the best and worst of all Actions have been done by great Men: Perhaps they have not picked private Pockets, but they have done worse; they have often disturbed, deceived, and pillaged the World: And he who is capable of the highest Mischief, is capable of the meanest: He who plunders a Country of a Million of Money, would in suitable Circumstances steal a Silver Spoon; and a Conqueror, who steals and pillages a Kingdom, would, in an humbler Fortune, rife a Portmanteau, or rob an Orchard.

Political Jealousy, therefore, in the People, is a necessary and laudable Passion. But in a Chief Magistrate, a Jealousy of his People is not so justifiable, their Ambition being only to preserve themselves; whereas it is natural for Power to be striving to enlarge itself, and to be encroaching upon those that have none. The most laudable Jealousy of a Magistrate is to be jealous for his People; which will shew that he loves them, and has used them well: But to be jealous of them, would denote that he has evil Designs against them, and has used them ill. The People's Jealousy tends to preserve Liberty; and the Prince's to destroy it. Venice is a glorious Instance of the former, and so is England; and all Nations who have lost their Liberty, are melancholy Proofs of the latter.

Power is naturally active, vigilant, and distrustful; which Qualities in it push it upon all Means and Expedients to fortify itself, and upon destroying all Opposition, and even all Seeds of Opposition, and make it restless as long as any Thing stands in its Way. It would do what it pleases, and have no Check. Now, because Liberty chastises and shortens Power, therefore Power would extinguish Liberty; and consequently Liberty has too much Cause to be exceeding jealous, and always upon her Defence. Power has many Advantages over her; it has generally numerous Guards, many Creatures, and much Treasure; besides, it has more Craft and Experience, less Honesty and Innocence: And whereas Power can, and for the most part does, subsist where Liberty is not, Liberty cannot subsist without Power; so that she has, as it were, the Enemy always at her Gates.

Some have said, that Magistrates being accountable to none but God, ought to know no other Restraint. But this Reasoning is as frivolous as it is wicked; for no good Man cares how many Punishments and Penalties lie in his Way to an Offence which he does not intend to commit: A Man who does not mean to commit Murder, is not sorry that Murder is punished with Death. And as to wicked Men, their being accountable to God, whom they do not fear, is no Security to us against their Folly and Malice; and to say that we ought to have no Security against them, is to insult common Sense, and give the Lie to the first Law of Nature, that of Self-Preservation. Human Reason says, that there is no Obedience, no Regard due to those Rulers, who govern by no Rule but their Lust. Such Men are no Rulers; they are Outlaws; who, being at Defiance with God and Man, are protected by no Law of God, or of Reason. By what Precept, moral or divine, are we forbid to kill a Wolf, or burn an infected Ship? Is it unlawful to prevent Wickedness and Misery, and to resist the Authors of them? Are Crimes sanctified by their Greatness? And is he who robs a Country, and murders Ten Thousand, less a Criminal, then he who steals single Guineas, and takes away single Lives? Is there any Sin in preventing, and restraining, or resisting the greatest Sin that can be committed, that of oppressing and destroying Mankind by wholesale? Sure there never were such open, such shameless, such selfish Impostors, as the Advocates for lawless Power! It is a damnable Sin to oppress Them; yet it is a damnable Sin to oppose Them when They oppress, or gain by Oppression of others! When they are hurt themselves ever so little, or but think themselves hurt, they are the loudest of all Men in their Complaints, and the most outrageous in their Behaviour: But when others are plundered, oppressed, and butchered, Complaints are Sedition; and to seek Redress, is Damnation. Is not this to be the Authors of all Wickedness and Falsehood?

To conclude: Power, without Control, appertains to God alone; and no Man ought to be trusted with what no Man is equal to. In Truth there are so many Passions, and Inconsistencies, and so much Selfishness, belonging to human Nature, that we can scarce be too much upon our Guard against each other. The only Security which we can have that Men will be honest, is to make it their Interest to be honest; and the best Defence which we can have against their being Knaves, is to make it terrible to them to be Knaves. As there are many Men wicked in some Stations, who would be innocent in others; the best Way is to make Wickedness unsafe in any Station.

P. S. This Letter is the Sequel of that upon Human Nature; and both are intended for an Introduction to a Paper which I intend to write upon the Restraints which all wise Nations put upon their Magistrates. [Trenchard and Gordon]

**Number 59**
**Saturday, December 30, 1721.**
*Liberty proved to be the unalienable Right of all Mankind.*

SIR,

I Intend to entertain my Readers with Dissertations upon Liberty, in some of my succeeding Letters; and shall, as a Preface to that Design, endeavour to prove in this, that Liberty is the unalienable Right of all Mankind.

All Governments, under whatsoever Form they are administered, ought to be administered for the Good of the Society; when they are otherwise administered, they cease to be government, and become

Usurpation. This being the End of all Government, even the most despotick have this Limitation to their Authority: In this Respect, the only Difference between the most absolute Princes and limited Magistrates, is, that in free Governments there are Checks and Restraints appointed and expressed in the Constitution itself: In despotick Governments, the People submit themselves to the Prudence and Discretion of the Prince alone: But there is still this tacit Condition annexed to his Power, that he must act by the unwritten Laws of Discretion and Prudence, and employ it for the sole Interest of the People, who give it to him, or suffer him to enjoy it, which they ever do for their own Sakes.

Even in the most free Governments, single Men are often trusted with discretionary Power: But they must answer for that Discretion to those that trust them. Generals of Armies and Admirals of Fleets have often unlimited Commissions; and yet are they not answerable for the prudent Execution of those Commissions? The Council of Ten, in Venice, have absolute Power over the Liberty and Life of every man in the State: But if they should make use of that Power to slaughter, abolish, or enslave the Senate; and, like the Decemviri of Rome, to set up themselves; would it not be lawful for those, who gave them that Authority for other Ends, to put those Ten unlimited Traytors to Death, any Way that they could? The Crown of England has been for the most part entrusted with the sole Disposal of the Money given for the Civil List, often with the Application of great Sums raised for other publick Uses; yet, if the Lord-Treasurer had applied this Money to the Dishonour of the King, and Ruin of the People (though by the private Direction of the Crown itself ) will any Man say that he ought not to have compensated for his Crime, by the Loss of his Head and his Estate?

I have said thus much, to show that no Government can be absolute in the Sense, or rather Nonsense, of our modern Dogmatizers, and indeed in the Sense too commonly practised. No barbarous Conquest; no extorted Consent of miserable People, submitting to the Chain to escape the Sword; no repeated and hereditary Acts of Cruelty, though called Succession, no Continuation of Violence, though named Prescription; can alter, much less abrogate, these fundamental Principles of Government itself, or make the Means of Preservation the Means of Destruction, and render the Condition of Mankind infinitely more miserable than that of the Beasts of the Field, by the sole Privilege of that Reason which distinguishes them from the Brute Creation.

Force can give no Title but to Revenge, and to the Use of Force again; nor could it ever enter into the Heart of any Man, to give another Power over him, for any other End but to be exercised for his own Advantage And if there are any Men mad or foolish enough to pretend to do otherwise, they ought to be treated as Idiots or Lunaticks; and the Reason of their Conduct must be derived from their Folly and Frenzy.

All Men are born free; Liberty is a Gift which they receive from God himself; nor can they alienate the same by Consent, though possibly they may forfeit it by Crimes. No Man has Power over his own Life, or to dispose of his own Religion; and cannot consequently transfer the Power of either to any body else. Much less can he give away the Lives and Liberties, Religion or acquired Property of his Posterity, who will be born as free as he himself was born, and can never be bound by his wicked and ridiculous Bargain.

The Right of the Magistrate arises only from the Right of private Men to defend themselves, to repel Injuries, and to punish those who commit them: That Right being conveyed by the Society to their publick Representative, he can execute the same no further than the Benefit and Security of that Society requires he should When he exceeds his Commission, his Acts are as extrajudicial as are those of any private Officer usurping an unlawful Authority, that is, they are void; and every Man is answerable for the Wrong which he does. A Power to do Good can never become a Warrant for doing Evil.

But here arises a grand Question, which has perplexed and puzzled the greatest Part of Mankind: Yet, I think, the Answer to it easy and obvious. The Question is, who shall be Judge whether the Magistrate acts justly, and pursues his Trust? To this it is justly said, That if those who complain of him are to judge him, then there is a settled Authority above the Chief Magistrate, which Authority must be itself the Chief Magistrate; which is contrary to the Supposition; and the same Question and Difficulty will recur again upon this new Magistracy. All this I own to be absurd; and I aver it to be at least as absurd to affirm, That the Person accused is to be the decisive Judge of his own Actions, when it is certain that he will always judge and determine in his own Favour; and thus the whole Race of Mankind will be left helpless under the heaviest Injustice, Oppression, and Misery, that can afflict human Nature.

But if neither Magistrates, nor they who complain of Magistrates, and are aggrieved by them, have a Right to determine decisively, the one for the other; and if there be no common established Power, to which both are subject; then every Man interested in the Success of the Contest, must act according to the Light and Dictates of his own Conscience, and inform it as well as he can. Where no Judge is nor can be appointed, every Man must be his own; that is, when there is no stated Judge upon Earth, we must have Recourse to Heaven, and obey the Will of Heaven, by declaring ourselves on that which we think the juster Side.

If the Senate and People of Rome had differed irreconcilable, there could have been no common Judge in the World between them; and consequently no Remedy but the last. For that Government consisting in the Union of the Nobles and the People, when they differed, no Man could determine between them; and therefore every Man must have been at Liberty to provide for his own Security, and the general Good, in the best manner he was able. In that Case the common Judge ceasing, every one was his own: The Government becoming incapable of acting, suffered a political Demise: The Constitution was dissolved; and there being no Government in Being, the People were in the State of Nature again.

The same must be true, where two absolute Princes, governing a Country, come to quarrel, as sometimes two Caesars in Partnership did, especially towards the latter End of the Roman Empire; or where a Sovereign Council govern a Country, and their Votes come equally to be divided. In such a Circumstance, every Man must take that Side which he thinks most for the publick Good, or choose any proper measures for his own Security: For, if I owe my Allegiance to two Princes agreeing, or to the Majority of a Council; when between these Princes there is no longer any Union, nor in that Council any Majority, no Submission can be due to that which is not; and the Laws of Nature and Self-Preservation must take place, where there are no other.

The Case is still the same, when there is any Dispute about the Titles of absolute Princes, who govern independently on the States of a Country, and call none. Here too every Man must judge for himself what Party he will take, to which Of the Titles he will adhere; and the like private Judgment must guide him, whenever a Question arises whether the said Prince be an Idiot or a Lunatick, and consequently whether he be capable or incapable of Government. Where there are no States, there can be no other way of judging; but by the Judgment of private Men the Capacity of the Prince must be judged, and his Fate determined. Lunacy and Idiotism are, I think, allowed by all to be certain Disqualifications for Government; indeed they are as much so, as if he were deaf, blind, and dumb, or even dead. He who can neither execute an Office, nor appoint a Deputy, is not fit for one.

Now I would fain know, why private Men may not as well use their Judgment in an Instance that concerns them more; I mean that of a tyrannical Government, of which they hourly feel the sad Effects, and sorrowful Proofs; whereas they have not by far the equal Means of coming to a Certainty about the natural Incapacity of their Governor. The Persons of great Princes are known but to few of their Subjects, and their Parts to much fewer; and several Princes have, by the Management of their Wives, or Ministers, or Murderers, reigned a good while after they were dead. In Truth, I think it is as much the Business and Right of the People to judge whether their Prince be good or bad, whether a Father or an Enemy, as to judge whether he be dead or alive; unless it be said (as many such wise Things have been said) that they may judge whether he can govern them, but not whether he does; and that it behoves them to put the Administration in wiser Hands, if he be a harmless Fool, but it is impious to do it, if he be only a destructive Tyrant; that Want of Speech is a Disqualification, but Want of Humanity, none.

That Subjects were not to judge of their Governors, or rather for themselves in the Business of Government, which of all human Things concerns them most, was an Absurdity that never entered into the Imagination of the wise and honest Ancients: Who, following for their Guide that everlasting Reason, which is the best and only Guide in human Affairs, carried Liberty, and human Happiness, the legitimate Offspring and Work of Liberty, to the highest Pitch that they were capable of arriving at. But the above Absurdity, with many others as monstrous and mischievous, were reserved for the Discovery of a few wretched and dreaming Mahometan and Christian Monks, who, ignorant of all Things, were made, or made themselves, the Directors of all Things; and bewitching the World with holy Lies and unaccountable Ravings, dressed up in barbarous Words and uncouth Phrases, bent all their Fairy Force against common Sense and common Liberty and Truth, and founded a pernicious, absurd, and visionary Empire upon their Ruins. Systems without Sense, Propositions without Truth, Religion without Reason, a rampant Church without Charity, Severity without Justice, and Government without Liberty or Mercy, were all the blessed Handy-works of these religious clad-men, and godly

Pedants; who, by pretending to know the other World, cheated and confounded this. Their Enmity to common Sense, and Want of it, were their Warrants for governing the Sense of all mankind By Lying, they were thought the Champions of the Truth; and by their Fooleries, Impieties, and Cruelty, were esteemed the Favourites and Confidents of the God of Wisdom, Mercy, and Peace.

These were the Men, who, having demolished all Sense and human Judgment, first made it a Principle, that People were not to judge of their Governor and Government, nor to meddle with it; nor to preserve themselves from publick Destroyers, falsely calling themselves Governors: Yet these Men, who thus set up for the Support and Defenders of Government, without the common Honesty of distinguishing the Good from the Bad, and Protection from Murder and Depredation, were at the same Time themselves the constant and avowed Troublers of every Government which they could not direct and command; and every Government, however excellent, which did not make their Reveries its own Rules, and themselves alone its peculiar Care, has been honoured with their professed Hatred; whilst Tyrants and publick Butchers, who flattered them, have been deified This was the poor State of Christendom before the Reformation; and I wish I could say, of no Parts of its since.

This barbarous Anarchy in Reasoning and Politicks, has made it necessary to prove Propositions which the Light of Nature had demonstrated. And, as the Apostles were forced to prove to the misled Gentiles, that they were no Gods which were made with Hands; I am put to prove, that the People have a Right to judge, whether their Governors were made for them, or they for their Governors? Whether their Governors have necessary and natural Qualifications? Whether they have any Governors or no? And whether, when they have none, every man must not be his own? I therefore return to Instances and Illustrations from Facts which cannot be denied; though Propositions as true as Facts may, by those especially who are defective in Point of Modesty or Discernment.

In *Poland*, according to the Constitution of that Country, it is necessary, we are told, that, in their Diets, the Consent of every Man present must be had to make a Resolve effectual: And therefore, to prevent the cutting of People's Throats, they have no Remedy but to cut the Throats of one another; that is, they must pull out their Sabres, and force the refractory members (who are always the Minority) to submit.

And amongst us in *England*, where a Jury cannot agree, there can be no Verdict; and so they must fast till they do, or till one of them is dead, and then the Jury is dissolved.

This, from the Nature of Things themselves, must be the constant Case in all Disputes between Dominion and Property. Where the Interest of the Governors and that of the Governed clash, there can be no stated Judge between them To appeal to a foreign Power, is to give up the Sovereignty; for either Side to submit, is to give up the Question: And therefore, if they themselves do not amicably determine the Dispute between themselves, Heaven alone must In such case, Recourse must be had to the first Principles of Government itself; which being a Departure from the State of Nature, and a Union of many Families forming themselves into a political Machine for mutual Protection and Defence, it is evident, that this formed Relation can continue no longer than the Machine subsists and can act; and when it does not, the Individuals must return to their former State again. No Constitution can provide against what will happen, when that Constitution is dissolved. Government is only an Appointment of one or more Persons, to do certain Actions for the Good and Emolument of the Society; and if the Persons thus interested will not act at all, or act contrary to their Trust, their Power must return of Course to those who gave it.

Suppose, for Example, the Grand Monarch, as he was called, had bought a neighbouring Kingdom, and all the Lands in it, from the Courtiers, and the Majority of the People's Deputies; and amongst the rest, the Church-Lands, into the Bargain, with the Consent of their Convocation or Synod, or by what other Name that Assembly was called; would the People and Clergy have thought themselves obliged to have made good this Bargain, if they could have helped it? I dare say that neither would; but, on the contrary, that the People would have had the Countenance of these reverend Patriots to have told their Representatives in round Terms, that they were chosen to act for the Interest of those that sent them, and not for their own; that their Power was given them to protect and defend their Country, and not to sell and enslave it.

This Supposition, as wild as it seems, yet is not absolutely and universally impossible. King John actually sold the Kingdom of England to his Holiness: And there are People in all Nations ready to sell their Country at Home; and such can never have any to withhold them from selling it Abroad.

It is foolish to say, that this Doctrine can be mischievous to Society, at least in any Proportion to the wild Ruin and fatal Calamities which must befal, and do befal the World, where the contrary Doctrine is maintained: For, all Bodies of Men subsisting upon their own Substance, or upon the Profits of their Trade and Industry, find their Account so much in Ease and Peace, and have justly such terrible Apprehensions of Civil Disorders, which destroy every thing that they enjoy; that they always bear a Thousand Injuries before they return One, and stand under the Burthens as long as they can bear them; as I have in another Letter observed.

What with the Force of Education, and the Reverence which People are taught, and have been always used to pay to Princes; what with the perpetual Harangues of Flatterers, the gaudy Pageantry and Outside of Power, and its gilded Ensigns, always glittering in their Eyes; what with the Execution of the Laws in the sole Power of the Prince; what with all the regular Magistrates, pompous Guards and standing Troops, with the fortified Towns, the Artillery, and all the Magazines of War, at his Disposal; besides large Revenues, and Multitudes of Followers and Dependants, to support and abet all that he does: Obedience to Authority is so well secured, that it is wild to imagine, that any Number of Men, formidable enough to disturb a settled State, can unite together and hope to overturn it, till the publick Grievances are so enormous, the Oppression so great, and the Disaffection so universal, that there can be no Question remaining, whether their Calamities be real or imaginary, and whether the Magistrate has protected or endeavoured to destroy his People.

This was the Case of *Richard* II. *Edward* II. and *James* II. and will ever be the Case under the same Circumstances. No Society of Men will groan under Oppressions longer than they know how to throw them off; whatever unnatural Whimsies and Fairy Notions idle and sedentary Babblers may utter from Colleges and Cloisters; and teach to others, for vile Self-Ends, Doctrines, which they themselves are famous for not practising.

Upon this Principle of People's judging for themselves, and resisting lawless Force, stands our late happy Revolution, and with it the just and rightful Title of our most excellent Sovereign King George, to the Scepter of these Realms; a Scepter which he has, and I doubt not will ever sway, to his own Honour, and the Honour, Protection, and Prosperity of us his People.

## Number 62.
## Saturday, January 20, 1721.

*An Enquiry into the Nature and Extent of Liberty; with its Loveliness and Advantages, and the vile Effects of Slavery.*

SIR,

I Have shewn, in a late Paper, wherein consists the Difference between Free and Arbitrary Governments, as to their frame and Constitution; and in this and the following I shall show their different Spirit and Effects. But first I shall shew wherein Liberty itself consists.

By Liberty, I understand the Power which every man has over his own Actions, and his Right to enjoy the Fruit of his Labour, Art, and Industry, as far as by it he hurts not the Society, or any members of it, by taking from any Member, or by hindering him from enjoying what he himself enjoys. The Fruits of a Man's honest Industry are the just Rewards of it, ascertained to him by natural and eternal Equity, as is his Title to use them in the Manner which he thinks fit: And thus, with the above Limitations, every Man is sole Lord and Arbiter of his own private Actions and Property. A Character of which no Man living can divest him but by Usurpation, or his own Consent.

The entering into political Society, is so far from a Departure from his natural Right, that to preserve it was the sole Reason why Men did so; and mutual Protection and Assistance is the only reasonable Purpose of all reasonable Societies. To make such Protection practicable, Magistracy was formed, with Power to defend the Innocent from Violence, and to punish those that offered it; nor can there be any other Pretence for Magistracy in the World. In order to this good End, the Magistrate is intrusted with conducting and applying the united Force of the Community; and with exacting such a Share of every Man's Property, as is necessary to preserve the Whole, and to defend every Man and his Property from foreign and domestick Injuries. These are the Boundaries of the Power of the Magistrate, who deserts his Function whenever he breaks them. By the Laws of Society, he is more limited and restrained than any Man amongst them; since, while they are absolutely free in all their Actions, which purely concern themselves; all his Actions, as a publick Person, being for the Sake of Society, must refer to it, and answer the Ends of it.

It is a mistaken notion in Government, that the Interest of the Majority is only to be consulted, since in Society every Man has a Right to every Man's Assistance in the Enjoyment and Defence of his private Property; otherwise the greater number may sell the lesser, and divide their Estates amongst themselves; and so, instead of a Society, where all peaceable Men are protected, become a Conspiracy of the many against the Minority. With as much Equity may one Man wantonly dispose of all, and Violence may be sanctified by mere Power.

And it is as foolish to say, that Government is concerned to meddle with the private Thoughts and Actions of Men, while they injure neither the Society, nor any of its members Every Man is, in Nature and Reason, the Judge and Disposer of his own domestick Affairs; and, according to the Rules of Religion and Equity, every Man must carry his own Conscience So that neither has the Magistrate a Right to direct the private Behaviour of Men; nor has the Magistrate, or any body else, any manner of Power to model People's Speculations, no more than their Dreams. Government being intended to protect Men from the Injuries of one another, and not to direct them in their own Affairs, in which no one is interested but themselves; it is plain, that their Thoughts and domestick Concerns are exempted entirely from its Jurisdiction In Truth, Mens Thoughts are not subject to their own Jurisdiction.

Idiots and Lunaticks indeed, who cannot take Care of themselves, must be taken Care of by others. But whilst Men have their five Senses, I cannot see what the Magistrate has to do with Actions by which the Society cannot be affected; and where he meddles with such, he meddles impertinently or tyrannically. Must the Magistrate tie up every Man's Legs, because some Men fall into Ditches? Or, must he put out their Eyes, because with them they see lying Vanities? Or, would it become the Wisdom and Care of Governors to establish a travelling Society, to prevent People, by a proper Confinement, from throwing themselves into Wells, or over Precipices; Or to endow a Fraternity of Physicians and Surgeons all over the nation, to take Care of their Subjects Health, without being consulted; and to vomit, bleed, purge, and scarify them at Pleasure, whether they would or no, just as these established Judges of Health should think fit? If this were the Case, what a Stir and Hubbub should we soon see kept about the established Potions and Lancets? Every Man, Woman, or Child, though ever so healthy, must be a Patient, or woe be to them! The best Diet and Medicines would soon grow pernicious from any other Hand; and their Pills alone, however ridiculous, insufficient, or distasteful, would be attended with a Blessing.

Let People alone, and they will take Care of themselves, and do it best; and if they do not, a sufficient Punishment will follow their Neglect, without the Magistrate's Interposition and Penalties. It is plain, that such busy Care and officious Intrusion into the personal Affairs, or private Actions, Thoughts, and Imaginations of Men, has in it more Craft than Kindness; and is only a Device to mislead People, and pick their Pockets, under the false Pretence of the publick and their private God. To quarrel with any Man for his Opinions, Humours, or the Fashion of his Clothes, is an Offence taken without being given. What is it to a Magistrate how I wash my Hands, or cut my Corns; what Fashion or Colours I wear, or what Notions I entertain, or what Gestures I use, or what Words I pronounce, when they please me, and do him and my Neighbour no Hurt? As well may he determine the Colour of my Hair, and controul my Shape and Features.

True and impartial Liberty is therefore the Right of every Man to pursue the natural, reasonable, and religious Dictates of his own Mind; to think what he will, and act as he thinks, provided he acts not to the Prejudice of another; to spend his own Money himself, and lay out the Produce of his Labour his own Way; and to labour for his own Pleasure and Profit, and not for others who are idle, and would live and riot by pillaging and oppressing him, and those that are like him.

So that Civil Government is only a partial Restraint put by the Laws of Agreement and Society upon natural and absolute Liberty, which might otherwise grow licentious: And Tyranny is an unlimited Restraint put upon natural Liberty, by the Will of one or a few. Magistracy, amongst a free People, is the Exercise of Power for the Sake of the People; and Tyrants abuse the People, for the Sake of Power. Free Government is the protecting the People in their Liberties by stated Rules: Tyranny is a brutish Struggle for unlimited Liberty to one or a few, who would rob all others of their Liberty, and act by no Rule but lawless Lust.

So much for an Idea of Civil Liberty. I will now add a Word or two, to shew how much it is the Delight and Passion of Mankind; and then shew its Advantages.

The Love of Liberty is an Appetite so strongly implanted in the Nature of all Living Creatures, that even the Appetite of Self-preservation, which is allowed to be the strongest, seems to be contained in it; since by the Means of Liberty they enjoy the Means of preserving themselves, and of satisfying their Desires in the Manner which they themselves choose and like best. Many Animals can never be tamed, but feel the Bitterness of Restraint in the midst of the kindest Usage; and rather than bear it, grieve and starve themselves to Death; and some beat out their Brains against their Prisons.

Where Liberty is lost, Life grows precarious, always miserable, often intolerable. Liberty is, to live upon one's own Terms; Slavery is, to live at the mere Mercy of another; and a Life of Slavery is, to those who can bear it, a continual State of Uncertainty and Wretchedness, often an Apprehension of Violence, often the lingering Dread of a violent Death: But by others, when no other Remedy is to be had, Death is reckoned a good one. And thus, to many Men, and to many other Creatures, as well as Men, the Love of Liberty is beyond the Love of Life.

This Passion for Liberty in Men, and their Possession of it, is of that Efficacy and Importance, that it seems the Parent of all the Virtues: And therefore in free Countries there seems to be another Species of Mankind, than is to be found under Tyrants. Small Armies of *Greeks* and *Romans* despised the greatest Hosts of Slaves; and a Million of Slaves have been sometimes beaten and conquered by a few Thousand Freemen. Insomuch that the Difference seemed greater between them than between Men and Sheep. It was therefore well said by Lucullus, when, being about to engage the great King Tigrane's Army, he was told by some of his Officers, how prodigious great the same was, consisting of between Three and Four Hundred Thousand Men: No matter, said that brave Roman, drawing up his little Army of Fourteen Thousand, but Fourteen Thousand *Romans*: *No matter, the Lion never enquires into the Number of the Sheep.* And these Royal Troops proved no better; for the *Romans* had little else to do but to kill and pursue; which yet they could scarce do for laughing; so much more were they diverted than animated by the ridiculous Dread and sudden Flight of these Imperial Slaves and Royal Cowards.

Men eternally cowed and oppressed by haughty and insolent Governors, made base themselves by the Baseness of that Sort of Government, and become Slaves by ruling over Slaves, want Spirit and Souls to meet in the Field Freemen, who scorn Oppressors, and are their own Governors, or at least measure and direct the Power of their Governors.

Education alters Nature, and becomes stronger. Slavery, while it continues being a perpetual Awe upon the Spirits, depresses them, and sinks natural Courage; and Want and Fear, the concomitants of Bondage, always produce Despondency and Baseness; nor will Men in Bonds ever fight bravely, but to be free. Indeed, what else should they fight for; since every Victory that they gain for a Tyrant, makes them poorer and fewer; and, increasing his Pride, increases his Cruelty, with their own Misery and Chains?

Those, who, from Terror and Delusion, the frequent Causes and Certain Effects of Servitude, come to think their Governors greater than Men, as they find them worse, will be as apt to think themselves less: And when the Head and the Heart are thus both gone, the Hands will signify little. They who are used like Beasts, will be apt to degenerate into Beasts. But those, on the contrary, who, by the Freedom of their Government and Education, are taught and accustomed to think freely of Men and Things, find, by comparing one Man with another, that all Men are naturally alike; and that their Governors, as they have the same Face, Constitution, and Shape with themselves, and are subject to the same Sickness, Accidents, and Death, with the meanest of their People; so they possess the same Passions and Faculties of the Mind which their Subjects possess, and not better. They therefore scorn to degrade and prostrate themselves, to adore those of their own Species, however covered with Titles, and disguised by Power: They consider them as their own Creatures; and, as far as they surmount themselves, the Work of their own Hands, and only the chief Servants of the State, who have no more Power to do Evil than one of themselves, and are void of every Privilege and Superiority, but to serve them and the State. They know it to be a Contradiction in Religion and Reason, for any Man to have a Right to do Evil; that not to resist any Man's Wickedness, is to encourage it; and that they have the least Reason to bear Evil and Oppression from their Governors, who of all Men are the most obliged to do them Good. They therefore detest Slavery and despise or pity Slaves; and, adoring Liberty alone, as they who see its Beauty and feel its Advantages always will, it is no Wonder that they are brave for it.

Indeed Liberty is the divine Source of all human Happiness. To possess, in Security, the Effects of our Industry, is the most powerful and reasonable Incitement t[o] be industrious; And to be able to provide for our Children, and to leave them all that we have, is the best Motive to beget them. But where Property is precarious, Labour will languish. The Privileges of thinking, saying, and doing what we please, and of growing as rich as we can, without any other Restriction, than that by all this we hurt not the Publick, nor one another, are the glorious Privileges of Liberty; and its Effects, to live in Freedom, Plenty, and Safety.

These are Privileges that increase Mankind, and the H[a]ppiness of Mankind. And therefore Countries are generally peopled in Proportion as they are free, and are certainly happy in that Proportion: And upon the same Tract of Land that would maintain a Hundred Thousand Freemen in Plenty, Five Thousand Slaves would starve. In *Italy,* fertile *Italy,* Men die sometimes of Hunger amongst the Sheaves, and in a plentiful Harvest; for what they sow and reap is none of their own; and their cruel and greedy Governors, who live by the Labour of their wretched Vassals, do not suffer them to eat the Bread of their own Earning, nor to sustain their Lives with their own Hands.

Liberty naturally draws new People to it, as well as increases the old Stock; and Men as naturally run when they dare from Slavery and Wretchedness, whithersoever they can help themselves. Hence great Cities losing their Liberty become Desserts, and little Towns by Liberty grow great Cities; as will be fully proved before I have gone through this Argument. I will not deny, but that there are some great Cities of Slaves: But such are only Imperial Cities, and the Seats of great Princes, who draw the Wealth of a Continent to their Capital, the Center of their Treasure and Luxury. *Babylon, Antioch, Seleucia,* and *Alexandria,* were great Cities peopled by Tyrants; but peopled partly by Force, partly by the above Reason, and partly by Grants and Indulgencies. Their Power, great and boundless as it was, could not alone people their Cities; but they were forced to soften Authority by Kindness; and having brought the Inhabitants together by Force, and by driving them Captive like Cattle, could not keep them together, without bestowing on them many Privileges, to encourage the first Inhabitants to stay, and to invite more to come.

This was a Confession in those Tyrants, that their Power was mischievous and unjust; since they could not erect one great City, and make it flourish, without renouncing in a great measure their Power over it; which, by granting it these Privileges, in Effect they did. These Privileges were fixed Laws, by which the Trade and Industry of the Citizens were encouraged, and their Lives and Properties ascertained and protected, and no longer subjected to the Laws of mere Will and Pleasure: And therefore, while these free Cities, enjoying their own

Liberties and Laws, flourished under them, the Provinces were miserably harassed, pillaged, dispeopled, and impoverished, and the Inhabitants exhausted starved, butchered, and carried away captive.

This shews that all Civil Happiness and Prosperity is inseparable from Liberty; and that Tyranny cannot make Men, or Societies of Men, happy, without departing from its Nature, and giving them Privileges inconsistent with Tyranny. And here is an unanswerable Argument, amongst a Thousand others, against absolute Power in a single Man. Nor is there one Way in the World to give Happiness to Communities, but by sheltering them under certain and express Laws, irrevocable at any Man's Pleasure.

There is not, nor can be, any Security for a People to trust to the mere Will of one, who, while his Will is his Law, cannot protect them if he would. The Number of Sycophants and wicked Counsellors, that he will always and necessarily have about him, will defeat all his good Intentions, by representing Things falsely, and Persons maliciously; by suggesting Danger where it is not, and urging Necessity where there is none; by filling their own Coffers, under Colour of filling his, and by raising Money for themselves, pretending the publick Exigencies of the State; by sacrificing particular Men to their own Revenge, under Pretence of publick Security; and by engaging him and his People in dangerous and destructive Wars, for their own Profit or Fame; by throwing publick Affairs into perpetual Confusion, to prevent an Enquiry into their won Behaviour; and by making him jealous of his People, and his People of him, on purpose to manage and mislead both Sides.

By all these, and many more wicked Arts, they will be constantly leading him into cruel and oppressive Measures, destructive to his People, scandalous and dangerous to himself; but entirely agreeable to their own Spirit and Designs, Thus will they commit all Wickedness by their Master's Authority, against his Inclinations, and grow rich by the People's Poverty, without his Knowledge; and the Royal Authority will be first a Warrant for Oppression, afterwards a Protection from the Punishment due to it. for, in short, the Power of Princes is often little else but a Stalking-Horse to the Intrigues and Ambition of their Minister.

But if the Disposition of such a Prince be evil, what must be the forlorn Condition of his People, and what Door of Hope can remain for common Protection! The best Princes have often evil Counsello[r]s, the Bad will have no other: And in such a Case, what Bounds can be set to their Fury, and to the Havock they will make? The Instruments and Advisers of Tyranny and Depredation always thrive best and are nearest their Ends, when Depredation and Tyranny run highest: When most is plundered from the People, their Share is greatest; we may therefore suppose every Evil will befal such a People, without supposing extravagantly. No Happiness, no Security, but certain Misery, and a vile and precarious Life, are the blessed Terms of such a Government – A Government which necessarily introduces all Evils, and from the same Necessity neither must nor can redress any.

The Nature of his Education, bred up as he ever is in perpetual Flattery, makes him haughty and ignorant; and the Nature of his Government, which subsists by brutish Severity and Oppression, makes him cruel. He is inaccessible, but by his Ministers, whose Study and Interest will be to keep him from knowing or helping the State of his miserable People. Their Master's Knowledge in his own Affairs, would break in upon their Scheme and Power; they are not likely to lay before him Representations of Grievances caused by themselves; nor, if they be the Effects of his own Barbarity and Command, will he hear them.

Even where absolute Princes are not Tyrants, there Ministers will be Tyrants. But it is indeed impossible for an arbitrary Prince to be otherwise, since Oppression is absolutely necessary to his being so. Without giving his People Liberty, he cannot make them happy; and by giving them Liberty, he gives up his own Power, So that to be and continue arbitrary, he is doomed to be a Tyrant in his own Defence. The Oppression of the People, Corruption, wicked Counsellors, and pernicious Maxims in the Court, and every where Baseness, Ignorance, and Chains, must support Tyranny, or it cannot be supported. So that in such Governments there are inevitable Grievances, without possible Redress; Misery, with Mitigation or Remedy; whatever is good for the People, is bad for their Governors; and what is good for the Governors, is pernicious to the People.

**Saturday, January 27, 1721**
*Civil Liberty produces all Civil Blessings, and
how; with the baneful Nature of Tyranny.*

SIR,

I Go on with my Considerations upon Liberty, to show that all
Civil Virtue and Happiness, every moral Excellency, all Politeness, all
good Arts and Sciences, are produced by Liberty; and that all Wickedness, Baseness, and Misery, are immediately and necessarily produced
by Tyranny; which being founded upon the Destruction of every thing
that is valuable, desirable, and noble, must subsist upon Means suitable
to its Nature, and remain in everlasting Enmity to all Goodness and
every human Blessing.

By the Establishment of Liberty, a due Distribution of Property
and an equal Dist[r]ibution of Justice is established and secured. As
Rapine is the Child of Oppression, Justice is the Offspring of Liberty,
and her Handmaid; it is the Guardian of Innocence, and the Terror of
Vice: And when Fame, Honour, and Advantages, are the Rewards of
Virtue, she will be courted for the Dower which she brings; otherwise,
like Beauty without Wealth, she may be praised, but more probably
will be calumniated, envied, and very often persecuted; while Vice,
when it is gainful, like rich Deformity and prosperous Folly, will be
admired and pursued. Where Virtue is all its own Reward, she will be
seldom thought any; and few will buy That for a great Price, which will
sell for none. So that Virtue, to be followed, must be endowed, and her
Credit is best secured by her Interest; that is, she must be strengthened
and recommended by the publick Laws, and embellished by publick
Encouragements, or else she will be slighted and shunned.

Now the Laws which encourage and increase Virtue, are the fixed
Laws of general and impartial Liberty; Laws, which being the Rule of
every Man's Actions, and the Measures of every Man's Power, make
Honesty and Equity their Interest. Where Liberty is thoroughly established, and its Laws equally executed, every Man will find his Account
in doing as he would be done unto, and no Man will take from another
what he would not part with himself: Honour and Advantage will
follow the Upright, Punishment overtake the Oppressor. The Property
of the Poor will be as sacred as the Privileges of the Prince, and the Law
will be the only Bulwark of both. Every Man's honest Industry and
useful Talents, while they are employed for the Publick, will be

employed for himself; and while he serves himself, he will serve the P[u]blick: Publick and private Interest will secure each other; all will cheerfully give a Part to secure the Whole, and be brave to defend it.

These certain Laws therefore are the only certain Beginnings and Causes of Honesty and Virtue amongst Men. There may be other Motives, I own; but such as only sway particular Men. few enough, God knows: And universal Experience has shewn us, that they are not generally prevailing, and never to be depended upon. Now these Laws are to be produced by Liberty alone, and only by such Laws can Liberty be secured and increased: And to make Laws certainly good, they must be made by mutual Agreement, and have for their End the general Interest.

But Tyranny must stand upon Force; and the Laws of Tyranny being only the fickle Will and unsteady Appetite of one Man, which may vary every Hour; there can be no settled Rule of Right or Wrong in the variable Humours and sudden Passions of a Tyrant, who, though he may sometimes punish Crimes, perhaps more out of Rage than Justice, will be much more likely to persecute and oppress Innocence, and to destroy Thousands cruelly, for one that he protects justly. There are Instances of Princes, who, being out of Humour with a Favourite, have put to Death all that spoke well of him, and afterwards all that did not: Of Princes, who put some of their Ministers to Death, for using one or two of their Barbers and Buffoons ill; as they did others of their Ministers, for using a whole Country well: Of Princes, who have destroyed, a whole People, for the Crimes or Virtues of one Man; and who, having killed a Minion in a Passion, have, to revenge themselves upon those who had not provoked them, destroyed in the same unreasonable Fury, a Hundred of their Servants who had no Hand in it, as well as all that had; who yet would have been destroyed, had they not done it: Of Princes, who have destroyed Millions in single mad Projects and Expeditions: Of Princes, who have given up Cities and Provinces to the Revenge or Avarice of a vile Woman or Eunuch, to be plundered, or massacred, or burned, as he or she thought fit to direct: Of Princes, who, to gratify the Ambition and Rapine of a few sorry Servants, have lost the Hearts of their whole People, and detached themselves from their good Subjects, to protect these Men in their Iniquity, who yet had done them no other Service, but that of destroying their Reputation, and shaking their Throne.

Such are arbitrary Princes, whose Laws are nothing but sudden

Fury, or lasting Folly and Wickedness in uncertain Shapes. Hopeful Rules these, for the governing of Mankind, and making them happy! Rules which are none, since they cannot be depended upon for a Moment; and generally change for the worse, if that can be. A Subject worth Twenty Thousand Pounds to Day, may, by a sudden Edict issued by the dark Counsel of a Traytor, be a Beggar to Morrow, and lose his Life without forfeiting the same. The Property of the whole Kingdom shall be great, or little, or none, just at the Mercy of a Secretary's Pen, guided by a Child, or a Dotard, or a foolish Woman, or a favourite Buffoon, or a Gamester, or whoever is uppermost for the Day; the next Day shall alter entirely the Yesterday's Scheme, though not for the better; and the same Men, in different Humours, shall be the Authors of both. Thus in arbitrary Countries, a Law aged Two Days i[s] an old Law; and no Law is suffered to be a standing Law, but such as are found by long Experience to be so very bad, and so thoroughly destructive, that human Malice, and all the A[r]ts of a Tyrant's Court, cannot make them worse. A Court which never ceaseth to squeeze, kill, and oppress, till it has wound up human Misery so high, that it will go no further. This is so much Fact, that I appeal to all History and Travels, and to those that read them, whether in arbitrary Countries, both in *Europe* and out of it, the People do not grow daily thinner, and their Misery greater; and whether Countries are not peopled and rich, in Proportion to the Liberty which they enjoy and allow.

It has been long my Opinion, and is more and more so, that in slavish Countries the People must either throw off their cruel and destroying Government, and set up another in its Room, or in some Ages the Race of Mankind there will be extinct. Indeed, if it had not been for free States, that have repaired and prevented in many Places the Mischiefs done by Tyrants, the Earth had been long since a Dessert, as the finest Countries in it are at this Day by that Means. The Gardens of the World, the fruitful and lovely Countries of the lower *Asia*, filled formerly by Liberty with People, Politeness, and Plenty, are now gloriously peopled with Owls and Grasshoppers; and perhaps, here and there, at vast Distances, with Inhabitants not more valuable, and less happy; a few dirty Huts of Slaves groaning, starving, and perishing, under the fatherly Protection of the *Sultan*, a Prince of the most Orthodox Standard.

The Laws therefore of Tyrants are not Laws, but wild Acts of Will, counselled by Rage or Folly, and executed by Dragoons. And as these

Laws are evil, all Sorts of Evil must concur to support them. While the People have Common-Sense left, they will easily see whether they are justly governed, and well or ill used; whether they are protected or plundered: They will know that no Man ought to be the Director of the Affairs of All, without their Consent; that no Consent can give him unlimited Power over their Bodies and Minds; and that the Laws of Nature can never be entirely abrogated by positive Laws; but that, on the contrary, the entering into Society, and becoming subject to Government, is only the parting with natural Liberty, in some Instances, to be protected in the Enjoyment of it in others.

So that for any Man to have arbitrary Power, he must have it without Consent; or if it be unadvisedly given at first, they who gave it soon repent when they find its Effects. In Truth, all those Princes that have such Power,* by keeping up great Armies in Time of Peace, effectually confess that they rule without Consent, and dread their People, whose worse Enemies they undoubtedly are. An arbitrary Prince therefore must preserve and execute his Power by Force and Terror; which yet will not do, without calling in the auxiliary Aids and strict Allies of Tyranny, Imposture, and constant Oppression. Let this People be ever so low and miserable, if they be not also blind, he is not safe. He must have established Deceivers to mislead them with Lyes, to terrify them with the Wrath of God, in case they stir Hand or Foot, or so much as a Thought, to mend their doleful Condition; as if the good God as the Sanctifier of all Villainy, the Patron of the worst of all Villains! He must have a Band of standing Cut-throats to murder all Men who would sacrilegiously defend their own. And both his Cut-throats and his Deceivers must go Shares with him in his Tyranny.

Men will naturally see their Interests, feel their Condition; will quickly find that the Sword, the Rack, and the Spunge, are not Government, but the Height of Cruelty and Robbery; and will never submit to them, but by the united Powers of Violence and Delusion: Their Bodies must be chained, their Minds enchanted and deceived; the Sword kept constantly over their Heads, and their Spirits kept low with Poverty, before they can be brought to be used at the wanton and brutish Pleasure of the most dignified and lofty Oppressor. So that God must be belied, his Creatures must be fettered, frightened, deceived, and starved, and Mankind made base and undone, that one of the worst of them may live riotously and safely amongst his Whores, Bitches, and Buffoons.

*Trenchard and Gordon here once again indicate their dislike for the Ottoman Sultan and the Moslem faith.

Men, therefore, must cease to be Men, and in Stupidity and Tameness grow Cattle, before they can become quiet Subjects to such a Government; which is a Complication of all the Villainies, Falsehood, Oppression, Cruelty, and Depredation, upon the Face of the Earth: Nor can there be a more provoking, impudent, shocking, and blasp[h]emous Position, than to assert all this Group of Horrors, or the Author of them, to be of God's Appointment.

*If such Kings are by God appointed,*
*Satan may be the Lord's Anointed.*

And whoever scatters such Doctrine, ought, by all the Laws of God, Reason, and Self-preservation, to be put to Death as a general Poisoner, and Advocate for publick Destruction.

All Men own, that it is the Duty of a Prince to protect his People: And some have said, that it is their Duty to obey him, when he butchers them. - An admirable Consequence, and full of sweet Consolation! His whole Business and Office is to defend them, and to do them Good; therefore they are bound to let him destroy them.-Was ever such Impudence in an enlightened Country? It is perfectly agreeable to the Doctrines and Followers of Mahomet: But shall Englishmen, who make their own Laws, be told, that they have no Right to the common Air, to the Life and Fortune which God has given them, but by the Permission of an Officer of their own making; who is what he is only for their Sakes and Security, and has no more Right to these Blessings, nor to do Evil, than one of themselves? And shall we be told this by Men, who are eternally the first to violate their own Doctrines? Or shall they after this have the Front to teach us any Doctrine, or to recommend to us any one Virtue, when they have thus given up all Virtue and Truth, and every Blessings that Life affords? For there is no Evil, Misery, and Wickedness, which arbitrary Monarchies do not produce, and must produce; nor do they, nor can they, produce any certain, general, or diffusive Good.

I have shewn, in my last, that any arbitrary Prince cannot protect his People if he would; and I add here, that he dares not. It would disgust the Instruments of his Power, and the Sharers in his Oppression, who will consider the Property of the People as the Perquisites of their Office, and claim a privilege of being little Tyrants, for making him a great one: So that every Kindness to his Subjects will be a Grievance to his Servants; and he must assert and exercise his Tyranny to the Height for their sakes, or they will do it for him. And the Instances are rare, if any, of any absolute Monarch's protecting in earnest his People against the Depredations of his Ministers and Soldiers, but it has cost him his Life; as may be shewn by many Examples in the *Roman* History: For this the Emperor *Pertinax* was murdered, and so was *Galba*.

*Machiavel* has told us, that it is impossible for such a Prince to please both the People and his Soldiers: The one will not be satisfied without Protection, nor the other without Rapine: To comply with the People, he must give up his Power; to comply with his Soldiers, he must give up his People. So that to continue what he is, and to preserve himself from the Violence of his Followers, he must countenance all their Villainies and Oppression, and be himself no more than an Imperial Thief at the Head of a Band of Thieves; for which Character he is generally well qualified by the base and cruel Maxims of that Sort of Power, and by the vile Education always given to such a Prince by the worst and most infamous of all Men, their supple and lying Sycophants.

Even the Christian Religion can do but little or no Good in Lands of Tyranny, since Miracles have ceased; but is made to do infinite Harm, by being corrupted and perverted into a deadly Engine in the Hands of a Tyrant and his Impostors, to rivet his Subjects Chains, and to confirm them thorough Wretches, Slaves, and Ignorants. I cannot indeed say, that they have the Christian Religion at all amongst them, but only use its amiable Name to countenance abominable Falsehoods, Nonsense, and heavy Oppression; to defend furious and implacable Bigotry, which is the direct Characteristick and Spirit of *Mahometism*, and destroys the very Genius and first Principles of Christianity. All this will be further shewn hereafter. I shall conclude with observing, that arbitrary Monarchy is a constant War upon Heaven and Earth, against the Souls as well as Bodies and Properties of Men.

Gl am, &c.

# DAVID HUME

# OF THE LIBERTY OF THE PRESS
## (1742)

Nothing is more apt to surprise a foreigner than the extreme liberty which we enjoy in this country of communicating whatever we please to the public and of openly censuring every measure entered into by the king or his ministers. If the administration resolve upon war, it is affirmed that, either willfully or ignorantly, they mistake the interests of the nation; and that peace, in the present situation of affairs, is infinitely preferable. If the passion of the ministers lie toward peace, our political writers breathe nothing but war and devastation, and represent the specific conduct of the government as mean and pusillanimous. As this liberty is not indulged in any other government, either republican or monarchical-in Holland and Venice more than in France or Spain-it may very naturally give occasion to the question: *How it happens that Great Britain alone enjoys this peculiar privilege?* And whether the unlimited exercise of this liberty be advantageous or prejudicial to the public.

The reason why the laws indulge us in such a liberty seems to be derived from our mixed form of government, which is neither wholly monarchical nor wholly republican. It will be found, if I mistake not, a true observation in politics that the two extremes in government, liberty and slavery, commonly approach nearest to each other; and that, as you depart from the extremes and mix a little of monarchy with liberty, the government becomes always the more free, and on the other hand, when you mix a little of liberty with monarchy, the yoke becomes always the more grievous and intolerable. In a government, such as that of France, which is absolute and where law, custom, and religion concur, all of them, to make the people fully satisfied with their condition, the monarch cannot entertain any *jealousy* against his subjects and therefore is apt to indulge them in great *liberties*, both of speech and action. In a government altogether republican, such as that of Holland, where there is no magistrate so eminent as to give *jealousy to* the state, there is no danger in entrusting the magistrates with large discretionary powers; and though many advantages result from such powers, in preserving peace and order, yet they lay a considerable restraint on men's actions and make every private citizen pay a great respect to the government. Thus it seems evident that the two extremes of absolute monarchy and of a republic approach near to each other: in some material circumstances. In the *first* the magistrate has no jealousy of the people, in the *second* the people have none of the magistrate; which want of jealousy begets a mutual confidence and trust in both cases and produces a species of liberty in monarchies and of arbitrary power in republics....

[A]s the republican part of the government prevails in England, though with a great mixture of monarchy, it is obliged, for its own preservation, to maintain a watchful *jealousy* over the magistrates, to remove all discretionary powers, and to secure everyone's life and fortune by general and inflexible laws. No action must be deemed a crime but what the law has plainly determined to be such; no crime must be imputed to a man but from a legal proof before his judges, and even these judges must be his fellow subjects, who are obliged by their own interest to have a watchful eye over the encroachments and violence of the ministers. From these causes it proceeds that there is as much liberty, and even perhaps licentiousness, in Great Britain as there were formerly slavery and tyranny in Rome.

These principles account for the great liberty of the press in these kingdoms beyond what is indulged in any other government. It is apprehended that arbitrary power would steal in upon us were we not careful to prevent its progress and were there not an easy method of conveying the alarm from one end of the kingdom to the other. The spirit of the people must frequently be roused in order to curb the ambition of the court, and the dread of rousing this spirit must be employed to prevent that ambition. Nothing so effectual to this purpose as the liberty of the press, by which all the learning, wit, and genius of the nation may be employed on the side of freedom and everyone be animated to its defense. As long, therefore, as the republican part of our government can maintain itself against the monarchical, it will naturally be careful to keep the press open, as of importance to its own preservation.

Since, therefore, the liberty of the press is so essential to the support of our mixed government, this sufficiently decides the second question: *Whether this liberty be advantages or prejudicial,* there being nothing of greater importance in every state than the preservation of the ancient government, especially if it be a free one. But I would fain go a step further and assert that such a liberty is attended with so few inconveniences that it may be claimed as the common right of mankind and ought to be indulged them almost in every government except the ecclesiastical, to which, indeed, it would be fatal. We need not dread from this liberty any such ill consequences as followed from the harangues of the popular demagogues of Athens and tribunes of Rome. A man reads a book or pamphlet alone and coolly. There is none present from whom he can catch the passion by contagion. He is not hurried away by the force and energy of action. And should he be wrought up to never so seditious a humor, there is no violent resolution presented to him by-which he can immediately vent his passion. The liberty of the press, therefore, however abused, can scarce ever excite popular tumults or rebellion. And as to those murmurs or secret discontents it may occasion, it is better they should get vent in words, that they may come to the knowledge of the magistrate before it be too late, in order to his providing a remedy against them. Mankind, it is true, have always a greater propension to believe what is said to the disadvantage of their governors than the contrary; but this inclination is inseparable from them whether they have liberty or not. A whisper may fly as quick and be as pernicious as a pamphlet. Nay, it will be more pernicious where men are not accustomed to think freely or distinguish betwixt truth and falsehood.

It is a very comfortable reflection to the lovers of liberty that this peculiar privilege of *Britain* is of a kind that cannot easily be wrested from us and must last as long as our government remains in any degree free and independent It is seldom that liberty of any kind is lost all at once. Slavery has so frightful an aspect to men accustomed to freedom that it must steal in upon them by degrees and must disguise itself in a thousand shapes in order to be received. But if the liberty of the press ever be lost, it must be lost at once. The general laws against sedition and libeling are at present as strong as they possibly can be made. Nothing can impose a further restraint but either the clapping an imprimatur upon the press or the giving very large discretionary powers to the court to punish whatever displeases them. But these concessions would be such a barefaced violation of liberty that they will probably be the last efforts of a despotic government. We may conclude that the liberty of *Britain is* gone forever when these attempts shall succeed.

It must however be allowed that the unbounded liberty of the press, though it be difficult perhaps impossible to propose a suitable remedy for it, is one of the evils attending those mixed forms of government.

# MONTESQUIEU

# SPIRIT OF LAWS (1748)

*15.—That we should not regulate by the Principles of political Laws
those Things which depend on the Principles of civil Law*

As men have given up their natural independence to live under
political laws, they have given up the natural community of goods to
live under civil laws.

By the first, they acquired liberty; by the second, property. We
should not decide by the laws of liberty, which, as we have already said,
is only the government of the community, what ought to be decided by
the laws concerning property. It is a paralogism to say, that the good of
the individual should give way to that of the public; this can never take
place, except when the government of the community, or, in other
words, the liberty of the subject is concerned; this does not affect such
cases as relate to private property, because the public good consists in
everyone's having his property, which was given him by the civil laws,
invariably preserved.

Cicero maintains, that the Agrarian laws were unjust; because the
community was established with no other view than that everyone
might be able to preserve his property.

Let us, therefore, lay down a certain maxim, that whenever the
public good happens to be the matter in question, it is not for the
advantage of the public to deprive an individual of his property, or even
to retrench the least part of it by a law, or a political regulation. In this

case we should follow the rigor of the civil law, which is the palladium of property.

Thus when the public has occasion for the estate of an individual. it ought never to act by the rigor of political law; it is here that the civil law ought to triumph, which, with the eyes of a mother. regards every individual as the whole community.

If the political magistrate would erect a public edifice, or make a new road, he must indemnify those who are injured by it; the public is in this respect like an individual who treats with an individual. It is fully enough that it can oblige a citizen to sell his inheritance, and that it can strip him of the great privilege. which he holds from the civil law, of not being forced to alienate his possessions.

After the nations which subverted the Roman Empire had abused their very conquests, the spirit of liberty called them back to that of equity. They exercised the most barbarous laws with moderation: and if any one should doubt the truth of this, they need only read Beaumanoir's admirable work on jurisprudence. written in the twelfth century.

They mended the highways in his time as we do at present. He says, that when a highway could not be repaired. they made a new one as near the old as possible; but indemnified the proprietors at the expense of those who reaped any advantage from the road. They determined at that time by the civil law; in our days, we determine by the law of politics.

## Of the Power of Punishments

Experience shows that in countries remarkable for the lenity of their laws the spirit of the inhabitants is as much affected by slight penalties as in other countries by severer punishments.

If an inconvenience or abuse arises in the state, a violent government endeavors suddenly to redress it, and instead of putting the old laws in execution, it establishes some cruel punishment, which instantly puts a stop to the evil. But the spring of government hereby loses its elasticity the imagination grows accustomed to the severe as well as he milder punishment; and as the fear of the latter diminishes, they are soon obliged in every case to have recourse to the former. Robberies on the highway became common in some countries; in order to remedy this evil, they invented the punishment of breaking upon the wheel, :he terror of which put a stop for a while to this mischievous practice. But soon after robberies on the highways became as common as ever.

Desertion in our days has grown to a very great height; in consequence of which it was judged proper to punish those delinquents with death; and yet their number did not diminish. The reason is very natural: a soldier accustomed to venture his life, despises, or affects to despise, the danger of losing it. He is habituated to the fear of shame; it would have been therefore much better to have continued a punishment which branded him with infamy for life; the penalty was pretended to be increased, while it really diminished.

Mankind must not be governed with too much severity; we ought to make a prudent use of the means which nature has given us to conduct them. If we inquire into the cause of all human corruptions, we shall find that they proceed from the impunity of criminals, and not from the moderation of punishments.

Let us follow nature, who has given shame to man for his scourge; and let the heaviest part of the punishment be the infamy attending it.

But if there be some countries where shame is not a consequence of punishment, this must be owing to tyranny, which has inflicted the same penalties on villains and honest men.

And if there are others where men are deterred only by cruel punishments, we may be sure that this must, in a great measure, arise from the violence of the government which has used such penalties nor slight transgressions.

It often happens that a legislator, desirous of remedying an abuse, thinks of nothing else; his eves are open only to this object, and shut to its inconveniences. When the abuse is redressed, you see only the severity of the legislator; yet there remains an evil in the state that has sprung from this severity; the minds of the people are corrupted, and become habituated to despotism.

Lysander having obtained a victory over the Athenians, the prisoners were ordered to be tried, in consequence of an accusation brought against that nation of having thrown all the captives of two galleys down a precipice, and of having resolved in full assembly to cut off the hands of those whom they should chance to make prisoners. The Athenians were therefore all massacred, except Adymantes, who had opposed this decree. Lysander reproached Phylocles, before he was put to death, with having depraved the people's minds, and given lessons of cruelty to all Greece.

"The Argives," says Plutarch, "having put fifteen hundred of their citizens to death, the Athenians ordered sacrifices of expiation, that it might please the gods to turn the hearts of the Athenians from so cruel a thought."

There are two sorts of corruptions-one when the people do not observe the laws; the other when they are corrupted by the laws: an incurable evil, because it is in the very remedy itself.

### Of the just Proportion between Punishments and Crimes

It is an essential point, that there should be a certain proportion in punishments, because it is essential that a great crime should be avoided rather than a smaller, and that which is more pernicious to society rather than that which is less.

"An impostor, who called himself Constantine Ducas, raised a great insurrection at Constantinople. He was taken and condemned to be whipped; but upon informing against several persons of distinction, he was sentenced to be burned as a calumniator." It is very extraordinary that they should thus proportion the punishments between the crime of high treason and that of calumny.

This puts me in mind of a saying of Charles II, King of Great Britain. He saw a man one day standing in the pillory; upon which he asked what crime the man had committed. He was answered, "Please your majesty, he has written a libel against your ministers." "The fool!" said the King, "why did he not write against me? They would have done nothing to him."

"Seventy persons having conspired against the Emperor Basil, he ordered them to be whipped, and the hair of their heads and beards to be burned. A stag, one day, having taken hold of him by the girdle with his horn, one of his retinue drew his sword, cut the girdle. and saved him; upon which he ordered that person's head to be cut off, 'for having,' said he, 'drawn his sword against his sovereign.'" "Who could imagine that the same prince could ever have passed two such different judgments.

It is a great abuse amongst us to condemn to the same punishment a person that only robs on the highway and another who robs and murders. Surely, for the public security, some difference should be made in the punishment.

In China, those who add murder to robbery are cut in pieces: but not so the others; to this difference it is owing that though they rob in that country they never murder.

In Russia, where the punishment of robbery and murder is the same, they always murder. The dead, say they, tell no tales.

Where there is no difference in the penalty, there should be some in the expectation of pardon. In England they never murder on the highway, because robbers have some hopes of transportation, which is not the case in respect to those that commit murder.

Letters of grace are of excellent use in moderate governments. This power which the prince has of pardoning, exercised with prudence, is capable of producing admirable effects. The principle of despotic government, which neither grants nor receives any pardon, deprives it of these advantages.

## *Of the Simplicity of Criminal Laws and Indifferent Governments*

We hear it generally said that justice ought to be administered with us as in Turkey. Is it possible, then, that the most ignorant of all nations should be the most clearsighted on a point which it most behooves mankind to know?

If we examine the set forms of justice with respect to the trouble the subject undergoes in recovering his property or in obtaining satisfaction for an injury or affront, we shall find them doubtless too numerous: but if we consider them in the relation they bear to the liberty and *security* of every individual, we shall often find them too few; and be convinced *that* the trouble, expense, delays, and even the very dangers of our judiciary proceedings are the price that each subject pays for his liberty.

In Turkey, where little regard is shown to the honor, life, or estate of the subject, all causes are speedily decided. The method of determining them is a matter of indifference, provided they be determined. The pasha, after a quick hearing, orders which party he pleases to be bastinadoed, and then sends them about their business.

Here it would be dangerous to be of a litigious disposition; this supposes a strong desire of obtaining justice, a settled aversion, an active mind, and a steadiness in pursuing one's point. All this should be avoided in a government where fear ought to be the only prevailing sentiment, and in which popular disturbances are frequently attended with sudden and unforeseen revolutions. Here every man ought to know that the magistrate must not hear his name mentioned, and that his security depends entirely on his being reduced to a kind of annihilation.

But in moderate governments, where the life of the meanest subject is deemed precious, no man is stripped of his honor or property until after a long inquiry, and no man is bereft of life till his very country has attacked him an attack that is never made without leaving him all possible means of making his defence.

Hence it is that when a person renders himself absolute, he immediately thinks of reducing the number of laws. In a government thus constituted they are more affected with particular inconveniences than with the liberty of the subject, which is very little minded.

In republics, it is plain that as many formalities at least are necessary as in monarchies. In both governments they increase in proportion to the value which is set on the honor, fortune, liberty, and life of the subject.

In republican governments, men are all equal; equal they are also in despotic governments: in the former, because they are everything; in the latter, because they are nothing.

# WILLIAM BLACKSTONE

# THE NATURAL RIGHTS OF MANKIND AND FREEDOM OF THE PRESS

## Commentaries (1769)

13. Of a nature very similar to challenges are *libels, libelli famosi,* which, taken in their largest and most extensive sense, signify any writings, pictures, or the like, of an immoral or illegal tendency; but, in the sense under which we are now to consider them, are malicious defamations of any person, and especially a magistrate, made public by either printing, writing, signs, or pictures, in order to provoke him to wrath, or expose him to public hatred, contempt, and ridicule. The direct tendency of these libels is the breach of the public peace, by stirring up the objects of them to revenge, and perhaps to bloodshed. The communication of a libel to any one person is a publication in the eye of the law: and therefore the sending an abusive private letter to a man is as much a libel as if it were openly printed, for it equally tends to a breach of the peace. For the same reason is immaterial with respect to the essence of a libel, whether the matter of it be true or false; since the provocation, and not the falsity, is the thing to be published criminally: though, doubtless, the falsehood of it may aggravate its guilt, and enhance its punishment. In a civil action, we may remember, a libel must appear to be false, as well as scandalous; for, if the charge be true, the plaintiff has received no private injury, and has no ground to demand a compensation for himself, whatever offence it may be against the public peace: and therefore, Upon a civil action, the truth of

from William Blackstone, *Commentaries on the Common Law of England, I: 119-141* the accusation may be pleaded in bar of the suit. But, in a criminal prosecution, the tendency which all libels have to create animosities. and to disturb the public peace, is the sole consideration of the law. And therefore, in such prosecutions, the only facts to be considered are, first, the making or publishing of the book or writing: and secondly, whether the matter be criminal: and, if both these points are against the defendant, the offense against the public is complete. The punishment of such libellers, for either making, repeating, printing, or publishing the libel, is fine, and such corporal punishment as the court in their discretion shall inflict; regarding the quantity of the offence, and the quality of the offender. By the law of the twelve tables. at Rome, libels, which affected the reputation of another were made a capital offence: but, before the reign of Augustus, the punishment became corporal only. Under the emperor Valentinian it was again made capital, not only to write, but to publish, or even to omit destroying them. Our law, in this and many other respects, corresponds rather with the middle age of Roman jurisprudence, when liberty, learning, and humanity, were in their full vigour than with the cruel edicts that were established in the dark and tyrannical ages of the antient *decemviri,* or the late emperors.

In this, and the other instances which we have lately considered, where blasphemous, immoral, treasonable schismatical, seditious, or scandalous libels are punished the English law, some with a greater, others with a less degree of severity; the liberty of the press, properly understood, is by no means infringed or violated. The liberty the press is indeed essential to the nature of a free state but this consists in laying no *previous* restraints upon publications, and not in freedom from censure for criminal matter when published. Every freeman has an undoubted right to lay what sentiments he pleases before the public to forbid this, is to destroy the freedom of the press: but if he publishes what is improper, mischievous, or illegal he must take the consequence of his own temerity. To subject the press to the restrictive power of a licenser, as was formerly done, both before and since the revolution, is to subject all freedom of sentiment to the prejudices of one man, and make him the arbitrary and infallible judge of all controverted points in learning, religion, and government. But to punish (as the law does at present) any dangerous or offensive writings, which, when published, shall on a fair and impartial trial be adjudged of a pernicious tendency, is necessary for the preservation of peace good order, of government and religion, the only solid foundations of civil liberty. Thus the will of individuals is still left free; the abuse only of that free will is the object of legal punishment. Neither is any restraint hereby laid upon freedom of thought or enquiry: liberty of private sentiment is still left; the disseminating, or making public of bad sentiments, destructive of the ends of society, is the crime which society corrects. A man (says a fine writer on this subject) may be allowed to keep poisons in his close but not publicly to vend them as cordials. And to this we may add, that the only plausible argument heretofore used for restraining the just freedom of the press, ' that it was "necessary to prevent the daily abuse of it," will entirely lose it's force, when it is shewn (by a seasonable exertion of the laws) that the press cannot be abused to any bad purpose without incurring a suitable punishment: whereas it never can be used to any good one, when under the control  an inspector. So true will it be found, that to censure the licentiousness, is to maintain the liberty, of the press.

## Commentaries (1765)

For the principal aim of society is to protect individuals in the enjoyment of those absolute rights, which were vested in them by the immutable laws of nature; but which could not be preserved in peace without that mutual assistance and intercourse, which is gained by the institution of friendly and social communities. Hence it follows, that the first and primary end of human laws is to maintain and regulate these *absolute* rights of individuals. Such rights as are social and *relative* result from, and are posterior to, the formation of states and societies: so that to maintain and regulate these, is clearly a subsequent consideration. And therefore the principal view of human laws is, or ought always to be, to explain, protect, and enforce such rights as are absolute. which in themselves are few and simple; and. then, such rights as are relative, which arising from a variety of connexions, will be far more numerous and more complicated. These will take up a greater space in any code of laws, and hence may appear to be more attended to, though in reality they are not, than the rights of the former kind let us therefore proceed to examine how far all laws ought, and how far the laws of England actually do, take notice of these absolute rights, and provide for their lasting security.  The absolute rights of man, considered as a free agent, endowed with discernment to know

good from evil, and with power of closing those measures which appear
to him to be most desirable, are usually summed up in one general
appellation, and denominated the natural liberty of mankind. This
natural liberty consists properly in a power of acting as one thinks fit,
without any restraint or control, unless by the law of nature: being a
right inherent in us by birth, and one of the gifts of God to man at his
creation, when he endued him with the faculty of free-will. But every
man, when he enters into society, gives up a part of his natural liberty,
as the price of so valuable a purchase; and, in consideration of receiving
the advantages of mutual commerce, obliges himself to conform to
those laws, which the community has thought proper to establish. And
this species of legal obedience and conformity is infinitely more
desirable, than that wild and savage liberty which is sacrificed to obtain
it. For no man, that considers a moment, would wish to retain the
absolute and uncontrolled power of doing whatever he pleases: the
consequence of which is, that every other man would also have the
same power; and then there would be no security to individuals in any
of the enjoyments of life. Political therefore, or civil, liberty, which is
that of a member of society, is no other than natural liberty so far
restrained by human laws (and no farther) as is necessary and expedient
for the general advantage of the publick. Hence we may collect that the
law, which restrains a man from doing mischief to his fellow citizens,
thou diminishes the natural, increases the civil liberty of mankind: but
every wanton and causeless restraint of the will of the subject, whether
practiced by a monarch. a nobility, or a popular assembly, is a degree
of tyranny. Nay, that even laws themselves, whether made with or
without our consult. if they regulate and constrain our conduct in
matters of mere indifference, without any good end in view, are laws
destructive of liberty: whereas if and public advantage can arise from
observing such precepts, the control of our private inclinations, in one
or to particular points, will conduce to preserve our general freedom in
others of more importance; by supporting that state, of society, which
alone can secure our independence. Thus the statute of king Edward IV,
which forbad the fine gentlemen of those times (under the degree of a
lord) to wear pikes upon their shoes or boots of more than two inches
in length, was a law that savoured of oppression; because, however
ridiculous the fashion then in use might appear, the restraining it by
pecuniary penalties could serve no purpose of common utility. But the
statute of king Charles II, which prescribes a thing seemingly as

indifferent; via a dress for the dead, who are all ordered to be buried in woollen; is a law consistent with public liberty, for it encourages the staple trade, on which in great measure depends the universal good of the nation. So that laws, when prudently framed, are by no means subversive but rather introductive of liberty; for (as Mr. Locke has well observed) where there is no law, there is no freedom. But then, on the other hand, that constitution or frame of government, that system of laws, is alone calculated to maintain civil liberty, which leaves the subject entire master of his own conduct, except in those points wherein the public good requires some direction or restraint.

The idea and practice of this political or civil liberty flourish in their highest vigour in these kingdoms, where it falls little short of perfection, and can only be lost or destroyed by the folly or demerits of it's owner: the legislature, and of course the laws of England, being peculiarly adapted to the preservation of this inestimable blessing even in the meanest subject. Very different from the modern constitutions of other states, on the continent of Europe, and from the genius of the imperial law; which in general are calculated to vest an arbitrary and despotic power of controlling the actions of the subject in the prince, or in a few grandees. And this spirit of liberty is so deeply implanted in our constitution, and rooted even in our very soil, that a slave or a negro, the moment he lands in England, falls under the protection of the laws, and with regard to all natural rights becomes *eo instanti* a freeman The absolute rights of every Englishman (which, taken in a political and extensive sense, are usually called their liberties) as they are founded on nature and reason, so they are coeval with our form of government; though subject at times to fluctuate and change: their establishment (excellent as it is) being still human. At some times we have seen them depressed by overbearing and tyrannical princes; at others so luxuriant as even to tend to anarchy, a worse state than tyranny itself, as any government is better than none at all. But the vigour of our free constitution has always delivered the nation from these embarassments, and, as soon as the convulsions consequent on the struggle have been over, the ballance of our rights and liberties has settled to it's proper level; and their fundamental articles have been from time to time asserted in parliament. as often as they were thought to he in danger.

First, by the great charter of liberties, which was obtained, sword in hand, from king John; and afterwards, with some alterations, confirmed in parliament by king Henry the third, his son. Which charter contained very few new grants; but, as sir Edward Coke observes, was for the most part declaratory of the principal grounds of the fundamental laws of England. Afterwards by the statute called *confirmatio cartarum*, whereby the great charter is directed to be allowed as the common law; all judgments contrary to it are declared void; copies of it are ordered to be sent to all cathedral churches, and read twice a year to the people; and sentence of excommunication is directed to be as constantly denounced against all those that by word, deed, or counsel act contrary thereto, or in any degree infringe it. Next by a multitude of subsequent corroborating statutes, (sir Edward Coke, I think, reckons thirty two,) from the first Edward to Henry the fourth. Then after a long interval by *the petition of night;* which was a parliamentary declaration of the liberties of the people, assented to by king Charles the first in the beginning of his reign. Which was closely followed by the still more ample concessions made by that unhappy prince to his parliament, before the fatal rupture between them; and by the many salutary laws, particularly the *habeas corpus* act, passed under Charles the second. To these succeeded *the bill of rights,* or declaration delivered by the lords and commons to the prince and princess of Orange 13 February 1688; and afterwards enacted in parliament when they became king and queen: which declaration concludes in these remarkable words; "and they do claim, demand, and insist upon all and singular the premises, as their undoubted rights and liberties." And the act of parliament itself recognizes "all and singular the rights and liberties asserted and claimed in the said declaration to be the true, antient, and indubitable rights of the people of this kingdom." Lastly, these liberties were again asserted at the commencement of the present century, in the *act of settlement,* whereby the crown is limited to his present majesty's illustrious house and some new provisions were added at the same fortunate aera for better securing our religion, laws, and liberties; which the statute declares to be "the birthright of the people of England:" according to the antient doctrine of the common law.

Thus much for the *declaration* of our rights and liberties. The rights themselves thus defined by these several statutes, consist in a number of private immunities: which will appear, from what has been premised, to be indeed no other, than either this *residuum* of natural liberty, which is not required by the laws of society to be sacrificed to public convenience; or else those civil privileges, which society hath engaged to provide in lieu of the natural liberties so given up by individuals. These therefore were formerly, either by inheritance or purchase, the rights of all mankind; but, in most other countries of the world being now more or less debased and destroyed, they at present may be said to remain, in a peculiar and emphatical manner, the rights of the people of England. And these may be reduced to three principal or primary articles; the right of personal security. the right of personal liberty; and the right of private property: because as there is no other known method of compulsion, or of abridging man's natural free will, but by an infringement or diminution of one or other of these important rights, the preservation of these, inviolate, may justly be said to include the preservation of our civil immunities in their largest and most extensive sense.

I. The right of personal security consists in a person's legal and uninterrupted enjoyment of his life, his limbs, his body, his health, and his reputation. 1. Life is the immediate gift of God, a right inherent by nature in every individual; and it begins in contemplation of law as soon as an infant is able to stir in the mother's womb. For if a woman is quick with child, and by a potion, or otherwise, killeth it in her womb; or if any one beat her, whereby the child dieth in her body, and she is delivered of a dead child; this, though not murder, was by the antient law homicide or manslaughter. But at present it is not looked upon in quite so atrocious a light, though it remains a very heinous misdemesnor. An infant *in ventre sa mere,* or in the mother's womb, is supposed in law to be born for many purposes. It is capable of having a legacy, or a surrender of a copyhold estate made to it. It may have a guardian assigned to it; and it is enabled to have an estate limited to it's use, and to take afterwards by such limitation, as if it were then actually born. And in this point the civil law agrees with ours. 2. A man's limbs, (by which for the present we only understand those members which may be useful to him in fight, and the loss of which only amounts to mayhem by the common law) are also the gift of the wise creator; to enable man to protect himself from external injuries in a state of nature. To these therefore he has a natural inherent right; and they cannot be wantonly destroyed or disabled without a manifest breach of civil liberty. . .

1. This natural life being, as was before observed, the immediate donation of the great creator, cannot legally be disposed of or destroyed by any individual, neither by the person himself nor by any other of his fellow creatures, merely upon their own authority. Yet nevertheless it

may, by the divine permission, be frequently forfeited for the breach of those laws of society, which are enforced by the sanction of capital punishments; of the nature, restrictions, expedience, and legality of which, we may hereafter more conveniently enquire in the concluding book of these commentaries. At present, I shall only observe, that whenever the *constitution* of a state vests in any man, or body of men, a power of destroying at pleasure, without the direction of laws, the lives or members of the subject, such constitution is in the highest degree tyrannical: and that whenever any *laws* direct such destruction for light and trivial causes, such laws are likewise tyrannical, though in an inferior degree; because here the subject is aware of the danger he is exposed to, and may by prudent caution provide against it. The statute law of England does therefore very seldom, and the common law does never, inflict any punishment extending to life or limb, unless upon the highest necessity: and the constitution is an utter stranger to any arbitrary power of killing or maiming the subject without the express warrant of law. *"Nullus liber homo,* says the great charter, *aliquo modo destruatur, nisi per legale judicium parium suorum aut per legem terrae."* Which words, *"aliquo modo destruatur,"* according to sir Edward Coke, include a prohibition not only of *killing,* and *maiming,* but also of *torturing* (to which our laws are strangers) and of every oppression by colour of an illegal authority. And it is enacted by the statute 5 Edw. III. c. 9. that no man shall be forejudged of life or limb, contrary to the great charter and the law of the land: and again, by statute 28 Ed. III. c. 3. that no man shall be put to death, without being brought to answer by due process of law.

II. Next to personal security, the law of England regards, asserts, and preserves the personal liberty of individuals. This personal liberty consists in the power of locomotion, of changing situation, or removing one's person to whatsoever place one's own inclination may direct; without imprisonment or restraint, unless by due course of law. Concerning which we may make the same observations as upon the preceding article; that it is a right strictly natural; that the laws of England have never abridged it without sufficient cause; and, that in this kingdom it cannot ever be abridged at the mere discretion of the magistrate, without the explicit permission of the laws. Here again the language of the great charter is, that no freeman shall be taken or imprisoned, but by the lawful judgment of his equals, or by the law of the land. And many subsequent old statutes expressly direct, that no man shall be taken or imprisoned by suggestion or petition to the king or his council, unless it be by legal indictment, or the process of the common law. By the petition of right, 3 Car. I it is enacted, that no freeman shall be imprisoned or detained without cause shewn, to which he may make answer according to law. By 16 Car. 1. c. 10. if any person be restrained of his liberty by order or decree of any illegal court, or by command of the king's majesty in person, or by warrant of the council board, or of any of the privy council; he shall, upon demand of his counsel, have a writ of *habeas corpus, to* bring his body before the court of king's bench or common pleas; who shall determine whether the cause of his commitment be just, and thereupon do as to justice shall appertain. And by 31 Car. II. c. 2. commonly called *the habeas corpus act*, the methods of obtaining this writ are so plainly pointed out and enforced, that, so long as this statute remains unimpeached, no subject of England can be long detained in prison, except in those cases in which the law requires and justifies such detainer. And, lest this act should be evaded by demanding unreasonable bail, or sureties for the prisoner's appearance, it is declared by I W. & M. st. 2. c. 2. that excessive bail ought not to be required.

Of great importance to the public is the preservation of this personal liberty: for if once it were left in the power of any, the highest, magistrate to imprison arbitrarily whomever he or his officers thought proper, (as in France it is daily practiced by the crown) There would soon be an end of all other rights and immunities. Some have thought, that unjust attacks, even upon life, or property, at the arbitrary will of the magistrate, are less dangerous to the commonwealth, than such as are made upon the personal liberty of the subject. To bereave a man of life, or by violence to confiscate his estate, without accusation or trial, would be so gross and notorious an act of despotism, as must at once convene the alarm of tyranny throughout the whole kingdom. But confinement of the person, by secretly hurrying him to gaol, where his sufferings are unknown or forgotten; is a less public, a less striking, and therefore a more dangerous engine of arbitrary government. And yet sometimes, when the state is in real danger, even this may be a necessary measure. But the happiness of our constitution is, that it is not left to the executive power to determine when the danger of the state is so great, as to render this measure expedient. For the parliament only, or legislative power, whenever it sees proper, can authorize the crown, by suspending the *habeas corpus* act for a short and limited time, to imprison suspected persons without giving any reason for so doing. As the senate of Rome was wont to have recourse to a dictator, a magistrate of absolute authority, when they judged the republic in any imminent danger. The decree of the senate, which usually preceded the nomination of this magistrate, was called the *senatus consultum ultimae necessitatis.* In like manner this experiment ought only to be tried in cases of extreme emergency; and in these the nation parts with it's liberty for a while, in order to preserve it for ever.

The confinement of the person, in any wise, is an imprisonment. So that the keeping a man against his will in a private house, putting him in the stocks, arresting or forcibly detaining him in the street, is an imprisonment. And the law so much discourages unlawful confinement, that if a man is under *duress of imprisonment,* which we before explained to mean a compulsion by an illegal restraint of liberty, until he seals a bond or the like; he may alledge this duress, and avoid the extorted bond. But if a man be lawfully imprisoned, and either to procure his discharge, or on any other fair account, seals a bond or a deed, this is not by duress of imprisonment, and he is not at liberty to avoid it. To make imprisonment lawful, it must either be, by process from the courts of judicature, or by warrant from some legal officer, having authority to commit to prison; which warrant must be in writing, under the hand and seal of the magistrate, and express the causes of the commitment, in order to be examined into (if necessary) upon a *habeas corpus.* If there be no cause expressed, the gaoler is not bound to detain the prisoner. For the law Judges in this respect, saith sir Edward Coke, like Festus the Roman governor; that it is unreasonable to send a prisoner, and not to signify withal the crimes alleged against him.

III. The third absolute right, inherent in every Englishman, is that of property: which consists of the free use, enjoyment, and disposal of all his acquisitions, without any control or diminution, save only by the laws of the land. The original of private property is probably founded in nature. as will be more fully explained in the second book of the ensuing commentaries: but certainly the modifications under which we at present find it, the method of conserving it in the present owner, and of translating it from man to man, are entirely derived from society; and are some of those civil advantages, in exchange for which every individual has resigned a part of his natural liberty. The laws of England are therefore, in point of honor and justice, extremely watchful in ascertaining and protecting this right. Upon this principle the great charter has declared that no freeman shall be disseised, or divested, of his freehold, or of his liberties, or free customs, but by the judgment of his peers, or by the law of the land. And by a variety of antient statutes it is enacted, that no man's lands or goods shall be seised into the king's hands, against the great charter, and the law of the land; and that no man shall be disinherited, nor put out of his franchises or freehold, unless he be duly brought to answer, and be forejudged by course of law; and if any thing be done to the contrary, it shall be redressed, and holden for none.

So great moreover is the regard of the law for private property, that it will not authorize the least violation of it; no, not even for the general good of the whole community. If a new road, for instance, were to be made through the grounds of a private person, it might perhaps be extensively beneficial to the public; but the law permits no man, or set of men, to do this without consent of the owner of the land. In vain may it be argued, that the good of the individual ought to yield to that of the community; for it would be dangerous to allow any private mall, or even any public tribunal, to be the judge of this common good, and to decide whether it be expedient or no. Besides, the public good is in nothing more essentially interested, than in the protection of every individual's private rights, as modelled by the municipal law. In this, and similar cases the legislature alone can, and indeed frequently does, interpose, and compel the individual to acquiesce. But how does it interpose and compel? Not by absolutely stripping the subject of his property in an arbitrary manner; but by giving him a full indemnification and equivalent for the injury thereby sustained. The public is now considered as an individual, treating with an individual for an exchange. All that the legislature does is to oblige the owner to alienate his possessions for a reasonable price; and even this is an exertion of power, which the legislature indulges with caution, and which nothing but the legislature can perform.

In the three preceding articles we have taken a short view of the principal absolute rights which appertain to every Englishman. But in vain would these rights be declared, ascertained, and protected by the dead letter of the laws, if the constitution had provided no other method to secure their actual enjoyment. It has therefore established certain other auxiliary subordinate rights of the subject, which serve principally as barriers to protect and maintain inviolate the three great and primary rights, of personal security, personal liberty, and private property. These are,

1. The constitution, powers, and privileges of parliament, of which I shall treat at large in the ensuing chapter.

2. The limitation of the king's prerogative, by bounds so certain and notorious, that it is impossible he should exceed them without the consent of the people. Of this also I shall treat in it's proper place. The former of these keeps the legislative power in due health and vigour, so as to make it improbable that laws should be enacted destructive of general liberty: the latter is a guard upon the executive power, by restraining it from acting either beyond or in contradiction to the laws, that are framed and established by the other.

3. A third subordinate right of every Englishman is that of applying to the courts of justice for redress of injuries. Since the law is in England the supreme arbiter of every man's life, liberty, and property, courts of justice must at all times be open to the subject, and the law be duly administered therein. The emphatical words of *magna carta*, spoken in the person of the king, who in judgment of law (says sir Edward Coke) is ever present and repeating them in all his courts, are these; *"mulli vendemus, nulli negabimus, aut differemus rectum vel justitiam*: and therefore every subject," continues the same learned author, "for injury done to him *in bonis, in terris, vel persona,* by any other subject, be he ecclesiastical or temporal without any exception, may take his remedy by the course of the law, and have justice and right for the injury done to him, freely without sale, fully without denial, and speedily without delay." It were endless to enumerate all the *affirmative* acts of parliament wherein justice is directed to be done according to the law of the land: and what law is, every subject knows; or may know if he pleases: for it depends not upon the arbitrary will of any judge; but is permanent, fixed, and unchangeable, unless by authority of parliament.

Not only the substantial part, or judicial decisions, of the law, but also the formal part, or method of proceeding, cannot be altered but by parliament: for if once those outworks were demolished, there would be no inlet to all manner of innovation in the body of the law itself. The king, it is true, may erect new courts of justice; but then they must proceed according to the old established forms of the common law. For which reason it is declared in the statute 16 Car. I. C. 10. upon the dissolution of the court of starchamber, that neither his majesty, nor his privy council, have any jurisdiction, power, or authority by English bill, petition, articles, libel (which were the course of proceeding in the starchamber, borrowed from the civil law) or by any other arbitrary way whatsoever, to examine, or draw into question, determine or dispose of the lands or goods of any subjects of this kingdom: but that the same ought to be tried and determined in the ordinary courts of justice, and by *course of law*.

4. If there should happen any uncommon injury, or infringement of the rights before mentioned, which the ordinary course of law is too defective to reach, there still remains a fourth subordinate right appertaining to every individual, namely, the right of petitioning the king, or either house of parliament, for the redress of grievances. In Russia we are told that the czar Peter established a law, that no subject might petition the throne, till he had first petitioned two different ministers of state. In case he obtained justice from neither, he might then present a third petition to the prince; but upon pain of death, if found to be in the wrong. The consequence of which was, that no one dared to offer such third petition; and grievances seldom falling under the notice of the sovereign, he had little restrained from nothing, but what would be pernicious either opportunity to redress them. The restrictions, for some there are, which are laid upon petitioning in England, are of a nature extremely different; and while they promote the spirit of peace, they are no check upon that of liberty.

5. The fifth and last auxiliary right of the subject, that I shall at present mention, is that of having arms for their defence, suitable to their condition and degree, and such as are allowed by law. Which is also declared by the same statute I W. & M. st. 2. c. 2. and is indeed a public allowance, under due restrictions, of the natural right of resistance and self-preservation, when the sanctions of society and laws are found insufficient to restrain the violence of oppression.    In these several articles consist the rights, or, as they are frequently termed, the liberties of Englishmen: liberties more generally talked of, than thoroughly understood; and yet highly necessary to be perfectly known and considered by every man of rank or property, lest his ignorance of the points whereon it is founded should hurry him into faction and licentiousness on the one hand, or a pusillanimous indifference and criminal submission on the other. And we have seen that these rights consist, primarily, in the free enjoyment of personal security. of personal liberty, and of private property. So long as these remain inviolate, the subject is perfectly free; for every species of compulsive tyranny and oppression must act in opposition to one or other of these

rights, having no other object upon which it can possibly be employed. To preserve these from violation, it is necessary that the constitution of parliaments be supported in it's full vigor; and limits certainly known, be set to the royal prerogative. And, lastly, to vindicate these rights, when actually violated or attacked, the subjects of England are entitled. In the first place, to the regular administration and free course of justice in the courts of law; next to the right of petitioning the king and parliament for redress of grievances; and lastly to the right of having and using arms for self-preservation and defence. And all these rights and liberties it is our birthright to enjoy entire; unless where the laws of our country have laid them under necessary restraints. Restraints in themselves so gentle and moderate, as will appear upon farther enquiry, that no man of sense or probity would wish to see them slackened. For all of us have it in our choice to do who hath not scrupled to profess, even in the very bosom of his native country, that the English is the only nation in the world, where political or civil liberty is the direct end of it's constitution. Recommending therefore to the student in our laws a farther and more accurate search into this extensive and important title, I shall close my remarks upon it with the expiring wish of the famous father Paul to his country, "ESTO PERPETUA!"

# EDMUND BURKE

# SPEECH ON CONCILIATION WITH THE COLONIES

22 Mar. 1775

In this character of the Americans, a love of freedom is the predominating feature which marks and distinguishes the whole: and as an ardent is always a jealous affection, your colonies become suspicious, restive, and untractable, whenever they see the least attempt to wrest from them by force, or shuffle from them by chicane, what they think the only advantage worth living for. This fierce spirit of liberty is stronger in the English colonies probably than in any other people of the earth; and this from a great variety of powerful causes; which, to understand the true temper of their minds, and the direction which this spirit takes, it will not be amiss to lay open somewhat more largely.

First, the people of the colonies are descendants of Englishmen. England, Sir, is a nation, which still I hope respects, and formerly adored, her freedom. The colonists emigrated from you when this part of your character was most predominant; and they took this bias and direction the moment they parted from your hands. They are therefore not only devoted to liberty, but to liberty according to English ideas, and on English principles. Abstract liberty, like other mere abstractions, is not to be found. Liberty inheres in some sensible object; and every nation has formed to itself some favourite point, which by way of eminence becomes the criterion of their happiness. It happened, you know, Sir, that the great contests for freedom in this country were from the earliest times chiefly upon the question of taxing. Most of the contests in the ancient commonwealths turned primarily on the right of election of magistrates; or on the balance among the several orders of the state. The question of money was not with them so immediate. But in England it was otherwise. On this point of taxes the ablest pens, and most eloquent tongues, have been exercised; the greatest spirits have acted and suffered. In order to give the fullest satisfaction concerning the importance of this point, it was not only necessary for those who in argument defended the excellence of the English constitution, to insist on this privilege of granting money as a dry point of fact, and to prove, that the right had been acknowledged in ancient parchments, and blind usages, to reside in a certain body called a House of Commons. They went much farther; they attempted to prove, and they succeeded, that in theory it ought to be so, from f the particular nature of a House of Commons, as an immediate representative of the people; whether the old records had delivered this oracle or not. They took infinite pains to inculcate, as a fundamental principle, that in all monarchies the people must in effect themselves, mediately or immediately, possess the power of granting their own money, or no shadow of liberty could subsist. The colonies draw from you, as with their life-blood, these ideas and principles. Their love of liberty, as with you, fixed and attached on this specific point of taxing. Liberty might be safe, or might be endangered, in twenty other particulars, without their being much pleased or alarmed. Here they felt its pulse; and as they found that beat, they thought themselves sick or sound. I do not say whether they were right or wrong in applying your general arguments to their own case. It is not easy indeed to make a monopoly of theorems and corollaries. The fact is, that they did thus apply those general arguments; and your mode of governing them, whether through lenity or indolence, through wisdom or mistake, confirmed them in the imagination, that they, as well as you, had an interest in these common principles.

They were further confirmed in this pleasing error by the form of their provincial legislative assemblies. Their governments are popular in a high degree; some are merely popular; in all, the popular representative is the most weighty; and this share of the people in their ordinary government never fails to inspire them with lofty sentiments, and with a strong aversion from whatever tends to deprive them of their chief importance.

If anything were wanting to this necessary operation of the form of government, religion would have given it a complete effect: Religion, always a principle of energy, in this new people is no way worn out or impaired; and their mode of professing it is also one main cause of this free spirit. The people are Protestants; and of that kind which is the most adverse to all implicit submission of mind and opinion. This is a persuasion not only favourable to liberty, but built upon it. I do not think, Sir, that the reason of this averseness in the dissenting churches, from all that looks like absolute government, is so much to be sought in their religious tenets, as in their history. Every one knows that the Roman Catholic religion is at least coeval with most of the governments where it prevails; that it has generally gone hand in hand with them, and received great favour and every kind of support from authority. The Church of England too was formed from her cradle under the nursing care of regular government. But the dissenting interests have sprung up in direct opposition to all the ordinary powers of the world; and could justify that opposition only on a strong claim to natural liberty. Their very existence depended on the powerful and unremitted assertion of that claim. All Protestantism, even the most cold and passive, is a sort of dissent. But the religion most prevalent in our northern colonies is a refinement on the principle of resistance; it is the dissidence of dissent, and the Protestantism of the Protestant religion. This religion, under a variety of denominations agreeing in nothing but in the communion of the spirit of liberty, is predominant in most of the northern provinces; where the Church of England, notwithstanding its legal rights, is in reality no more than a sort of private sect, not composing most probably the tenth of the people. The colonists left England when this spirit was high, and in the emigrants was the highest of all; and even that stream of foreigners, which has been constantly flowing into these colonies, has, for the greatest part, been composed of dissenters from the establishments of their several countries, and have brought with them a temper and character far from alien to that of the people with whom they mixed. Sir, I can perceive by their manner, that some gentlemen object to the latitude of this description; because in the southern colonies the Church of England forms a large body, and has a regular establishment. It is certainly true. There is, however, a circumstance attending these colonies, which, in my opinion, fully counterbalances this difference, and makes the spirit of liberty still more high and haughty than in those to the northward. It is, that in Virginia and the Carolinas they have a vast multitude of slaves. Where this is the case in any part of the world, those who are free, are by far the most proud and jealous of their freedom. Freedom is to them not only an enjoyment, but a kind of rank and privilege. Not seeing there, that freedom, as in countries where it is a common blessing, and as broad and general as the air, may be united with much abject toil, with great misery, with all the exterior of servitude, liberty looks, amongst them, like something that is more noble and liberal. I do not mean, Sir, to commend the superior morality of this sentiment, which has at least as much pride as virtue in it; but I cannot alter the nature of man. The fact is so; and these people of the southern colonies are much more strongly, and with a higher and more stubborn spirit, attached to liberty, than those to the northward. Such were all the ancient commonwealths; such were our Gothic ancestors; such in our days were the Poles; and such will be all masters of slaves, who are not slaves themselves. In such a people, the haughtiness of domination combines with the spirit of freedom, fortifies it, and renders it invincible.

Permit me, Sir, to add another circumstance in our colonies, which contributes no mean part towards the growth and effect of this untractable spirit. I mean their education. In no country perhaps in the world is the law so general a study. The profession itself is numerous and powerful; and in most provinces it takes the lead. The greater number of the deputies sent to the congress were lawyers. But all who read, and most do read, endeavour to obtain some smattering in that science. I have been told by an eminent bookseller, that in no branch of his business, after tracts of popular devotion, were so many books as those on the law exported to the plantations. The colonists have now fallen into the way of printing them for their own use. I hear that they have sold nearly as many of Blackstone's Commentaries in America as in England. General Gage marks out this disposition very particularly in a letter on your table. He states, that all the people in his government are lawyers, or smatterers in law; and that in Boston they have been enabled, by successful chicane, wholly to evade many parts of one of your capital penal constitutions. The smartness of debate will say, that this knowledge ought to teach them more clearly the rights of legislature, their obligations to obedience, and the penalties of rebellion. All this is mighty well. But my honourable and learned friend on the floor, who condescends to mark what I say for animadversion, will disdain that ground. He has heard, as well as I, that when great honours and great emoluments do not win over this knowledge to the service of the state, it is a formidable adversary to government. If the spirit be not tamed and broken by these happy methods, it is stubborn and litigious. *Abeunt stuolia in mores*. This study renders men acute, inquisitive, dexterous, prompt in attack, ready in defence, full of resources. In other countries, the people, more simple, and of a less mercurial cast, judge of an ill principle in government only by an actual grievance; here they antici-pate the evil, and judge of the pressure of the grievance by the badness of the principle. They augur misgovernment at a distance; and snuff the approach of tyranny in every tainted breeze. The last cause of this disobedient spirit in the colonies is hardly less powerful than the rest, as it is not merely moral, but laid deep in the natural constitution of things. Three thousand miles of ocean lie between you and them. No contrivance can prevent the effect of this distance in weakening government. Seas roll, and months pass, between the order and the execution; and the want of a speedy explanation of a single point is enough to defeat a whole system. Then, Sir, from these six capital sources; of descent, of form of government; of religion in the northern provinces; of manners in the southern; of education; of the remoteness of situation from the first mover of government; from all these causes a fierce spirit of liberty has grown up. It has grown with the growth of the people in your colonies, and increased with the increase of their wealth; a spirit, that unhappily meeting with an exercise of power in England, which, however lawful, is not reconcilable to any ideas of liberty, much less with theirs, has kindled this flame that is ready to consume us. I do not mean to commend either the spirit in this excess, or the moral causes which produce it. Perhaps a more smooth and accommodating spirit of freedom in them would be more acceptable to us. Perhaps ideas of liberty might be desired, more reconcilable with an arbitrary and boundless authority. Perhaps we might wish the colonists to be persuaded, that their liberty is more secure when held in trust for them by us (as their guardians during a perpetual minority) that with any part of it in their own hands. The question is, not whether their spirit deserves praise or blame, but what, in the name of God, shall we do with it?

For, in order to prove that the Americans have no right to their liberties, we are every day endeavoring to subvert the maxims which preserve the whole spirit of our own. To prove that the Americans ought not to be free, we are obliged to depreciate the value of freedom itself; and we never seem to gain a paltry advantage over them in debate, without attacking some of those principles, or deriding some of those feelings, for which our ancestors have shed their blood.

# RICHARD PRICE

# CIVIL LIBERTY, FREE GOVERNMENT AND SLAVERY

*Of the Value of Liberty, and the Excellence of a Free Government.*

Having shown in the preceding section what liberty is, the next question to be considered is how far it is valuable.

Nothing need be said to show the value of the three kinds of liberty which I have distinguished under the names of physical, moral, and religious liberty. They are, without doubt, the foundation of all the happiness and dignity of men, as reasonable and moral agents, and the subjects of the Deity. It is, in like manner, true of civil liberty that it is the foundation of the whole happiness and dignity of men as members of civil society and the subjects of civil government. First, it is civil liberty, or such free government as I have described, that alone can give just security against oppression. One government is better than another in proportion as it gives more of this security. It is on this account that the supreme government of the Deity is perfect. There is not a possibility of being oppressed or aggrieved by it. Subjection to it is the same with complete freedom.

Were there any men on whose superior wisdom and goodness we might absolutely depend, they could not possess too much power and the love of liberty itself would engage us to fly to them, and to put ourselves under their direction. But such are the principles that govern human nature such the weakness and folly of men, such their love of domination, selfishness, and depravity, that none of them can be raised

From Richard Price, *Observations on the Nature of Civil Liberty, the Principles of Government, and the Justice and Policy of the War with America* to an elevation above others without the utmost danger. The constant experience of the world has verified this and proved that nothing intoxicates the human mind as much as power and that men, when they have got possession of it, have seldom failed to employ it in grinding their fellow-men and gratifying the vilest passions. In the establishment, therefore, of civil government I would be preposterous to rely on the discretion of any men. If a people would obtain security against oppression, they must seek it in themselves and never part with the powers of government out of their own hands. It is there only they can be safe. A people will never oppress themselves or invade their own rights. But if they trust the arbitrary will of any body or succession of men they trust enemies and it may be depended on that the worst evils will follow.

It follows from hence that a free government is the only government which is consistent with the ends of government. Men combine into communities and institute government to obtain the peaceable enjoyment of their rights and to defend themselves against injustice and violence. And when they endeavour to secure these ends by such a free government as I have described, improved by such arrangements as may have a tendency to preserve it from confusion, and to concentrate in it as much as possible of the wisdom and force of the community, in this case, it is a most rational and important institution. But when the contrary is done and the benefit of government are sought by establishing a government of men, and not of laws made with common consent, it becomes a most absurd institution. It is seeking a remedy for oppression in one quarter by establishing it in another and avoiding the outrages of little plunderers by constituting a set of great plunderers. It is, in short, the folly of giving up liberty in order to maintain liberty and, in the very act of endeavouring to secure the most valuable rights, to arm a body of enemies with power to destroy them.

I can easily believe that mankind, in the first and rude state of society might act thus irrationally. Absolute governments, being the simplest forms of government, might be the first that were established. A people having experienced the happy effects of the wisdom or the valour of particular men, might be led to trust them with unlimited power as their rulers and legislators. But they would soon find reason to repent. And the time, I hope may come when mankind in general, taught by long and dear experience, and weary of the abuses of power under slavish governments, will learn to detest them, and never to give up that self-government which, whether we consider men in their private or collective capacities, is the first of all the blessings they can possess. Again, free governments are the only governments which will give scope to the exertion of the powers of men and are favourable to their improvement. The members of free states, knowing their rights to be secure, and that they shall enjoy without molestation the fruits of every acquisition they can make, are encouraged and incited to industry. Being at liberty to push their researches as far as they call into all subjects and to guide themselves by their own judgments in all their religious and civil concerns, while they allow others to do the same, error and superstition must lose ground. Conscious of being their own governors, bound to obey no laws except such as they have given their consent to, and subject to no control from the arbitrary will of any of their fellow citizens, they possess an elevation and force of mind which must make them great and happy. How different is the situation of the vassals of despotic power. Like cattle insured to the yoke, they are driven on in one track, afraid of speaking or even thinking on the most interesting points, looking up continually to a poor creature who is their master, their powers fettered, and some of the noblest springs of action in human nature rendered useless within them. There is nothing indeed more humiliating than that debasement of mankind which takes place in such situations.

It has been observed of free governments that they are often torn by violent contests which render them dreadful scenes of distress and anarchy. But it ought to be considered that this has not been owing, to the nature of such governments but to their having been ill-modelled and lacking those arrangements and supplemental checks which are necessary to constitute a wise form of government. There is no reason to doubt but that free governments may be so contrived as to exclude the greatest part of the struggles and tumults which are arisen in free states and, as far as they cannot be excluded, they will do more good than harm. They will occasion the display of powers and produce exertions which can never be seen in the still scenes of life. They are the active efforts of health and vigour and always tend to preserve and purify. Whereas, on the contrary, the quiet which prevails under slavish governments, and which may seem to be a recommendation of them, proceeds from an ignominious tameness and stagnation of the human faculties. It is the same with the stillness of midnight or the silence and torpor of death.

Further, free governments are the only governments which are consistent with the natural equality of mankind. This is a principle which, in my opinion, has been assumed, with the greatest reason, by some of the best writers on government. But the meaning of it is not that all the subordinations in human life owe their existence to the institution of civil government. The superiorities and distinctions arising from the relation of parents to their children, from the differences in the personal qualities and abilities of men, and from servitudes founded on voluntary compact must have existed in a state of nature, and would now take place were all men so virtuous as to leave no occasion for civil government. The maxim, therefore, "that all men are naturally equal," refers to their state when grown up to maturity and become independent agents, capable of acquiring property, and of directing their own conduct. And the sense of it is that no one of them is constituted by the author of nature the vassal or subject of another or has any right to give law to him or, without his consent, to take away any part of his property or to abridge him of his liberty. In a state of nature one man may have received benefits from another; and this would lay the person obliged under an obligation of gratitude, but it would not make his benefactor his master or give him a right to judge for him what grateful returns he ought to make and to extoll these from him. In a state of nature, also, one may possess more strength, or more knowledge or more property than another, and this would give him weight and influence but it would not give him ally degree of authority. There would not be one human being who would be bound to obey him. A person, likewise in a state of nature, might let out his labour or give up to another, on certain stipulated terms, the direction of his conduct, ;and this would so far bring him into the station of a servant; but being done by himself, and on such terms only as he chooses to consent to, it is an *instance* of his liberty; and he will always have it in his power to quit the service he has chosen or to enter into another.

This equality or independence of men is one of their essential rights. It is the same with that equality or independence which now actually takes place among the different states or kingdoms of the world with respect to one another. "Mankind came with this right from the hands of their Maker." But all governments which are not free are totally inconsistent with it. They imply that there are some of mankind who are born with, an inherent right of dominion and that the rest are born under an obligation to subjection, and that civil government, instead of being founded on any compact, is nothing but the exercise of this right. Some such sentiments seem to be now reviving in this country and even to be growing, fashionable. Most of the writers against the *Observations on Civil Liberty* argue on the supposition of a right in the few to govern the many independently of their own choice. Some of these writers have gone so far as to assert, in plain Language, that civil governors derive their power immediately from the Deity and are his agents or representatives, accountable to him only. And one courtly writer, in particular, has honoured them with the appellation of *our political gods*. Probably this is the idea of civil governors entertained by the author of the *Remarks on the Acts of the Thirteenth Parliament of Great Britain*, for it is not easy to imagine on what other ground he can assert that property and civil rights are derived from civil governors and their gifts to mankind.

If these sentiments are just, civil governors are indeed an awful order of beings; and it becomes us to enquire with anxiety who they are and how we may distinguish them from the rest of mankind. Shall we take for such all, whether men or women, whom we find in actual possession of civil power, whatever may be their characters or however they may have acquired their power? This is too extravagant to be asserted. It would legalize the *American* Congress. There must then be some pretenders among civil governors and it is necessary we should know how to discover them. It is incredible that the Deity should not have made this easy to us by some particular marks and distinctions which point out to our notice his real viceregents, just as he has pointed out man, by his figures and superior powers, to be the governor of the lower creatures. In particular, these persons must be possessed of wisdom and goodness superior to those of the rest of mankind for, without this, a grant of the powers they are supposed *to* possess would be nothing but a grant of power to injure and oppress without remedy and without bounds. But this is a test by which they cannot be tried. It would leave but few of them in possession of the places they hold and the rights they claim. It is not in the high ranks of life or among the great and mighty that we are to seek wisdom and goodness. These love the shade and fly from observation. They are to be found chiefly in the middle ranks of life and among the contemplative and philosophical who decline pubic employments and look down with  pity on the scramble for power among mankind and the restlessness and misery of ambition. It *is* proper to add that it has never been hitherto understood that any superiority in intellectual and moral qualifications lays the foundation of a claim to dominion.

It *is* not then, by their superior endowments, that the Deity intended to point out to us the few whom he has destined to command the many. But in what other manner could they be distinguished? Must we embrace Sir Robert Filmer's patriarchal scheme? One would have thought that Mr. Locke has said more than enough to expose this stupid scheme. One of my opponents, however, has adopted it; and the necessary inference from it is that, as there is but now one lineal descendent from Adam's eldest son, there can be but one rightful monarch of the world. But I will not abuse my reader's patience by saying more on this subject. I am sorry that in this country there should be any occasion for taking notice of principles so absurd and at the same time so pernicious. I say *pernicious* for they imply that King James the Second was deposed at the Revolution unlawfully and impiously, that the present King is an usurper, and that the present government, being derived from rebellion and treason, has no right to our allegiance.

Without all doubt, it is the choice of the people that makes civil governors. The people are the spring of all civil power, and they have a right to modify it as they please.

Mankind being naturally equal according to the foregoing explanation, civil government, in its genuine intention, is an institution for maintaining that equality by defending it against the encroachments of violence and tyranny. All the subordinations and distinctions in society previous to its establishment, it leaves as it found them, only confirming and protecting them. It makes no man master of another. It elevates no person above his fellow citizens. On the contrary, it levels all by fixing all in a state of subjection to one common authority. The authority of the laws. The will of the community. Taxes are given, not imposed. Laws are regulations of common choice, not injunctions of superior power. The authority of magistrates is the authority of the state, and their salaries are wages paid by the state for executing its will and doing its business. They do not govern the state. It is the state governs them and, had they just ideas of their own stations, they would consider themselves as no less properly servants of the public than the labourers who work upon its roads or the soldiers who fight its battles. A king, in particular, is only the first executive officer, the creature of the law, and as much accountable and subject to the law as the meanest peasant. And were kings properly attentive to their duty, and as anxious as they should be about performing it, they could not easily avoid sinking under the weight of their charge.

# PART II

*"Every spot of the world is overrun with oppression. Freedom hath been hunted around the globe. Asia and Africa have long expelled her. Europe regards her like a stranger, and England hath given her warning to depart. O receive the fugitive, and prepare in time an assylum for mankind."*

—Thomas Paine
*Common Sense*

# AMERICAN CONCEPTIONS OF LIBERTY IN THE REVOLUTIONARY ERA

The issue of liberty galvanized the American colonists like none other as the Revolution approached. What was earlier a philosophical debate over the nature of liberty and government now took an urgent turn. The burning issues of economic and political freedom impacted on the lives of the colonists all the more heavily, in face of the acts of a distant parliament in London. Indeed viewed as oppressive, these enactments included the imposition of taxation, including the notorious Stamp Act of 1764, and a variety of other trade restrictions designed to dampen economic competition in the new world. Most notably, however, such burdens were enacted without the representative voice of the colonists themselves in Parliament.

Other objections to parliamentary acts, represented in these selections, involve the tenure of appointed judges at the pleasure of the crown, the right to self-government itself, slavery and religious freedom. And we hear in these writings both an echo of the past, the rich and ancient heritage of Anglo-American liberty, and a strong foreward projection of those values that would shape the new order, a written constitution and a Bill of Rights.

In a piece by Joseph Galloway [though of uncertain authorship], we see espoused the strong conviction of the necessity of an independent judiciary. The security of impartial laws, administered by fair and impartial judges beholden to no higher authority but that of the law itself, was considered as among the most vital rights of all Englishmen. Only the fair and impartial administration of the laws could secure for them the adequate protections of their liberties and properties. They regarded their rights to property and security as among the most ancient of liberties afforded to any freeborn Englishman on either side of the Atlantic. Judges who must depend upon the pleasure and political authority of another are thereby hindered in the enforcement of the very fundamental rights they are charged to protect. That our early ministers of justice had to serve at the pleasure of kings and governors soon became an issue of contention in the Anglo-American struggle. Our framers and founders simply felt that human nature and liberty itself are too frail to withstand the onslaughts of power and prerogative upon the independence of our courts.

Thomas Fitch wrote of a most central issue in the Anglo-American struggle and American concept of liberty at the time of the Revolution. It is indeed one that echoes down through the centuries to this day: taxation without representation. The issue was governed fundamentally by the conviction that no government can properly rule over a free people with laws passed and imposed without their consent. Popular consent, through representatives assembled in parliament or legislature, was the key principle here. That no law could issue forth or be repealed, no burden imposed upon the people without their consent or that of their representatives assembled, was the paramount concern. Fitch and others reasoned forth from the basic premise that this and other natural rights attach to all Englishmen everywhere. They carried their rights with them across the Atlantic; they did not shed them upon reaching the shores of a new land. It was the conviction among the colonists, moreover, that they could not truly and substantially enjoy their rights without the authority to legislate laws for themselves.

American colonists felt some additional pride and support in their belief thay they did, in effect, *earn* their right to self-government and the preservation of their ancient liberties. They felt so in view of a century and more of loyalty and obedience in service to the crown, as pioneering settlers and civilizers of a new and an untamed land. By an appeal to the precedents of the common law and a deep sense of the nature of their enterprise in the new world, our early American forefathers made their case for liberty. They had but to appeal to the authority of tradition itself, to the sanctity it gave to old rights even in a new land and a new world.

The early Americans talked a good deal about what we would today refer to as natural law. Natural law includes natural rights. These include the most fundamental rights and freedoms that we have always enjoyed under the federal Constitution. As originally understood, however, such "natural" rights were seen as so basic and fundamental that no legislative body could grant or deny them. Because such rights naturally attach to every man by virtue of his or her humanity, not even a written constitution could grant or take back these basic freedoms. Such was indeed the view of James Otis, a lawyer who asserted that individual natural rights arise out of nature. They do not somehow vanish when individuals come together in forming a civil society. *All* men and women are freeborn by nature. This includes Afro-Americans no less than white Europeans, Christians no less than Jews, Muslims and Bhuddists, and, of course, colonial subjects no less than natural born Englishmen. The laws of God and nature thus afford an equality of liberty for all, are of universal application, and remain unalterable by the laws of man.

Query: Just what is the *philosophical* origin of American liberty and the idea that it must be equally afforded to all freeborn persons? Whence comes it and what is its proper sense and application? Ought such basic liberties to be conceived as equal to those enjoyed by a free and sovereign people, as were natural-born Englishmen in the mother country itself?

History teaches us, as Stephen Hopkins points out, that the inhabitants of the Greek and Roman colonies enjoyed their rights and liberties on full equality with those of their mother countries. Recognized rights and liberties were of equally good currency in the most remote corners of the empire. American British subjects should, therefore,be able to claim the very same rights to possess property and to enjoy their liberties as their English brethren accross the sea. Indeed at this time, the British were among the most renown and tenacious of their liberties of any peoples on the face of the earth. Thus along with Locke, Otis, Jefferson and others, Hopkins considered the basic rights to life, liberty and property as natural rights indeed, as the inherent and "inalienable" rights of man. These are the birthrights of every freeborn human being; they are not subject to the grace of a monarch or denial by a legislative body. Such a hallowed conception translated into some rather specific and concrete demands by the colonists in their relations with the mother land. Among these demands were those of what we might call political due process. Hopkins recognized the necessity of general laws, of acts and regulations enacted for the good of all. These might include external trade restrictions on the high seas no less than internal, domestic regulations affecting trade. It was contended, however, that the colonists did have a crucial right to be heard through their own representatives in Parliament. As evidenced in the Stamp Act, the Sugar Act and several other such restrictions, Parliament imposed these burdens in restraint of trade without affording notice to or the opportunity of a hearing for those who would sustain the burden of their enactments. The power of a representative body must not exceed that of its constituents, on this view, and it must assuredly not act without their consent.

It was the deep and abiding thought of the early Americans that one who is bound to the will and whims of another is little more than an abject slave to the other. However wise the master, however benevolent the king or his agents, the fact remains that the servant is without property and liberty in its use and enjoyment. With a long record of loyal obedience to the crown, the revolutionary generation of Americans felt all the more justified in the assertion of their rights and liberties. They "carried" their rights along with them in coming to the new world. They had not forfeited any of them in crossing the sea to settle on these shores. And they possessed the strength and resolve to exercise those rights in the vast new continent that lay before them.

Benjamin Rush was a Philadelphia physician who spoke even more specifically to the issue of slavery in America. The very idea of slavery, he writes, is an assault to the human understanding and the dignity of man. It is essentially a foreign idea and one that is innately alien to the Anglo-American conscience and tradition. As an institution in practice in the colonies, it amounts to an outrage. Indeed it is an outrage against human nature itself, a nature which evidences no mark of inferiority as among the races of mankind. There is moreover, as Hopkins argues, no support to be found in scripture for the practice of slavery. Slave labor is essentially stolen labor, stolen from those entitled by nature to the fruits of their labor and to freedom itself. It is as such the "peculiar institution", one that divides and degrades the community of freeborn humanity. It was an institution which, as Hopkins points out, had destroyed the lives and liberties of countless negroes in America. It should thus have no place in the new nation, conceived in liberty and equality.

We know, of course, than America had to wait a century more before the legal abolition of slavery, and this only after a bloody civil war. We can see in our Thirteenth Amendment, enacted after the Civil

War, a flat prohibition of involuntary servitude accross the board. It is broadly applicable to all sectors of public and private life in the United States today.

Alexander Hamilton lends further support to the natural rights idea of liberty so prevalent among the early Americans. Natural law, as properly conceived, is eternal and unchangeable. It is indeed "obligatory upon all mankind", more binding than the mere "parchment barriers" of charters, constitutions and even bills of rights. No man-made law could be valid, even a written constitution, if it contradicts the natural law and the natural rights of mankind to life, liberty and property. This is again consistent with the viewpoints taken in earlier writings and with traditional conceptions of right in the common laws of England. For Hamilton, however, a proponent of a strong central government, it is the very purpose of government to protect and preserve such fundamental rights. This includes, of course, the constitutional right to free self-government, and self-government among a free people could only be effective if it were strong.

Among the most eloquent and moving pieces ever written in behalf of liberty is that of Thomas Paine's *Common Sense*. Paine echoes the convictions of Locke in his conception of limited government, charged with the specific obligation of protecting the few fundamental rights afforded to all human beings. In the absence of perfection and universal virtue among mankind, however, the necessary evil of government must exist to secure those precious liberties that are the birthright of each. Paine does place great faith, however, in the wisdom of the people who, through their elected and representative bodies, would serve as an effective check against the tyranny of a king. As kings and hereditary rule are the bane of all mankind for Paine, we needed merely a pure and strong republican form of government to foreclose the possibility of tyranny by an executive head. The reader will judge whether Paine's faith in popular wisdom and restraint could ever have been quite adequate in the absence of an equally strong executive officer and an independent judiciary.

It is the thought thus evidenced in these early writings that galvanized the revolutionary generations of early America. Concepts of liberty, of enormous motivating power, thus paved the way for the great national discussion and debates to follow. It remained only to win their independence, to fight the war, to forge a new government worthy of a free people and a sovereign nation. It remained to draft the blueprint, to write the federal Constitution that would meld together a loose confederation of states in the common cause of freedom and nationhood. It was indeed a momentous time, an era that called for nothing less than a new charter of liberty: a federal constitution and a Bill of Rights.

# JOSEPH GALLOWAY

# LETTER TO THE PEOPLE OF PENNSYLVANIA, &c.

*WHOEVER* has made himself acquainted with ancient history and looked into the original design of government will find that one of its chief and principal ends was to secure the persons and properties of mankind from private injuries and domestic oppression.*

In forming a plan of government completely to answer these excellent purposes, the fundamental laws and rules of the constitution, which ought never to be infringed, should be made alike distributive of justice and equity, and equally calculated to preserve the sovereign's prerogative and the people's liberties. But power and liberty ever being *opponents,* should the work stop here the constitution would bear a near analogy to a ship without rudder, rigging, or sails, utterly incapable of answering the end of its construction. For though the wisest and best laws were enacted to fix the bounds of power and liberty, yet without a due care in constituting persons impartially to execute them, the former by its influence and encroachments on liberty would soon become tyranny, and the latter by the like extent of its limits might possibly degenerate into licentiousness. In both cases, the condition of mankind would be little mended, scarcely better than in their original state of nature and confusion, before any civil polity was agreed upon.

The men therefore who are to settle the contests between prerogative and liberty, who are to ascertain the bounds of sovereign power and to determine the rights of the subject, ought certainly to be perfectly

---

*This piece, of uncertain authorship, was possibly written by Joseph Galloway in 1760, and appears in Bernard Bailyn's *Pamphlets of the American Revolution:* 1750-1776 (Harvard University Press, 1965).

free from the influence of either. But more especially of the former, as history plainly evinces that it is but too apt to prevail over the ministers of justice by its natural weight and authority, notwithstanding the wisest precautions have been used to prevent it.

The necessity of this independent state of justice is rendered apparent by the slightest consideration of human frailty. Consider men as they really are, attended with innumerable foibles and imperfections, ever liable to err, and you will find but very few who are so obstinately just as to be proof against the enticing baits of honor and interest. The love of promotion and private advantage are passions almost universal, and admit of the most dangerous extremes. The one in excess generally produces the most servile obedience, the other, intolerable avarice and a base dereliction of virtue. That which we love and engages our attention we are ever ready to purchase at any *price*. Thus an inordinate lover of promotion, sooner than part with it, would surrender up his regard for justice, his duty to his country and to his GOD for its preservation. And the avaricious man, sooner than lose his pelf, would part with his honor, his reputation, I had almost said his life. And such is the influence of this dread of parting with that which we esteem, whatever it be, that it so effectually chains down the powers of the human soul that it cannot be said to enjoy freedom of judgment, scarcely freedom of thought.

Of this truth the abject promises and servile conduct of the great Lord *Bacon* exhibit an irrefragable proof. It was but rational to think that a man of his extensive abilities and capacious soul, that could comprehend all the beauties of rectitude and justice at a view, would at least preserve in his public station an independent and unperverted judgment. And yet his virtue fell a victim to his love of promotion. He begged for preferment with the same low servility that the necessitous pauper would beg for daily bread. His promise to the King in order to obtain the chancellor's place was "That when a direction was once given, it should be pursued and performed." And when he succeeded in his wishes, his conduct with respect to the court and its arbitrary measures showed that he strictly fulfilled his engagement.

Whoever has read the form of a commission *during pleasure* and considered its limitations must certainly be surprised that a generous mind would accept of a tenure so servile and so incompatible with the very nature of justice. He can be but a *tenant at will* of a grantor at best, and for the most part of an attorney general, or perhaps some other favorite in the several counties. The terms of tenure are *until our further will and pleasure shall be made known,* which by a natural construction, if we may call reason and experience to our aid, is no longer than you gratify us, our favorites and creatures, in your determinations, let our *will and pleasure* therein be ever so illegal, ever so partial and unjust.

That some men of independent circumstances, happy in the possession of virtue, have accepted of those commissions and acted uprightly I will not pretend to dispute. They are remarkable instances of public integrity, and merit the highest commendation. They are among mankind as a comet among the stars, rarely to be seen. But generally to look for strict impartiality and a pure administration of justice, to expect that power should be confined within its legal limits and right and justice done to the subject by men who are dependent, is to ridicule all laws against bribery and corruption, and to say that human nature is insensible of the love or above the lure of honor, interest, or promotion.

With what freedom and justness do the modern writers of a certain great nation complain against the multiplicity of ministerial officers who hold their commissions *during pleasure;* and what renders that freedom so justifiable and those complaints so just but the misfortunes the nation has suffered by the weight these *creatures* have thrown into the scale of power by paying an implicit obedience to its commands and a devoted adherence to its measures. If, then, such are the dangerous effects of a dependency in the ministerial officers whose conduct is circumscribed by positive laws and checked by the superior courts of justice, how much more so must a dependency of the judicial officers be where everything is left in the power and to the discretion of the judge on whose breath the security of all property and the liberty of the people depend? Must it not produce more dangerous consequences? Will it not bring on inevitable ruin?

But further to illustrate the necessity of an independent state of justice in every community where the security of property and the happiness of mankind is the object of its *polity,* numerous instances might be adduced from the histories of *Europe* in which it has been the principal policy of the most arbitrary princes who have conceived a design of quelling the spirit of liberty and enslaving their subjects to their *will and pleasure to* draw over to their party the ministers of the law. By this means, having effectually superseded the execution of the laws and subdued the power which alone could check a tyrannical exercise of prerogative, they have let loose every instrument of oppression and left nothing in the community able to oppose the torrent. Attempts of this kind have frequently succeeded, and sometimes in reigns when the judges have been as independent as the law could make them. If so, how much more easily is this policy pursued and executed when the judges hold their offices on the servile tenure of *during pleasure*.

Without wandering into foreign history, a few examples from that of our mother country and our own province will best suit my purpose, as they are more familiar and adapted to your circumstances.

By this kind of policy, RICHARD II broke over every barrier of law and prostrated the fence which the wisdom of ages had planted round the constitution.

The opinion subscribed by all the judges in *England* touching the commission for inspecting the public revenues of the same reign is an evincing evidence of this truth. The Parliament, observing the immense profusion of the public treasure by the ministers of RICHARD, the great want of economy in his household, a number of pensions granted to his creatures, his numerous favorites grown rich amidst a national penury and distress, saw the necessity of an inquiry into and reformation of these abuses, and appointed a committee of eleven noblemen for that purpose whose authority was confirmed by an act of Parliament. But this being inconsistent with the King's arbitrary plan, he no sooner received the supplies but in a most solemn manner he protested against it, and pursued every measure in his power to enslave the nation. His detestable scheme was to intimidate and corrupt the several sheriffs to return a packed Parliament of his own tools; the city of *London* was to furnish him with men and money, and the judges of the courts were to *pervert the laws* and sacrifice the *rights of the nation*.

But he failed in all his reliances, save on the prostituted judges: the sheriffs informed him that the people would never give up that *most valuable privilege*, the *freedom of elections*. The city of *London* excused herself from acting her part in the horrid scene. But the judges, overawed and corrupted, justified all his measures. In the opinion I have mentioned above, they declared that the commission and statute aforesaid were derogatory to the King's prerogative; that the persons who moved for them procured or prevailed on His Majesty to assent to them should be punished with *death;* that the King in all matters to be treated of in Parliament had a right to *direct and command* from the beginning to the end thereof; that if they acted contrary to the King's *pleasure* made known therein, they were to be punished as traitors; that he could whenever he pleased remove any of his judges and officers, and *justify* or punish them for their offenses; and that the Lords and Commons could not impeach them for any of their crimes; with many other things equally subversive of the laws of the land and the very being of the constitution. An opinion so evidently infamous and servile that it cannot call for the least remark. I shall therefore only observe that *Belknap,* Chief Justice, after he had signed it, not being resolute enough to be steady nor so vicious as to want remorse for violating his oath, the cause of truth, and his country, declared "that he wanted nothing but a hurdle, a horse, and a halter to bring him to the death he deserved."

The same plan of policy was pursued by CHARLES I. He removed Sir *Robert Heath,* Lord Chief Justice, from his office because he could not approve of and justify his conduct, and Sir *John Finch,* a most abject tool of the court became his successor.

Thus by removing *at his pleasure* men of virtue and integrity from the courts of law and placing in their stead such as would serve his arbitrary purposes, he procured a set of judges entirely devoted to his will. Under the sanction of their opinion, he issued forth his proclamations, and enforced an obedience to them as the fundamental laws of the land; while those very laws, by which not public and private property only but the very existence of the constitution itself was preserved, were dispensed with. So far did he carry this policy that it was common for the secretaries of state to send letters to the judges to lay aside the laws against papists, while the persons that dared to disobey his arbitrary proclamations were proceeded against with more rigor than if they had violated the fundamental laws of the kingdom.

The same measure was taken to justify and support that infamous violation of the subject's right, the imposition of ship money. The judges were first closeted, flattered, threatened, and intimidated, until they were prevailed on to subscribe to all opinions directly inconsistent with the laws of the land and the liberties of the nation.

No *Englishman* can ever forget the unheard of barbarities committed by Judge *Jeffreys,* that murdering instrument of the court of James II.

Nor will that successful attempt of the same King to procure a set of judges that should determine not according to law but his tyrannical directions ever to be effaced from the minds of *Britons.* He first closeted them agreeable to the example of his predecessor CHARLES, and would have made an express bargain with them *that they should continue in their commissions, provided they would maintain his pretended prerogative of dispensing with penal laws.* But four of them discovered great dissatisfaction at the proposal, and particularly Sir *Thomas Jones* plainly told him "He would not do what he required of him." His Majesty answered, "He would have twelve judges of his own opinion." Sir *Thomas* replied, "Twelve judges, Sir, you may possibly find, but not twelve lawyers." But to convince him of his mistake, the King in a few days appointed four such *creatures* from the bar, in the room of the four worthy judges, as effectually answered his purpose; and eleven out of twelve confirmed, as far as their opinions could confirm, his illegal power of dispensing with the laws of their country?

Many other instances of this nature might be brought from the history of your forefathers to demonstrate the necessity of creating the office of a judge *independent of power;* and to show that an increase of prerogative, a perversion of the laws, a suspension of your natural rights, and a violation of the fundamentals of an *English* constitution have often been effected by this kind of policy, this undue and *illegal influence* on the courts of justice.

Thus it is evident of justice, from the slightest consideration of the frailty of human nature, and from ancient modern observation that your rights and properties have been utterly insecure while your judges have been under the influence of and subject to the pleasure of your rulers, and that your welfare and happiness have been merely ideal when the laws of the land, those impregnable bulwarks of your safety, have either been suspended or not executed.

Having shown you that a security of your rights and properties was the chief end of your entering into society, and that that security cannot be obtained without an independent and uninfluenced judicature, it becomes an indispensable duty to take some pains to convince you that this *security is* your undoubted privilege as *Englishmen,* of which you cannot be divested without violence to your ancient rights and the principles of an *English* government.

To trace this important privilege to its original source, it will be necessary to follow me back; to the first dawn of the present constitution of *England,* there to learn the precarious situation of property and the wise remedy that was framed to give it a permanent security.

Before the time of the great ALFRED, that wise founder of the

*English* government, the care of the several counties was committed to the nobility. They acted in a double capacity, as leaders of the troops and judges of the people's properties; and, being frequently absent on military duty, they were obliged to leave the administration of their civil affairs to prefects or deputies who, holding their authority during the pleasure of the lords, and the lords being the *creatures* and *dependents* of the crown, in all their determinations paid a devoted obedience to the *directions of their superiors* and the voice of prerogative, while the execution of the laws and the rights of the subject were the least of their concern. The nation at this time had property, but no safety in the enjoyment. They had some degree of liberty, but held it as *tenants at will* of the crown, of the nobility, or their favorites; they had laws, but no protection from the hostile hand of the domestic oppressor. In this unfortunate and desponding situation did the great father of public virtue find liberty and property — the two principal objects of all good laws. A generous compassion for the distressed state of the nation induced him to alter the constitution wherever he found it inconsistent with the welfare and happiness of his people. The *security of property,* without which private felicity is a mere chimera, engrossed his chief attention. He was the author of the excellent institution of trials by jurors, that solid pillar of *English* liberty. He altered the former dependent state of justice by appointing and commissionating judges as *independent of the crown* that they might ever after remain free from its influence and deaf to every solicitation but the convictions of truth. He did not, perhaps, like our modern politicians, see no advantage in an impartial administration of justice, but well knew from late experience that justice must be a stranger to the land whose form of government could not ensure safety to the liberties and properties of the people.

The office of a judge being thus wisely established, numerous instances might be drawn from the *English* history to demonstrate that the ministers of justice were not removable at *the pleasure of the crown.*

EDWARD I, a prince remarkable for his excellent schemes of distributive justice, and as cautious as the good ALFRED lest his prerogative should oppress the law, was determined to purge the civil polity from the gross pollutions it had contracted from former reigns. But before he could displace a set of the most venal and corrupted judges, he was under a necessity from the *nature* of their commissions to impeach them before the nobility and convict them of their offenses.

In the arbitrary reign of JAMES I, Lord Chief Justice *Coke,* who at that time had become very odious to the King by a virtuous opposition to his measures and had also incurred the public indignation by his extreme avarice, was convicted of one of the most trifling articles exhibited against him, on his own confession, which served *as a pretense* for the removing him from his offices.

Agreeable to this excellent policy of the common law, ever since the latter end of the eighth century the judges have held their commissions *during their good behavior,* a few instances to the contrary made by the encroachments of power excepted: even in the most arbitrary reigns of CHARLES and JAMES II, the judges were commissionated in this legal and constitutional form, reigns in which power had so great an ascendancy that had it not been consistent with the ancient common law and the usage and custom of ages, the rights of the nation had not met with so great a favor. The forms of the commissions of Sir *Robert Hyde* and Sir *Robert Forster,* who held them *during good behavior,* are to be seen in the reports of CHARLES'S reign. And Sir *Robert Archer,* sometime before having unjustly incurred the displeasure of CHARLES, received it supersedes to his commission as one of the judges, but with virtuous resolution he refused to surrender his patent without a trial, and continued in his office during his life.

The next thing worthy of your attention is how far this invaluable policy, so often suspended by arbitrary power, was restored and confirmed by your predecessors, the first settlers of this province. They had drank of the bitter cup of despotic authority; they had suffered the mischiefs of perverted law; they had seen their liberties both civil and religious bend under its weight; they resolved therefore to seek a more hospitable country, but would not venture their lives and estates in this *desert* land without some security against any encroachment on this *in estimable part* of their mother constitution. They wisely foresaw great danger of an invasion thereof in a province where an immense quantity of *property was to* attend a large extent of *power,* where the same person who was to enjoy the powers of government was likewise to be an *universal landlord* possessed of many millions of acres with all their increasing advantages and emoluments; that this property at the same time it produced contests would create power and influence, and if those contests were to be decided, though not immediately by the proprietary himself yet mediately by his deputies whose dignity, office, and estate depended on his breath, their conditions and circumstances by their removal would be rendered worse, and the safety of their persons and properties more precarious. It was therefore expressly stipulated and solemnly covenanted by *William Penn* with the first adventurers before their departure from their native country, that "He would nominate and appoint such persons for *judges,* treasurers, masters of the rolls, sheriffs, justices, as were most fitly qualified for those employments; to whom he would make and grant commissions for the said offices respectively, to hold them for so long time as every such person should *well behave himself* in the office or place to him respectively granted, and no longer."

Thus secured, as they thought, in the enjoyment of their liberties and estates, they surrendered up every social connection of their native land under the vain expectation of enjoying this privilege agreed on before their departure. But how righteously this fundamental rule of your constitution has been observed, the late dependent state of your magistracy (whose commissions have been granted during the *governor's pleasure),* the partiality and favor that have been shown to a favorite attorney to whose influence they have been shown for their offices and whose will their continuance therein depended, the many instances of men of integrity being displaced from the Seat of justice because of their virtuous opposition to the measures of power, and the partial distribution of offices to creatures and tools, are so many incontestable testimonies of a manifest breach of public faith with your predecessors and you their posterity.

If your ancestors here were not wanting in their endeavors to secure you from the mischiefs of perverted law and to transmit to you an upright administration of justice, the Parliament of your mother country have not been less careful in this respect. At the time of the happy Revolution, that famous opportunity of overcoming the usurpations of former reigns and restoring the constitution to its ancient freedom, many of the national rights were revived and confirmed by the *Bill of Rights.* And yet, such was the haste and zeal of the Parliament to settle the essentials of the present government that many important matters were neglected, among which may be accounted a restitution of the courts of judicature to their ancient *independency.* But this error was not long undiscovered. The Parliament called to mind the mischiefs the nation had suffered in the slavish opinion of the judges in the case of ship money; the arbitrary removal of Justices *Powell* and *Holloway* for acting consistent with their oaths and consciences in the

case of the five bishops; they remembered that such was the influence
of JAMES II with the judges whom he commissioned *during his
pleasure* that juries were packed, the subject held to excessive bail, the
laws of liberty violated and dispensed with, expensive fines imposed,
cruel punishments inflicted, the spirit of liberty worn out, and many
innocents condemned. Without the spirit of divination, they plainly
foresaw that the same train of fatal consequences must attend the
liberties of the nation should their judges remain subject to the same
influence. They therefore, as soon as it became necessary to make a
farther limitation of the succession of the crown in the Protestant line,
gladly embraced the happy opportunity of rectifying former mistakes
and of making a further security for the ancient rights and liberties of
the subject. They resolved that the *one* should go hand in hand with the
*other*. And by the act which settled the further limitation of the crown,
it is, among other things, expressly declared that the judges' commissions shall be made as long *as they should behave themselves well in
their offices,* and their salaries shall be ascertained and established.

Here it is worthy your information, *first,* that the rights and
liberties claimed and declared by the Bill of Rights, that second Magna
Carta, and the Act of Settlement created no innovation of the ancient
constitution. The Parliament had no design to change but only to restore
the ancient laws and customs of the realm, which were the true and
indubitable rights and liberties of the people of England. This appears
as well from the Bill of Rights and the resolves which preceded the Act
of Settlement as from the act itself. From whence it follows that this
right of the people to have their judges indifferent men and independent
of the crown is not of a late date but part of the ancient constitution of
your government and inseparably inherent in the persons of every
freeborn Englishman; and that the granting commissions to the judges
during pleasure was then esteemed by the Parliament and truly was an
arbitrary and illegal violation of the people's ancient liberties.

SECONDLY, that those excellent laws were *intended to extend,*
and actually do extend, to all the King's subjects in *America.* That their
faith and allegiance are bound by them to the present most *excellent*
royal family, and of course that they are entitled to the rights and
liberties therein claimed, asserted, and confirmed. And yet your former
governors, as if they had been determined to revive and pursue the
wicked policy of those arbitrary reigns I have mentioned, and to throw
aside the worthy example of his present most gracious Majesty, have

acted as if those excellent laws were not to be executed, and the example of their sovereign unworthy of influencing their conduct. They have granted all the commissions of the judges *during their will and pleasure,* and like CHARLES and JAMES have occasionally removed such as dared oppose their arbitrary designs, and filled up their places with others who would ratify and support their measures, however unjust and illegal.

This being the case, what censure and blame would your representatives have merited had they not seized the first opportunity of rendering your *courts and judges independent.* An opportunity ordered; they passed a law limiting the number of judges, which before was unlimited, and left it in the power of a bad governor to create as many dependents as his measures should call for. It directs that the judges of the Supreme Court and Common Pleas shall hold their commissions during *their good behavior;* which before have often depended on the nod of a governor or an attorney general. And it ordains that the judges of the Common Pleas shall hold the orphans court; that in no instance your properties exceeding the value of , £5 should be determined by men *dependent* on power or its advocates; and the ministers of justice, who ought to be the ministers of your protection, may not be prevailed on either to pervert your laws or to give up your rights.

A law so full of advantages to the people one would imagine could not have an enemy; and yet we find there is nothing so virtuous but the enemies of virtue will decry. The principal objection against this law is that "It brings a great expense on the counties without any benefit accruing from it." Let us inquire what mighty burden will attend it in the county of *Philadelphia,* where the expense will be greatest. The judges have never sat above *five* days in the quarter at most, which, at *twenty shillings* per day, will amount to *one hundred pounds* per annum. *One hundred pounds* divided among 7000 taxables, which this county contains, will not make it *three pence half penny* per man. Is an expense so trifling equal to the advantages to be derived from such a law? Is that expense unnecessary which procures safety to your property and protection to your persons? Is an impartial administration of justice of so little moment to the people? For what purpose were the courts of judicature established? Was it that judgment should be given according to the nod and direction of a governor, or attorney general, or as the last shall happen to be employed? Or was it that they should be free from all fear, favor, or affection whatsoever? That their determinations might flow from an honest conscience, from an impartial and unbiased mind?

The enemies to this law, like all other persons who do not act upon principle, manifestly contradict their own constant practice. What man among them, who has a controversy with his neighbor, would not choose to have it determined by arbitrators at least as independent of his opponent as himself? I think I am safe in asserting that no man of common sense would submit his cause to the judgment of arbitrators who are the *tenant at will* or debtors of his antagonist, or to persons who are connected with him by blood or affinity or by obligations and favors conferred. Is it not a common objection at our courts of justice in the election of referees that the person named is of the same religious persuasion with the other party? Whence arises the objection but from a well-grounded suspicion that in some men even similitude of sentiments may create undue favor and attachment to the interest of one side and bias the private judgment and be the cause of injustice.

If this be the case between neighbor and neighbor, how does it stand between the proprietaries and the people of this province? Every freeholder is by contract their debtor, and therefore every one of them may, and many often will, have disputes and lawsuits with them respecting the many covenants contained in their grants and the quitrents. Does not the same reason which declares the use of indifferent arbitrators in the case of private persons loudly proclaim the necessity of independent men to settle the differences between power and property, between the proprietaries and the people? Have not men who are clothed with immense property and extensive power by the weight of these alone too great an opportunity of influencing the courts of justice without this unnatural and unreasonable dependency of the judges *on their pleasure?*

I have shown you in the reigns of CHARLES and JAMES that men of their fortune and the most extensive abilities have sacrificed their honor, their oaths, and their consciences on the altar of court influence; that they have violated the sacred office and trust of a judge, which were committed to them for the welfare of the people. Do you think it would be a difficult task to produce you examples of the like immolations in your own government? Have some of your past administrations been less oppressive and arbitrary than those of CHARLES and JAMES? Have not the royal grant and proprietary charter, the foundations of your constitution, been dispensed with and superseded by arbitrary edicts? Have not those edicts, which like the laws of the *Medes* and *Persians* were to alter not, chained down the judgments of your rulers and deprived them of their disertion in matters or Iegislation?

Have you known a scheme of power to deprive you of your properties in which your magistrates have not been concerned? Have you forgot the attempt to destroy the freedom of your elections, abetted and supported by the men who ought to have suppressed it? Have not your servants, as much your property as the money in your purses, been illegally enlisted by a former governor, and scarcely any could be found who dared to execute the laws made for its safety? What part did they act in preventing your houses (which by law are to every man a place of refuge and safety) from being made *barracks* for the soldiery? Did they execute the penal statute of our mother country against it, or did not some of them act a *shameful* neutrality while others united with power and in its very council abetted the illegal attempt? How *manfully* and *conscientiously* did they exert themselves in suppressing the rioters, those instruments of power, who were collected to frighten the representatives to surrender up your sacred rights, or were not some of them mixed with the mob, promoting and abetting their wicked design?

Where then is the difference? If CHARLES and JAMES dispensed with penal statutes in order to introduce *popery*, your former governors have dispensed with the laws and fundamentals of your liberties and privileges in order to introduce *slavery*. If the former influenced the determinations of the judges and thereby perverted the laws of the country your poperies by severe penalties have deprived the head of the executive as well as legislative authority of his discretion and reason. And your governors have so influenced the courts of justice to justify and support their despotic designs that you and your predecessors from the like dangerous policy have suffered equal mischief and the like misfortunes.

Should, then, the same illegal and arbitrary measures hereafter be pursued by some future son of oppression, should a design be formed of dispensing with your laws and of imposing unnecessary taxes and burdens *heavy to be borne* without the assent of your representatives, and the ministers of justice be thought the proper instruments of effecting these horrid purposes, how certain the success! how easy the task! while your judges are dependent on the *will of the oppressor*. Can you doubt that human nature, wearing the yoke engraved with the motto DURING PLEASURE, will not hold and practice the doctrine of *passive obedience* and *nonresistance* with respect to the destruction of your rights and privileges? If it should retain virtue enough not to be active in their ruin, will not the same cause ever produce the same effect? Will that which was once destructive now change its nature and become harmless and innocent? Has the poison of the asp ever lost its virulent quality? Will you then surrender up your sacred rights into the hands of power for protection? Will you suffer the safety of your persons, which is still more precious, to depend on the humor and caprice of your rulers and their favorites?

Consider, my countrymen, farther, are the Pennsylvanians men of more independent fortunes or of greater abilities? Do they inherit a greater share of inflexible virtue? And are they less liable to influence and corruption than the people of *England?* Has not fatal experience evidently demonstrated that the private property of your proprietaries, and their favorites will daily clash more and more with yours, more frequently and in a much greater degree than the private *interest* of your sovereign possibly can with that of his subjects. And yet has not the wise example and policy of a *British* Parliament thought it indispensably necessary, even there, that the judges should hold their commissions *during good behavior,* as independent of the crown as of the nation?

If those things be so, can the least spark of reason be offered why a *British* subject in *America* shall not enjoy the like safety, the same protection against domestic oppression? Is it because you have left your native land at the risk of your lives and fortunes to toil for your mother country, to load her with wealth, that you are to be rewarded with a loss of your privileges? Are you not of the same stock? Was the blood of your ancestors polluted by a change of soil? Were they freemen in *England* and did they become slaves by a six-weeks' voyage to America? Does not the sun shine as bright, our blood run as warm? Is not our honor and virtue as pure, our liberty as valuable, our property as dear, our lives as precious here as in England? Are we not subjects of the same King, and bound by the same laws, and have we not the same God for our protector?

What, then, can you think of those abject *Americans,* those slaves by principle, those traitors to their own and posterity's happiness, who, plunging the dagger into the vitals of their own liberty, do not blush at declaring that you are not *entitled to the same security of property, the same rights and privileges of the freeborn subjects of* England? *Let me* ask those enemies to your welfare, how much thereof are you entitled to? Who will measure out and distribute your poor pittance, your short allowance? Is a tenth, an hundredth, or a thousandth part to be the portion of your liberty? Abject, detestable thought! The poor *African,* who is taken captive in war and dragged an involuntary slave to Jamaica calls for your humanity and compassion; but the voluntary wretch that works out his own and posterity's slavish condition for the sake of a little present lucre, promotion, or power is an object deserving your deepest resentment, your highest inclination.

Ye who are not willfully blind to the advantages of this beneficial law, who for want of a little reflection have spoken derogatorily of its merits, let me rouse you from your lethargy and prevail on you to see through the perspective of truth your and your posterity's danger and approaching misery. What will avail the laws which are and shall be made for your protection if they are not impartially executed ? What will avail the virtuous struggles, the noble victories of your representatives over the attempts of your intestine enemies? What will avail the heavy taxes you labor under? the thousands you have exhausted? the blood and treasure you have expended to protect your persons and properties from foreign invaders, if they are not safe from the insidious designs of ambition and power, their ever vigilant and active foes, nor even from the artful attempts of a litigious neighbor who is in favor with the *great* or can first employ a favorite attorney?

Whatever, then, be the fate of the law which has occasioned this address to you, let me entreat you to insist on the enjoyment of this your native, your ancient, and indubitable right. 'Tis yours by the usage and custom of ages; 'tis yours by the rules of reason; 'tis yours by covenant with the first founder of your government; 'tis yours by the united consent of King, Lords, and Commons; 'tis yours by birthright and as *Englishman.* Complain, and remonstrate to your representatives incessantly, until they shall, like the great and good ALFRED, make a restitution of this your most important and essential right, the first and principal object of their concern; until they prevail on your governors to grant the judges commissions to the people of *Pennsylvania in* the same free and constitutional manner as your sovereign grants them to his subjects in *England* .

Be assured, if a privilege thus justly founded, so often ratified and confirmed, if an impartial and independent administration of justice is once wrested from your hands, neither the money in your pockets, nor the clothes on your backs, nor your inheritances, nor even your persons can remain long safe from violation. You will become slaves indeed, in no respect different from the sooty *Africans,* whose persons and properties are subject to the disposal of their tyrannical masters.

# JAMES FITCH

# TAXATION WITHOUT REPRESENTATION

REASONS, &c.

BY THE constitution, government, and laws of Great Britain, the English are free people. Their freedom consists principally if not wholly in this general privilege, that "no laws can be made or abrogated without their consent by their representatives in Parliament".

By the common law of England every commoner hath a right not to be subjected to laws made without his consent, and because such consent (by reason of the great inconvenience and confusion attending numbers in such transactions) cannot be given by every individual man in person, therefore is the power of rendering such consent lodged in the hands of representatives by them elected and chosen for that purpose. Their subjection, then, to their laws is not forced but voluntary.

As the chief excellency of the British constitution consists in the subjects' being bound only by such laws to which they themselves consent, as aforesaid, and as, in order to their enjoying that right, they are (agreeable to the constitution) necessarily vested with the power of electing their representatives, so this right or power is a fundamental privilege and so essential a part of the constitution that without it the subject cannot be said to be free: therefore, if he be hindered from voting in such election or obstructed in the lawful use of that real right or privilege, a suit will lie for him at common law.

None of the privileges included in those general rights (which in an especial manner denominate the British subjects a free people) is maintained with greater care and circumspection, and of which they are more jealous, than this particular, known, approved, and fixed one, that no tax, loan, or benevolence can be imposed on them but with their own consent by their representatives in Parliament. This privilege is of ancient date, and whenever it hath been encroached upon has been claimed, struggled for, and recovered as being essential for the preservation of the liberty, property, and freedom of the subject. For if the privilege of not being taxed without their consent be once alien from them, liberty and freedom are certainly gone with it. That power which can tax as it shall think proper may govern as it pleases; and those subjected to such taxations and government must be far, very far from being a free people. They cannot, indeed, be said to enjoy even so much as the shadow of English liberties.

Upon these general and fundamental principles, it is conceived that the Parliament (although it hath a general authority, a supreme jurisdiction over all His Majesty's subjects, yet as it is also the high and safe guardian of their liberties) doth not extend its taxations to such parts of the British dominions; as are not represented in that grand legislature of the nation; nor is it to be presumed that this wise and vigilant body will permit such an essential right, which is as the very basis of the constitution, in any instance ever to be violated. And upon the same principles (as is apprehended) those subordinate jurisdictions or governments which by distance are so separated from Great Britain that they are not and cannot be represented in Parliament have always been permitted to have and enjoy privileges similar to those of their fellow subjects in the mother country, that is, of being subjected only to taxations and by the particular legislatures wherein they are or may be represented by persons by them elected for that purpose, and consequently of not being taxed without their consent. Thus, in Ireland, taxes are laid by the Parliament of that kingdom; and in the colonies or plantations in America by the several Assemblies or legislatures therein.

These being the essential rights and privileges of the British constitution, founded on the principles of the common law, though in diverse respects particularly regulated by sundry statutes, *the King's subjects in the plantations* claim a general right to the substance and constitutional part of them as their birthright and inheritance. This claim is founded on such considerations as follow, viz.:

*First.* The people in the colonies and plantations in America are really, truly, and in every respect as much the King's subjects as those born and living in Great Britain are. "All persons born in any part of the

King's dominions and within his protection are his subjects, as all those born in Ireland, Scotland, Wales, the King's plantations, or on the English seas, who by their birth owe such an inseparable allegiance to the King that they cannot by any act of theirs renounce or transfer their subjection to any foreign prince." *4 Bac. 166.*

*Secondly.* All the King's subjects, both in Great Britain and in the colonies and plantations in America, have right to the same general and essential privileges of the British constitution, or those privileges which denominate them to be a free people.

As protection necessarily demands and binds to subjection and obedience to that authority and those laws whereby a people are protected, so subjection and obedience as necessarily and justly entitle to protection: these mutually imply, require, and support each other. The King, as political head of his subjects, stands equally related to them in that capacity, and is as really obligated to protect one subject as well as another; and as he has an interest in all his subjects, so they have an interest in him, regulated according to the political constitution. Though the particular and formal parts of the governments of the colonies may be various one from another and diverse from that of Great Britain, and such diversity of forms or establishments necessarily arise from their different situations and circumstances, yet both law and equity agree in this general principle, that all the King's subjects ought to be supported and protected in their rights and liberties, and especially in such as are fundamental and essential to their freedom. The subjects in Great Britain are under no greater or stronger obligations of submission and obedience to the crown than those in the colonies are; and surely, if the colonists are under the same obligations to submission and obedience with other their fellow subjects, it will not be easy to show that they have not the same right to be protected and secured in the enjoyment of every just and legal privilege.

Though the subjects in the colonies are situated at a great distance from their mother country, and for that reason cannot participate in the general legislature of the nation nor enjoy some particular formal immunities possessed by those at home, yet as they settled at this distance by royal license and under national encouragements and thereby enlarged the British dominions and commerce, which add riches and strength to the nation, and as they brought with them and constantly claimed the general principles, those fundamental principles which contain the essence and spirit of the common law of the nation, it may not be justly said they have lost their birthright by such their removal into America; for to suppose that those settlements, that the performance of such important and public services, should be prejudicial to the claim of the colonies to the general privileges of British subjects would be inconsistent both with law and reason, would naturally lead to unjust and absurd conclusions, inasmuch as those public national advantages would not have been promoted unless some of the King's subjects had planted, settled, and dwelt in his colonies abroad, and yet that such planting, settling, and living should subject the inhabitants to the loss of their essential rights as Englishmen would be to reward great, public, and meritorious services with great and unspeakable losses and disadvantages. And how inconsistent such measures and principles are with the honor and justice of the British crown and government may well deserve consideration. It therefore seems apparent that the King's subjects in the plantations have a right, and that it is for the honor of the crown and law that they should have a right, to the general and essential privileges of the British constitution, as well as the rest of their fellow subjects. And with regard to the colony of Connecticut in particular, there can be no question of its having such right, as these general privileges and immunities are fully and explicitly granted and declared to belong to them by the royal charter of incorporation given to the said colony by King Charles the Second in the fourteenth year of his reign, in which is contained this paragraph, viz.: "And further our will and pleasure is, and we do for us, our heirs and successors, ordain, declare, and grant unto the said governor and company and their successors that all and every the subjects of us, our heirs or successors, which shall go to inhabit within the said colony, and every of their children which shall happen to be born there, or on the seas in going thither or returning from thence, shall have and enjoy all liberties and immunities of free and natural subjects within any of the dominions of us, our heirs or successors, to all intents, constructions, and purposes whatsoever, as if they, and every of them, were born within the realm of England." Now whether these words are to be understood only as declarative of the privileges of the ancient common law of England and of the common rights of Englishmen settled by royal license and under the protection of the crown in a colony or plantation abroad and so evidential of the rights and immunities belonging to all the King's subjects in America, or whether they are to be considered as a grant and confirmation of such privileges and immunities to His Majesty's subjects of the colony of Connecticut in particular, they equally evince (as far as a royal declaration and grant can operate to that purpose) the truth of what is here pleaded for so far as respects the people of the said colony. Indeed these words (on the general principles of the common law) ought (as is apprehended) to be construed as containing a full declaration of the rights of the subject, and in order to remove all doubts about the same, a confirmation of them is annexed to or joined therewith. It may also be further observed that by this paragraph can't be meant or intended that the King's subjects within all his dominions should have or be governed by the same particular and formal laws or regulations, because their situations are in distant parts of the world, and their circumstances are so widely different that the same particular establishments and formal regulations which in one place might be good and wholesome for the people, in another would be unwholesome, prejudicial, and by no means answer the end of laws. But this declaration and confirmation denotes and imports (as is conceived) that all those general and essential rights which the free and natural subjects in the mother country are possessed of and vested with by virtue of the main, leading, and fundamental principles of the common law or constitution of the realm, the King's subjects in the said colony of Connecticut shall have and enjoy to all intents, constructions, and purposes whatsoever, that is, in such plenitude as always to be, and ever to be treated as, free and natural subjects.

*Thirdly.* In order that the King's subjects in the colonies and plantations in America might have and enjoy the like liberties and immunities as other their fellow subjects are favored with, it was and is necessary the colonies should be vested with the authority and power of legislation; and this they have accordingly assumed and exercised from their first regular settlement down to this time, and have been constantly owned and acknowledged therein, treated as having such authority, and protected in the same by the crown and the supreme legislature of the nation. Those corporations which by their situation and circumstances are privileged with the right of electing their representatives to bear a proportionable part in the general legislature of the nation, although they may be vested with authority to make bylaws and regulations within their own jurisdictions agreeable to the bounds and limits of the charters which institute and give them existence indeed are, and ought to be, immediately subject to the laws, orders, and taxes of such general legislature, as well as others, and that even without being expressly named, for this obvious and solid reason: because they are legally represented therein. But with regard to those corporations or governments which by their distance and situation have no possible opportunity of such a representation, the case is far otherwise. Whenever, therefore, acts are formed by the supreme legislature that are, in any respect, to extend to the governments abroad, they are made to be so extended by express words; and even such as are so extended to subjects who are not admitted a representation, or to bear a part in the legislation, may not improperly be said to be *sovereign acts,* or acts supported by the sovereign dominion of the makers of them. And as the exercise of such sovereign authority may be said (as is humbly conceived) to be in some measure an exception from the general rule by which British subjects (according to the constitution) arc governed, it is most justly to be presumed and relied upon that the supreme guardians of the liberties of the subjects will never extend that authority further than may be done without depriving any of the King's subjects of those privileges which are essential to their liberty and freedom or leave them in possession of such rights and liberties. It is a clear point that the colonies may not, they cannot, be represented in Parliament; and if they are not vested with legislative authority within themselves where they may be represented by persons of their own electing, it is plain they will not be represented in any legislature at all, and consequently if they are subjected to any laws it must be to such as they have never consented to either by themselves or any representatives, which will be directly contrary to that before-mentioned fundamental principle of the British constitution that "NO LAW CAN BE MADE OR ABROGATED WITHOUT THE CONSENT OF THE PEOPLE BY THEIR REPRESENTATIVES." It therefore appears that for the crown to govern the colonies and plantations abroad by and with the consent of the people represented in Assemblies or legislative bodies is properly and truly of government; and although this may not in every form and manner be exactly similar to the government at home, yet as near as the different situation therefore appears that for the crown to govern the colonies and plantations abroad by and with the consent of the people represented in Assemblies or legislative bodies is properly and truly to govern them agreeable to the British constitution of government; and although this may not in every form and manner be exactly similar to the government at home, yet as near as the different situation and circumstances admit w ill it agree with the fundamental principles thereof. That the colony of Connecticut (agreeable to these general principles) is vested with such a legislative authority appears by their charter full to that effect. By this charter the colony are empowered to meet in a General Assembly, consisting of a governor or deputy governor, assistants, and deputies, annually to be chosen by the freemen; and such Assembly is vested with authority from time to time to make, ordain, and establish all manner of wholesome and reasonable laws, statutes, and ordinances, directions and instructions not contrary to the laws of the realm of England; and every officer appointed for putting such laws, ordinances, etc., from time to time into due execution is sufficiently warranted and discharged against the King's Majesty, his heirs and successors, by a special clause in the same charter express to that purpose. By this royal patent it is therefore evident that a full power of legislation is granted to the colony, limited with a restriction that they conform or are not to act contrary to the general principles of the laws of the nation; and consequently, as when they exceed the bounds and limits prescribed in the charter their acts will be void, so when they conform and regulate their acts agreeable to the intent and meaning of it their acts may properly be said to have the royal approbation and assent. And these powers, rights, and privileges the colony has been in possession of for more than a century past. This power of legislation necessarily includes in it an authority to impose taxes or duties upon the people for the support of government and for the protection and defense of the inhabitants, as, without such authority, the general rights of legislation would be of no avail to them. These privileges and immunities, these powers and authorities, the colony claims not only in virtue of their right to the general principles of the British constitution and by force of the royal declaration and grant in their favor, but also as having been in the possession, enjoyment, and exercise of them for so long a time, and constantly owned, acknowledged, and allowed to be just in the claim and use thereof by the crown, the ministry, and the Parliament, as may evidently be shown by royal instructions, many letters and acts of Parliament, all supposing and being predicated upon the colony's having and justly exercising these privileges, powers, and authorities; and what better foundation for, or greater evidence of, such rights can be demanded or produced is certainly difficult to be imagined. These points being thus rendered so clear and evident, may it not thence be very justly inferred,

Fourthly, that charging stamp duties or other internal taxes on the colonies in America by Parliamentary authority will be an infringement of the aforementioned rights and privileges, and deprive the colonists of their freedom and inheritance so far as such taxations extend? The charging a tax on any particular part of the subject's estates in the plantations by authority of Parliament will doubtless be found nothing less than taking from them a part of their estates on the sole consideration of their being able to bear it, or of having a sufficiency left notwithstanding. It must certainly be admitted that the people thus charged do not consent, nor have any opportunity so to do. An express consent, either by themselves or representatives, can by no means be pretended; neither can their consent be argued from implication, as their subjection and allegiance to the crown are supposed to be according to the tenor of the laws of the nation, for although the King is styled the head of the commonwealth, supreme governor, *parens patriae*, etc., yet he is still able to make the law of the land the rule of his government.

Therefore, in this case, as there can be no other implied consent than what the general principles of the law or constitution implies or what is included in the obligations to submission and obedience to laws, and as the general, fundamental principles of the British constitution or laws, which the Americans claim the privilege of, are quite the reverse of such implications and really imply and suppose the contrary, it follows that charging such taxes will be to take part of their estates from the people without their consent, either expressed or implied. It can't be said such charging would be founded on contract, as it might be where the subjects are represented in the legislature; neither may it be founded on a forfeiture, as there is no pretense of that kind in these cases; surely, then, there can be no right either to demand or receive a man's estate where both these are wanting.

If these internal taxations take place, and the principles upon which they must be founded are adopted and carried into execution, the colonies will have no more than a show of legislation left, nor the King's subjects in them any more than the shadow of true English liberty; for the same principles which will justify such a tax of a penny will warrant a tax of a pound, an hundred, or a thousand pounds, and so on without limitation; and if they will warrant a tax on one article, they will support one on as many particulars as shall be thought necessary to raise any sum proposed. And all such subjections, burdens, and deprivations, if they take place with respect to the King's subjects abroad, will be without their consent, without their having opportunity to be represented or to show their ability, disability, or circumstances. They will no longer enjoy that fundamental privilege of Englishmen whereby, in special, they are denominated a free people. The legislative authority of the colonies will in part actually be cut off; a part of the same will be taken out of their own Assemblies, even such part as they have enjoyed so long and esteem most dear. Nay, may it not be truly said in this case that the Assemblies in the colonies will have left no other power or authority, and the people no other freedom, estates, or privileges than what may be called a tenancy it will; that they have exchanged, or rather lost, those privileges and rights which, according to the national constitution, were their birthright and inheritance, for such a disagreeable tenancy? Will not such determinations amount to plain declarations to the colonies that although they have enjoyed those immunities and privileges heretofore, and been acknowledged and encouraged in the possession and use of them, yet now they must expect, for reasons of state, for some public utility, to part with them, and be brought under a kind of subjection not far from the very reverse of that freedom they justly claim and so highly value? May it not be inquired what reasons are or may be assigned for so different treatment of the subjects of the same most gracious King, of the same general state or community? May it not, upon the whole, be concluded that charging stamp duties or other internal duties by authority of Parliament, as has been mentioned, will be such an infringement of the rights, privileges, and authorities of the colonies that it may be humbly and firmly trusted and even relied upon that the supreme guardians of the liberties of the subject will not suffer the same to be done, and will not only protect them in the enjoyment of their just rights but treat them with great tenderness, indulgence, and favor?

Hereby it appears that this charter was granted upon valuable considerations, which adds weight and strength to the title on which the claim of the colony to the rights, immunities, and franchises therein granted and confirmed are founded, for here the considerations of large sums of money advanced, conquest made at the expense of the blood and treasure of the planters, eminent public national services performed and to be performed, and all to the enlargement of the King's dominions and for the increase of the national commerce, which the charter is a clear and full evidence of. The powers and privileges granted by this charter were properly the purchase of the people, and the granting was an instance of royal justice to them, though the grace and favor of the crown assuredly ought to be and hath been at all times humbly and gratefully acknowledged therein. Therefore, as there really were valuable considerations which were proper foundations for such a grant, it was doubtless judged to be for the honor of the crown to grant the powers of government with such ample and beneficial immunities and privileges as are allowed and given in and by the charter aforesaid; and these the people indeed look upon as the purchase of their ancestors, as a gracious and royal reward of the merit and services of their forefathers, and as one of the best inheritances they left to their children. Whether, therefore, it can be consistent with law or equity they should he deprived of such an inheritance or any part thereof, may be worthy of serious consideration; for if the right of a single person to vote in the election of a member of Parliament be so sacred in the eye of the law that to deprive him of it entitles to an action at common law for his damages and the violation of his privileges, as was adjudged in the House of Lords in the case of Ashby and White, how sacred then ought the powers, privileges, and immunities of a whole colony of loyal people, of all the freemen in it, to be looked upon and considered ? And of what importance is it they should be defended and protected therein? As the enjoyment of such privileges and liberties, of such a free constitution of government, naturally tends to promote loyalty and obedience in a people, so the inhabitants of the colony of Connecticut (without arrogating) may, with the strictest veracity, say and insist that none of the colonies in the British dominions have approved themselves more loyal and obedient to the King's Majesty or more forward and zealous for promoting his service than they have constantly done. These principles of loyalty and zeal, the natural result of liberty and freedom, have influenced the colony to exert itself with a becoming vigorous spirit and resolution in public and benevolent services whenever they have been called upon or applied to for that purpose. It hath not only defended itself in its infant state against the violent insurrections of the Indians who formerly lived near or dwelt among them, and at all times down to the present day against all its enemies, but also, as it increased in numbers and strength, hath from time to time afforded aid, succor, and relief to the neighboring colonies. It is found by ancient memorials that the colony of Connecticut united with, and, at large expense and to most remarkable effect, assisted the other colonies in carrying on the famous Indian war called the Narragansett War, which raged about the year 1675, when (after a shocking destruction of the English people, their infant towns and settlements) those barbarians were totally subdued and the distressed country thereby saved from impending ruin . . .

In these services, from the year 1735 to the year 1762 inclusive, the expenses of the colony, never and above the Parliamentary grants (which have been received with the most sensible and humble gratitude), amounts to upwards of four hundred thousand pounds, the large arrears of which sum will remain a heavy, distressing burden upon the people for many years to come.

Moreover, several thousands of the hardiest and most able young men, the hope and strength of the farmers, have been destroyed, lost, and enervated in the many distant arduous campaigns during the course of this terrible war. The husbandry of the country (its only resource) has suffered and still suffers extremely hereby; and the colony will not recover itself from these disadvantages in a long tract of time. And although by the success of the military operations in America, large, extensive, and most valuable acquisitions have been made to the British dominions, yet the colony of Connecticut gains nothing thereby further than as it may be said to be concerned in the common cause and general interest of the whole. It had no lands to recover or even to secure from the enemy, as some other governments had; it hath no immediate trade with the Indians, nor will its situation admit of any but what may, by some individuals, be carried on through and so subject to the control of other colonies. The profits of this trade have ever been mostly in the hands of those whose proximity gave them peculiar advantages for it. Nay, instead of receiving particular benefit by these events, the colony will rather suffer disadvantage thereby in the emigration of its inhabitants, already thinned, for settlement of the vacant lands in other provinces which are now secure from the enemy who formerly annoyed them. Therefore principles of loyalty and zeal for the King's service, principles of benevolence, humanity, and compassion for their fellow subjects in danger and distress, and the agreeable prospect, a laudable desire of enjoying quiet and peace in consequence of a general tranquility in the land, must be considered as the genuine motives and springs inducing the colony of Connecticut to exert itself in the manner and to the degrees before-mentioned. And now, when all these things are duly considered and viewed in a proper light, will it not be thought that the colony has good reason to hope and expect, in return for and in consequence of such services, if not to be indulged with greater and more extensive favors from the crown and nation, at least to be protected and secured in the full enjoyment of the rights and privileges essential to the freedom of Englishmen, instead of having those rights curtailed or infringed by charging on them a stamp duty, as proposed, or any other the like new and unprecedented taxation?

OBJECTION

Perhaps, after all that hath been offered, it will be objected by some that America ought, and is able, to bear a just proportion of the American expense, and that as the duty already charged will, they suppose, not be sufficient to defray that expense, it becomes necessary to make additions to the duties already laid.

ANSWER

*First. In order to obv*iate and answer this objection it may be necessary to enter a little into a consideration of the occasion and nature of those charges which by some are denominated American expenses. That expense which is occasioned merely for the defense and protection of the new governments and acquisitions, it is conceived, ought not to be charged upon the colonies in general, as it is truly no other than a national interest, or an interest of the particular new governments or acquisitions, and consequently ought, where it is not purely national, to be laid on those whose immediate profit is advanced thereby. The old colonies, especially New England, were at the sole charge of settling and defending themselves, and that they should now be compelled to contribute towards settling others under much better advantages in that regard than they were, will not fail of being esteemed hard and injurious. If the expense arises in defending and securing the fur trade and the outposts requisite for carrying on the same, to oblige these colonies which receive no immediate advantage by it to bear a proportionable part of the burden will also be hard and unequal, and especially if that trade is sufficiently profitable to support itself; if otherwise, why is there so much care and mighty attention constantly exercised towards it? If the expense occurs in holding and protecting the new and large acquisitions, wherefore should the colonies bear that when they have no interest in them? They do indeed properly belong to the crown, and will finally be disposed of and settled for the benefit of the crown and the nation in general, and not for the advantage of the colonies in particular. But,

Secondly. What America's proportionable part in the American expense will be is somewhat uncertain and difficult to determine. And in order to form any tolerable judgment in the case, it will be necessary to consider the wealth of the colonies compared with the mother country; their number of inhabitants compared with the extent of their own country; the nature of their climates, in some of which the cold seasons are of such long continuance as to occasion a consumption of the greatest part of their produce; their trade and commerce, the profits of which in general center in Great Britain; their business, advantages and disadvantages and other circumstances, such as their being, in a general way, obliged to spend so great a proportion of their labor in clearing, fencing, and preparing their lands for improvement; and that the surplus of their labor in many instances is but very little and in some nothing at all. The clear profits, therefore, to the colonies being so very inconsiderable, it must surely be found, on a just and reasonable computation, that their proportion of any general national expense, if anything, will be very small. But,

*Thirdly.* If, notwithstanding, it shall be judged necessary (which is even a difficult supposition) to make an addition to the charges on America, yet is it humbly conceived, for the reasons already offered, it will not by any means ever be thought proper or just, in order to effect that purpose, it should be done in a way that shall be an infringement on the constitutions of the colonies or that will deprive the subjects in them of some of those important liberties and privileges which, as Englishmen and freemen, they so justly value, and have a legal and equitable right to, as well as the rest of their fellow subjects. Revenues are never raised in Great Britain by a violation of the constitution or any part of it, but the liberties and privileges of the subjects are always saved and maintained in those cases. And why the Americans should not value their privileges at as high a rate as their fellow subjects in Great Britain do theirs, and wherefore the same justice is not due to the one as to the other, what sufficient reasons can possibly be assigned? Therefore, whatever may be done in this matter it is humbly trusted will surely be elected in such manner as to leave the legislatures of the colonies entire, and the people in the full possession and enjoyment of their just rights and immunities. This, it is conceived, might be effected by a duty (if thought necessary and proper) on the importation of

Negroes and on the fur trade, etc.; for although that on slaves may and doubtless will fall with most weight where the greatest numbers are imported, yet will none be charged thereby but such as voluntarily submit to it; and was such importation lessened, which might indeed be some disadvantage to a few individuals, yet probably it would be attended with many salutary effects both with respect to Great Britain and her colonies in general. And as a principal article of the expense in America must be for protecting, and securing the fur trade, what good reasons can be adduced wherefore that trade should not be so charged as to support itself? For (as hath been a!ready hinted) if it will not bear this charge, why is it still held and maintained at such great expense?

Having thus *shown that the English are a free people; that their freedom consists in these general privileges that* no laws can be made or abrogated without their consent by representatives, *and for that purpose have right to elect their representatives; that the American colonists are as really the King's subjects as loyal and have as much right to the general and fundamental privileges of the British constitution and to protect in the enjoyment thereof as the rest of their fellow subjects in the mother country; that in consequence hereof the colonies and plantations in America according to the general principles of the national constitution are vested with authority of legislation and have right to be represented in their Assemblies in whom that authority is lodged and with whose consent they are to be governed by the crown; that for the crown to govern these colonies and plantations by and with the consent of the people in such legislative assemblies is properly and truly to govern them agreeable to the national constitution, or that it is as conformable to the fundamental principles of the British government that the subjects in the colonies should be represented in Assemblies or legislative bodies as that the subjects in Great Britain should be represented in Parliament or the supreme legislature of the nation and that the government of the subjects, with the consent of their respective representatives, is founded on the sole general and essential principles of liberty; that charging stamp duties or internal taxes on the colony by authority of Parliament, will be inconsistent with those authorities and privileges which the colonies and the people in them legally enjoy, and have, with the approbation of the supreme power of the nation been in the use and possession of for a long course of years; as also the probability that such measures will in the event prove prejudicial to the national interest as well as hurtful to the colonies;*

*together with some matters and circumstances more directly and peculiarly in favor of the colony of Connecticut, and the especial public and benevolent services performed by it on many occasions, which may justly merit some favorable considerations; and answered such objections as might probably be made against the tenor of the reasonings and representations herein offered and laid down; it is now concluded that on account of these and such other weighty reasons as may occur a British Parliament whose design is to keep up that constitution, support the honor and prerogative of the crown and maintain the privileges of the people, will have a tender regard for the rights and immunities of the king's subjects in the American colonies, and charge no internal taxations upon them without their consent.*

# OXENBRIDGE THACHER

## SENTIMENTS OF
## A BRITISH AMERICAN

IT WELL becomes the wisdom of a great nation, having been highly successful in their foreign wars and added a large extent of country to their dominions, to consider with a critical attention their internal state lest their prosperity should destroy them.

Great Britain at this day is arrived to an heighth of glory and wealth which no European nation hath ever reached since the decline of the Roman Empire. Everybody knows that it is not indebted to itself alone for this envied power: that its colonies, placed in a distant quarter of the earth, have had their share of efficiency in its late successes, as indeed they have also contributed to the advancing and increasing its grandeur from their very first beginnings.

In the forming and settling, therefore, the internal polity of the kingdom, these have reason to expect that their interest should be considered and attended to, that their rights, if they have any, should be preserved to them, and that they should have no reason to complain that they have been lavish of their blood and treasure in the late war only to bind the shackles of slavery on themselves and their children.

No people have been more wisely jealous of their liberties and privileges than the British nation. It is observed by *Vattel* that "their present happy condition hath cost them seas of blood; but they have not purchased it too dear."

The colonies, making a part of this great empire, having the same British rights inherent in them as the inhabitants of the island itself, they cannot be disfranchised or wounded in their privileges but the whole body politic must in the end feel with them.

The writer of this, being a native of an English colony, will take it for granted that the colonies are not the mere property of the mother state; that they have the same rights as other British subjects. He will also suppose that no design is formed to enslave them, and that the justice of the British Parliament will finally do right to every part of their dominions.

These things presupposed, he intends to consider the late act made in the fourth year of his present Majesty entitled *An Act for Granting Certain Duties in the British Colonies and Plantations* in America, etc., to show the real subjects of grievance therein to the colonists, and that the interest of Great Britain itself may finally be greatly affected thereby. There is the more reason that this freedom should be indulged after the act is passed inasmuch as the colonies, though greatly interested therein, had no opportunity of being heard while it was pending.

[I.] The first objection is that a tax is thereby laid on several commodities, to be raised and levied in the plantations, and to be remitted home to England. This is esteemed a grievance inasmuch as the same are laid without the consent of the representatives of the colonists. It is esteemed an essential British right that no person shall be subject to any tax but what in person or by his representative he hath a voice in laying. The British Parliament have many times vindicated this right against the attempts of Kings to invade it. And though perhaps it may be said that the House of Commons, in a large sense, are the representatives of the colonies as well as of the people of Great Britain, yet it is certain that these have no voice in their election. Nor can it be any alleviation of heir unhappiness that if this right is taken from them, it is taken by that body who have been the great patrons and defenders of it in the people of Great Britain.

Besides, the colonies have ever supported a subordinate government among themselves.

Being placed at such a distance from the capital, it is absolutely impossible they should continue a part of the kingdom in the same sense as the corporations there are. For this reason, from their beginning there hath been a subordinate legislature among them subject to the control of the mother state; and from the necessity of the case there must have been such, their circumstances and situation being in many respects so different from that of the parent state they could not have subsisted without this. The colonies have always been taxed by their own representatives and in their respective legislatures, and have supported an entire domestic government among themselves. Is it just, then, they should be doubly taxed? That they should be obliged to bear the whole charges of their domestic government, and should be as subject to the taxes of the British Parliament as those who have no domestic government to support?

The reason given for this extraordinary taxation, namely, that this war was undertaken for the security of the colonies, and that they ought therefore to be taxed to pay the charge thereby incurred, it is humbly apprehended is without foundation. For —

(1) It was of no less consequence to Great Britain than it was to the colonies that these should not be overrun and conquered by the French. Suppose they had prevailed and gotten all the English colonies into their possession: how long would Great Britain have survived their fate! Put the case that the town of Portsmouth or any other seaport had been besieged and the like sums expended in its defense, could any have thought that town ought to be charged with the expense?

(2) The colonies contributed their full proportion to those conquests which adorn and dignify the late and present reign. One of them in particular raised in one year seven thousand men to be commanded by His Majesty's general, besides maintaining many guards and garrisons on their own frontiers. All of them by their expenses and exertions in the late war have incurred heavy debts, which it will take them many years to pay.

(3) The colonies are no particular gainers by these acquisitions. None of the conquered territory is annexed to them. All are acquisitions accruing to the crown. On account of their commerce, they are no gainers: the northern colonies are even sufferers by these cessions. It is true they have more security from having their throats cut by the French while the peace lasts; but so have also all His Majesty's subjects.

(4) Great Britain gaineth immensely by these acquisitions. The command of the whole American fur trade and the increased demand for their wooden manufactures from their numerous new subjects in a country too cold to keep sheep: these are such immense gains as in a commercial light would refund the kingdom, if every farthing of the expense of reducing Canada were paid out of the exchequer.

But to say the truth, it is not only by the taxation itself that the colonists deem themselves aggrieved by the act we are considering.

For—.

II. The power therein given to courts of admiralty alarms them greatly. The common law is the birthright of every subject, and trial by jury a most darling privilege. So deemed our ancestors in ancient times, long before the colonies were begun to be planted. Many struggles had they with courts of admirality, which, like the element they take their name from, have divers times attempted to innundate the land. Hence the statutes of *Richard II*, of *Henry IV*, and divers other public acts. Hence the watchful eye the reverend sages of the common law, have kept over these courts. Now by the act we are considering, the colonists are deprived of these privileges: of the common law, for these judges are supposed to be connusant only of the civil law; of juries, for all here is put in the breast of one man. He judges both law and fact, and his decree is final; at least it cannot be reversed on this side the Atlantic. In this particular the colonists are put under a quite different law from all the rest of the King's subjects: jurisdiction is nowhere else given to courts of admiralty of matters so foreign from their connusance. In some things the colonists have been long subject to this cruel yoke, and have indeed fully experienced its galling nature. Loud complaints have been long made by them of the oppressions of these courts, their exhorbitant fees, and the little justice the subject may expect from them in cases of seizures. Let me mention one thing that is notorious: these courts have assumed (I know not by what law) a commission of five per cent to the judge on all seizures condemned. What chance does the subject stand for his right upon the best claim when the judge, condemning, is is to have an hundred or perhaps five hundred pounds, and acquitting, less than twenty shillings? If the colonists should be thought partial witnesses in this case, let those of the inhabitants of Great Britain who have had the misfortune to be suitors or to have any business in these dreadful courts be inquired of.

There have been times when the legislature of Great Britain appeared to be as sensible of the bad conduct of these courts as we are now. I mean when the statute of 6 Anne c. 37 and some later ones to the same purpose were made, wherein the remedy they have given is as extraordinary as the power given those courts. For in those statutes the judge of admiralty is subjected to a penalty of five hundred pounds, to be recovered by the aggrieved suitor at common law. These only refer to cases of prizes, and give no remedy in cases of seizures, where their power is not only decisive but in many respects uncontrollable.

Meantime, can the colonists help wondering and grieving that the British legislature should vest with such high powers over them courts in whom they appear to have so little confidence?

But in the act we are considering, the power of these courts is even much enlarged and made still more grievous. For it is thereby enacted that the seizor may inform in any court of admiralty for the particular colony, or in any court of admiralty to be appointed over- all America, at his pleasure. Thus a malicious seizor may take the goods of any man, ever so lawfully and duly imported, and carry the trial of the cause to a thousand miles distance, where for mere want of ability to follow, the claimer shall be incapable of defending his right. At the same time an hardship is laid upon the claimer; his claim is not to be admitted or heard until he find sureties to prosecute, who are to be of known ability in the place where security is given. And he, being unknown in a place so distance from home, whatever be his estate, shall be incapable of producing such sureties.

III. The empowering commanders of the King's ships to seize and implead, as is done in this act and a former act and by special commission from the commissioners of the customs, is another great hardship on the colonies. The knowledge of all the statutes relating to the customs, of the prohibitions on exports and imports, and of various intricate cases arising on them, requires a good lawyer. How can this science ever be expected from men educated in a totally different way, brought up upon the boisterous element and knowing no law aboard their ships but their own will? Here perhaps it will be said, this is not peculiar to the colonies. The power to these commanders is given in all parts of the dominions as well as in the colonies: why should they complain of being under the same law as the other subjects? I answer, There is this great essential difference between the cases: in Great Britain no jurisdiction is given to any other than the common law courts; there too the subjects are near the throne, where, when they are oppressed, their complaints may soon be heard and redressed; but with respect to the colonies, far different is the case! Here it is their own courts that try the cause! Here the subject is far distant from the throne! His complaints cannot soon be heard and redressed....

The present decree, however unjust, deprives him even of the means of seeking redress. The judge with his troop and the proud captain have divided his wealth; and he hath nothing to do but to hang himself or to go a begging in a country of beggars.

There is yet another very great objection the colonists make to this act, of no less weight than the other three. It is this:

IV. Whereas it is good law that all officers seizing goods seize at their peril, and if the goods they seize are not liable to forfeiture they must pay the claimant his cost, and are liable to his action besides, which two things have been looked upon as proper checks of exorbitant wanton power in the officer: both these checks are taken off. They, the officers, may charge the revenue with the cost, with the consent of four of the commissioners of the customs. And if the judge of admirality will certify that there was probable cause of seizure, no action shall be maintained by the claimant though his goods on trial appear to be ever so duly imported and liable to no sort of forfeiture, and he hath been forced to expend ever so much in the defense of them. This last regulation is in the act peculiarly confined to America.

Much more might be said on these subjects, but I aim at brevity.

Let it now be observed that the interest of Great Britain is finally greatly affected by these new regulations. We will not here insist on the parental tenderness due from Great Britain to us and suggest she must suffer from sympathy with her children, who have been guilty of no undutiful behavior towards her but on the contrary have greatly increased her wealth and grandeur and in the last war have impoverished themselves in fighting her battles. We will suppose her for this little moment to have forgot the bowels of a mother.

Neither will we dwell long on the importance of the precedent. The consideration of a million and half of British subjects disfranchised or put under regulations alien from our happy constitution: what pretense it may afford to after ministers to treat the inhabitants of the island itself after the same manner. We will suppose for the present that at a thousand leagues distance, across the water, the inhabitants of the capital will not be endangered by a conflagration of all the colonies.

Nor will we mention any possible danger from the alienation of the affections of the colonies from their mother country in case of a new war. We will suppose them to have that reverence for the English name they are allowed to retain that they will be as lavish of what blood and treasure remains to them now they are cut off from all these privileges as when they could please themselves with the surest hope of holding them inviolable.

What we are now considering is how the mere present self-interest of Great Britain is affected by these new regulations....

THESE are the sentiments of a British American, which he ventures to expose to the public with an honest well-meant freedom. Born in one of the colonies and descended from ancestors who were among the first planters of that colony, he is not ashamed to avow a love to the country that gave him birth; yet he hath ever exulted in the name of Briton. He hath ever thought all the inhabitants in the remotest dominions of Great Britain interested in the wealth, the prosperity, and the glory of the capital. And he desireth ever to retain these filial sentiments.

If the objections he proposeth are of any weight, he trusts the meanness and distance of the proposer shall not diminish that weight — that those great minds who can comprehend the whole vast machine in one view will not deem it below them to inspect a single small wheel that is out of order.

He concludes all with his most ardent wishes that the happy island of Great Britain may grow in wealth, in power, and glory to yet greater degrees; that the conquests it makes over foreign enemies may serve the more to protect the internal liberties of its subjects; that her colonies now happily extended may grow in filial affection and dutiful submission to her mother; and that she in return may never forget her parental affections. That the whole English empire, united by the strongest bands of love and interests, formidable to the tyrants and oppressors of the earth, may retain its own virtue, and happily possess immortality.

# JAMES OTIS

# OF THE NATURAL RIGHTS
# OF COLONISTS

In order to form an idea of the natural rights of the colonists, I presume it will be granted that they are men, the common children of the same Creator with their brethren of Great Britain. Nature has placed all such in a state of equality and perfect freedom to act within the bounds of the laws of nature and reason without consulting the will or regarding the humor, the passions, or whims of any other man, unless they are formed into a society or body politic. This it must be confessed is rather an abstract way of considering men than agreeable to the real and general course of nature. The truth is, as has been shown, men come into the world and into society at the same instant. But this hinders not but that the natural and original rights of each individual may be illustrated and complained in this way better than in any other. We see here, by the way, a probability that this abstract consideration of men, which has its use in reasoning on the principles of government, has insensibly led some of the greatest men to imagine some real general state of nature agreeable to this abstract conception, antecedent to and independent of society. This is certainly not the case in general, for most men become members of society from their birth, though separate independent states are really in the condition of perfect freedom and equality with regard to each other, and so are any number of individuals who separate themselves from a society of which they have formerly been members, for ill treatment or other good cause, with express design to found another. If in such case there is a real interval between the separation and the new conjunction, during such interval the individuals are as much detached and under the law of nature only as would be two men who should chance to meet on a desolate island.

The colonists are by the law of nature freeborn, as indeed all men are, white or black. No better reasons can be given for enslaving those of any color than such as Baron Montesquieu has humorously given as the foundation of that cruel slavery excercised over the poor Ethiopians, which threatens one day to reduce both Europe and America to the ignorance and barbarity of the darkest ages. Does it follow that 'tis right to enslave a man because he is black? Will short curled hair like wool instead of Christian hair, as 'tis called by those whose hearts are as hard as the nether millstone, help the argument? Can any logical inference in favor of slavery be drawn from a flat nose, a long or a short face? Nothing better can be said said in favor of a trade that is the most shocking violation of the law of nature, has a direct tendency to diminish the idea of the inestimable value of liberty, and makes every dealer in it a tyrant, from the director of an African company to the petty chapman in needles and pins on the unhappy coast. It is a clear truth that those who every day barter away other men's liberty will soon care little for their own. To this cause must be imputed that ferocity, cruelty, and brutal barbarity that has long marked the general character of the sugar islanders. They can in general form no idea of government but that which in person or by an overseer, the joint and several proper representative of a creole and of the d____l, is exercised over ten thousand of their fellow men, born with the same right to freedom and the sweet enjoyments of liberty and life as their unrelenting taskmasters, the overseers and planters.

Is it to be wondered at if when people of the stamp of a creolean planter get into power they will not stick for a little present gain at making their own posterity, white as well as black, worse slaves if possible than those already mentioned ?

There is nothing more evident, says Mr. Locke, than "that creatures of the same species and rank, promiscuously born to all the same advantages of nature and the use of the same faculties, should also be equal one among another without subordination and subjection, unless the master of them all should by any manifest declaration of his will set one above another and confer on him by an evident and clear appointment an undoubted right to dominion and sovereignty." "The natural liberty of man is to be free from any superior power on earth, and not to be under the will or legislative authority of man, but only to have the law of nature for his rule." This is the liberty of independent states; this is the liberty of every man out of society and who has a mind to live so; which liberty is only abridged in certain instances, not lost to those who are born in or voluntarily enter into society; this gift of God cannot be annihilated.

The colonists, being men, have a right to be considered as equally entitled to all the rights of nature with the Europeans, and they are not to be restrained in the exercise of any of these rights but for the evident good of the whole community. By being or becoming members of society they have not renounced their natural liberty in any greater degree than other good citizens, and if 'tis taken from them without their consent they are so far enslaved. They have an undoubted right to expect that their best good will ever be consulted by their rulers, supreme and subordinate, without any partial views confined to the particular interest of one island or another. Neither the riches of Jamaica nor the luxury of a metropolis should ever have weight enough to break the balance of truth and justice. Truth and faith belong to men as men from men, and if they are disappointed in their just expectations of them in one society they will at least wish for them in another. If the love of truth and justice, the only spring of sound policy in any state, is not strong enough to prevent certain causes from taking place, the arts of fraud and force will not prevent the most fatal effects.

In the long run, those who fall on arbitrary measures will meet with their deserved fate. The law of nature was not of man's making, nor is it in his power to mend it or alter its course. He can only perform and keep or disobey and break it. The last is never done with impunity, even in this life, if it is any punishment for a man to feel himself depraved, to find himself depraved, to find himself degraded by his own folly and wickedness from the rank of a virtuous and good man to that of a brute, or to be transformed from the friend, perhaps father, of his country to a devouring lion or tiger. The unhappy revolutions which for ages have distressed the human race have been all owing to the want of a little wisdom, common sense, and integrity in the administration of those whom, by their stations, God had in kindness to the world rendered able to do a great deal for the benefit of mankind with the exertion of a small portion of private and public virtue.

# STEPHEN HOPKINS

# THE RIGHTS OF COLONIES EXAMINED

Liberty is the greatest blessing that men enjoy, and slavery the heaviest curse that human nature is capable of. This being so makes it a matter of the utmost importance to men which of the two shall be their portion. Absolute liberty is, perhaps, incompatible with any kind of government. The safety resulting from society, and the advantage of just and equal laws, hath caused men to forego some part of their natural liberty, and submit to government. This appears to be the most rational account of its beginning, although, it must be confessed, mankind have by no means been agreed about it. Some have found its origin in the divine appointment; others have thought it took its rise from power; enthusiasts have dreamed that dominion was founded in grace. Leaving these points to be settled by the descendants of Filmer, Cromwell, and Venner, we will consider the British constitution as it at present stands, on Revolution principles, and from thence endeavor to find the measure of the magistrate's power and the people's obedience.

This glorious constitution, the best that ever existed among men, will be confessed by all to be- founded by compact and established by consent of the people. By this most beneficent compact British subjects are to be governed only agreeable to laws to which themselves have some way consented, and are not to be compelled to part with their property but as it is called for by the authority of such laws. The former is truly liberty; the latter is really to be possessed of property and to have something that may be called one's own.

On the contrary, those who are governed at the will of another, or of others, and whose property may be taken from them by taxes or otherwise without their own consent and against their will, are in the

miserable condition of slaves. "For liberty solely consists in an independency upon the will of another; and by the name of slave we
understand a man who can neither dispose of his person or goods, but
enjoys all at the will of his master," says Sidney on government. These
things premised, whether the British American colonies on the continent are justly entitled to like privileges and freedom as their fellow
subjects in Great Britain are, shall be the chief point examined. In
discussing this question we shall make the colonies in New England,
with whose rights we are best acquainted, the rule of our reasoning, not
in the least doubting but [that] all the others are justly entitled to like
rights with them

New England was first planted by adventurers who left England,
their native country, by permission of King CHARLES I, and at their
own expense transported themselves to America, with great risk and
difficulty settled among savages, and in a very surprising manner
formed new colonies in the wilderness. Before their departure the terms
of their freedom and the relation they should stand in to the mother
country in their emigrant state were fully settled: they were to remain
subject to the King and dependent on the kingdom of Great Britain. In
return they were to receive protection and enjoy all the rights and
privileges of freeborn Englishmen.

This is abundantly proved by the charter given to the Massachusetts colony while they were still in England, and which they received
and brought over with them as the authentic evidence of the conditions
they removed upon. The colonies of Connecticut and Rhode Island also
afterwards obtained charters from the crown, granting them the like
ample privileges. By all these charters, it is in the most express and
solemn manner granted that these adventurers, and their children after
them forever, should have and enjoy all the freedom and liberty that the
subjects in England enjoy; that they might make laws for their own
government suitable to their circumstances, not repugnant to, but as
near as might be agreeable to the laws of England; that they might
purchase lands, acquire goods, and use trade for their advantage, and
have an absolute property in whatever they justly acquired. These, with
many other gracious privileges were granted them by several kings;
and they were to pay as an acknowledgment to the crown only one fifth
part of the ore of gold and silver that should at any time be found in the
said colonies, in lieu of, and full satisfaction for, all dues and demands
of the crown and kingdom of England upon them.

There is not anything new or extraordinary in these rights granted to the British colonies. The colonies from all countries, at all times, have enjoyed equal freedom with the mother state. Indeed, there would be found very few people in the world willing to leave their native country and go through the fatigue and hardship of planting in a new uncultivated one for the sake of losing their freedom. They who settle new countries must be poor and, in course, ought to be free. Advantages, pecuniary or agreeable, are not on the side of emigrants, and surely they must have something in their stead.

To illustrate this, permit us to examine what hath generally been the condition of colonies with respect to their freedom. We will begin with those who went out from the ancient commonwealths of Greece, which are the first, perhaps, we have any good account of. Thucydides, that grave and judicious historian, says of one of them, "they were not sent out to be slaves, but to be the equals of those who remain behind"; and again, the Corinthians gave public notice "that a new colony was going to Epidamnus, into which all that would enter, should have equal and like privileges with those who stayed at home." This was uniformly the condition of all the Grecian colonies; they went out and settled new countries; they took such forms of government as themselves chose, though it generally nearly resembled that of the mother state, whether democratical or oligarchical. ''Tis true, they were fond to acknowledge their original, and always confessed themselves under obligation to pay a kind of honorary respect to, and show a filial dependence on, the commonwealth from whence they sprung. Thucydides again tells us that the Corinthians complained of the Corcyreans, "from whom, though a colony of their own, they had received some contemptuous treatment, for they neither payed them the usual honor on their public solemnities, nor began with a Corinthian in the distribution of the sacrifices, which is always done by other colonies." From hence it is plain what kind of dependence the Greek colonies were under, and what sort of acknowledgment they owed to the mother state.

If we pass from the Grecian to the Roman colonies, we shall find them not less free. But this difference may be observed between them, that the Roman colonies did not, like the Grecian, become separate states governed by different laws, but always remained a part of the mother state; and all that were free of the colonies were also free of Rome, and had right to an equal suffrage in making all laws and appointing all officers for the government of the whole commonwealth. For the truth of this we have the testimony of St. Paul, who though born at Tarsus, yet assures us he was born free of Rome. And Grotius gives us the opinion of a Roman king concerning the freedom of colonies: King Tullus says, "for our part, we look upon it to be neither truth nor justice that mother cities ought of necessity and by the law of nature to rule over their colonies."

When we come down to the latter ages of the world and consider the colonies planted in the three last centuries in America from several kingdoms in Europe, we shall find them, says Pufendorf, very different from the ancient colonies, and gives us an instance in those of the Spaniards. Although it be confessed these fall greatly short of enjoying equal freedom with the ancient Greek and Roman ones, yet it will be said truly, they enjoy equal freedom with their countrymen in Spain: but as they are all under the government of an absolute monarch, they have no reason to complain that one enjoys the liberty the other is deprived of. The French colonies will be found nearly in the same condition, and for the same reason, because their fellow subjects in France have also lost their liberty. And the question here is not whether all colonies, as compared one with another, enjoy equal liberty, but whether all enjoy as much freedom as the inhabitants of the mother state; and this will hardly be denied in the case of the Spanish, French, or other modern foreign colonies.

By this it fully appears that colonies in general, both ancient and modern, have always enjoyed as much freedom as the mother state from which they went out. And will anyone suppose the British colonies in America are an exception to this general rule? Colonies that came out from a kingdom renowned for liberty, from a constitution founded on compact, from a people of all the sons of men the most tenacious of freedom; who left the delights of their native country, parted from their homes and all their conveniences, searched out and subdued a foreign country with the most amazing travail and fortitude, to the infinite advantage and emolument of the mother state; that removed on a firm reliance of a solemn compact and royal promise and grant that they and their successors forever should be free, should be partakers and sharers in all the privileges and advantages of the then English, now British constitution.

If it were possible a doubt could yet remain, in the most unbelieving mind, that these British colonies are not every way justly and fully entitled to equal liberty and freedom with their fellow subjects in

Europe, we might show that the Parliament of Great Britain have always understood their rights in the same light.

By an act passed in the-thirteenth year of the reign of his late Majesty, King George II, entitled An Act For Naturalizing Foreign Protestants, etc., and by another act, passed in the twentieth year of the same reign, for nearly the same purposes, by both which it is enacted and ordained "that all foreign Protestants who had inhabited and resided for the space of seven years or more in any of His Majesty's colonies in America" might, on the conditions therein mentioned, be naturalized, and thereupon should "be deemed, adjudged, and taken to be His Majesty's natural-born subjects of the kingdom of Great Britain to all intents, constructions, and purposes, as if they, and every one of them, had been or were born within the same." No reasonable man will here suppose the Parliament intended by these acts to put foreigners who had been in the colonies only seven years in a better condition than those who had been born in them or had removed from Britain thither, but only to put these foreigners on an equality with them; and to do this, they are obliged to give them all the rights of natural-born subjects of Great Britain.

From what hath been shown, it will appear beyond a doubt that the British subjects in America have equal rights with those in Britain; that they do not hold those rights as a privilege granted them, nor enjoy them as a grace and favor bestowed, but possess them as an inherent, indefeasible right, as they and their ancestors were freeborn subjects, justly and naturally entitled to all the rights and advantages of the British constitution.

And the British legislative and executive powers have considered the colonies as possessed of these rights, and have always heretofore, in the most tender and parental manner, treated them as their dependent, though free, condition required. The protection promised on the part of the crown, with cheerfulness and great gratitude we acknowledge, hath at all times been given to the colonies. The dependence of the colonies to Great Britain hath been fully testified by a constant and ready obedience to all the commands of his present Majesty and his royal predecessors, both men and money having been raised in them at all times when called for with as much alacrity and in as large proportions as hath been done in Great Britain, the ability of each considered. It must also be confessed with thankfulness that the first adventurers and their successors, for one hundred and thirty years, have fully enjoyed all the freedoms and immunities promised on their first removal from England. But here the scene seems to be unhappily changing: the British ministry, whether induced by a jealousy of the colonies by false informations, or by some alteration in the system of political government, we have no information; whatever hath been the motive, this we are sure of: the Parliament in their last session passed an act limiting, restricting, and burdening the trade of these colonies much more than had ever been done before, as also for greatly enlarging the power and jurisdiction of the courts of admiralty in the colonies; and also came to a resolution that it might be necessary to establish stamp duties and other internal taxes to be collected within them. This act and this resolution have caused great uneasiness and consternation among the British subjects on the continent of America: how much reason there is for it we will endeavor, in the most modest and plain manner we can, to lay before our readers.

In the first place, let it be considered that although each of the colonies hath a legislature within itself to take care of its interests and provide for its peace and internal government, yet there are many things of a more general nature, quite out of the reach of these particular legislatures, which it is necessary should be regulated, ordered and governed. One of this kind is the commerce of the whole British empire, taken collectively, and that of each kingdom and colony in it as it makes a part of that whole. Indeed, everything that concerns the proper interest and fit government of the whole commonwealth, of keeping the peace, and subordination of all the parts towards the whole and one among another, must be considered in this light. Amongst these general concerns, perhaps, money and paper credit, those grand instruments of all commerce, will be found also to have a place. These, with all other matters of a general nature, it is absolutely necessary should have a general power to direct them, some supreme and overruling authority with power to make laws and form regulations for the good of all, and to compel their execution and observation. It being necessary some such general power should exist somewhere, every man of the least knowledge of the British constitution will be naturally led to look for and find it in the Parliament of Great Britain. That grand and august legislative body must from the nature of their authority and the necessity of the thing be justly vested with this power. Hence it becomes the indispensable duty of every good and loyal subject cheerfully to obey and patiently submit to all the acts, laws, orders, and regulations that may be made and passed by Parliament for directing and governing all these general matters.

Here it may be urged by many, and indeed with great appearance of reason, that the equity, justice, and beneficence of the British constitution will require that the separate kingdoms and distant colonies who are to obey and be governed by these general laws and regulations ought to be represented, some way or other, in Parliament, at least whilst these general matters are under consideration. Whether the colonies will ever be admitted to have representatives in Parliament, whether it be consistent with their distant and dependent state, and whether if it were admitted it would be to their advantage, are questions we will pass by, and observe that these colonies ought in justice and for the very evident good of the whole commonwealth to have notice of every new measure about to be pursued and new act that is about to be passed, by which their rights, liberties, or interests will be affected. They ought to have such notice, that they may appear and be heard by their agents, by counsel, or written representation, or by some other equitable and effectual way.

The colonies are at so great a distance from England that the members of Parliament can generally have but little knowledge of their business, connections, and interest but what is gained from people who have been there; the most of these have so slight a knowledge themselves that the informations they can give are very little to be depended on, though they may pretend to determine with confidence on matters far above their reach. All such kind of informations are too uncertain to be depended on in the transacting business of so much consequence and in which the interests of two millions of free people are so deeply concerned. There is no kind of inconveniency or mischief can arise from the colonies having such notice and being heard in the manner above mentioned; but, on the contrary, very great mischiefs have already happened to the colonies, and always must be expected, if they are not heard before things of such importance are determined concerning them.

Enlarging the power and jurisdiction of the courts of vice-admiralty in the colonies is another part of the same act, greatly and justly complained of. Courts of admiralty have long been established in most of the colonies, whose authority were circumscribed within moderate territorial jurisdictions; and these courts have always done the business necessary to be brought before such courts for trial in the manner it ought to be done and in a way only moderately expensive to the subjects; and if seizures were made or informations exhibited without reason or contrary seizures were made or informations exhibited without reason or contrary to law, the informer or seizor was left to the justice of the common law, there to pay for his folly or suffer for his temerity. But now this course is quite altered, and a customhouse officer may make a seizure in Georgia of goods ever so legally imported, and carry the trial to Halifax at fifteen hundred miles distance; and thither the owner must follow him to defend his property; and when he comes there, quite beyond the circle of his friends, acquaintance, and correspondents, among total strangers, he must there give bond and must find sureties to be bound with him in a large sum before he shall be admitted to claim his own goods; when this is complied with, he hath a trial and his goods acquitted. If the judge can be prevailed on (which it is very well known may too easily be done) to certify there was only probable cause for making the seizure, the unhappy owner shall not maintain any action against the illegal seizor for damages or obtain any other satisfaction, but he may return to Georgia quite ruined and undone in conformity to an act of Parliament. Such unbounded encouragement and protection given to informers must call to everyone's remembrance Tacitus' account of the miserable condition of the Romans in the reign of Tiberius their emperor, who let loose and encouraged the informers of that age. Surely if the colonies had been fully heard before this had been done, the liberties and properties of the Americans would not have been so much disregarded.

The resolution of the House of Commons, come into during the same session of Parliament, asserting their rights to establish stamp duties and internal taxes to be collected in the colonies without their own consent, hath much more, and for much more reason, alarmed the British subjects in America than anything that had ever been done before. These resolutions, carried into execution, the colonies cannot help but consider as a manifest violation of their just and long-enjoyed rights. For it must be confessed by all men that they who are taxed at pleasure by others cannot possibly have any property, can have nothing to be called their own. They who have no property can have no freedom, but are indeed reduced to the most abject slavery, are in a condition far worse than countries conquered and made tributary, for these have only a fixed sum to pay, which they are left to raise among themselves in the way that they may think most equal and easy, and having paid the stipulated sum the debt is discharged, and what is left is their own. This is much more tolerable than to be taxed at the mere will of others, without any bounds, without any stipulation and agreement, contrary to their consent and against their will. If we are told that those who lay these taxes upon the colonies are men of the highest character for their wisdom, justice, and integrity, and therefore cannot be supposed to deal hardly, unjustly, or unequally by any; admitting and really believing that all this is true, it will make no alteration in the nature of the case. For one who is bound to obey the will of another is as really a slave though he may have a good master as if he had a bad one; and this is stronger in politic bodies than in natural ones, as the former have perpetual succession and remain the same; and although they may have a very good master at one time, they may have a very bad one at another. And indeed, if the people in America are to be taxed by the representatives of the people in Britain, their malady is an increasing evil that must always grow greater by time. Whatever burdens are laid upon the Americans will be so much taken off the Britons; and the doing this will soon be extremely popular, and those who put up to be members of the House of Commons must obtain the votes of the people by promising to take more and more of the taxes off them by putting it on the Americans. This must most assuredly be the case, and it will not be in the power even of the Parliament to prevent it; the people's private interest will be concerned and will govern them; they will have such, and only such, representatives as will act agreeable to this their interest; and these taxes laid on Americans will be always a part of the supply bill, in which the other branches of the legislature can make no alteration. And in truth, the subjects in the colonies will be taxed at the will and pleasure of their fellow subjects in Britain. How equitable and how just this may be must be left to every impartial man to determine.

But it will be said that the monies drawn from the colonies by duties and by taxes will be laid up and set apart to be used for their future defense. This will not at all alleviate the hardship, but serves only more strongly to mark the servile state of the people. Free people have ever thought, and always will think, that the money necessary for their defense lies safest in their own hands, until it be wanted immediately for that purpose. To take the money of the Americans, which they want continually to use in their trade, and lay it up for their defense at a thousand leagues distance from them when the enemies they have to fear are in their own neighborhood, hath not the greatest probability of friendship or of prudence.

It is not the judgment of free people only that money for defending them is safest in their own keeping, but it hath also been the opinion of the best and wisest kings and governors of mankind, in every age of the world, that the wealth of a state was most securely as well as most profitably deposited in the hands of their faithful subjects. Constantine, emperor of the Romans, though an absolute prince, both practiced and praised this method. "Diocletian sent persons on purpose to reproach him with his neglect of the public, and the poverty to which he was reduced by his own fault. Constantine heard these reproaches with patience; and having persuaded those who made them in Diocletian's name, to stay a few days with him, he sent word to the most wealthy persons in the provinces that he wanted money and that they had now an opportunity of showing whether or no they truly loved their prince. Upon this notice everyone strove who should be foremost in carrying to the exchequer all their gold, silver, and valuable effects; so that in a short time Constantine from being the poorest became by far the most wealthy of all the four princes. He then invited the deputies of Diocletian to visit his treasury, desiring them to make a faithful report to their master of the state in which they should find it. They obeyed; and, while they stood gazing on the mighty heaps of gold and silver, Constantine told them that the wealth which they beheld with astonishment had long since belonged to him, but that he had left it by way of depositum in the hands of his people, adding, the richest and surest treasure of the prince was the love of his subjects. The deputies were no sooner gone than the generous prince sent for those who had assisted him in his exigency, commended their zeal, and returned to everyone what they had so readily brought into his treasury."

We are not insensible that when liberty is in danger, the liberty of complaining is dangerous; yet a man on a wreck was never denied the liberty of roaring as loud as he could, says Dean Swift. And we believe no good reason can be given why the colonies should not modestly and soberly inquire what right the Parliament of Great Britain have to tax them. We know such inquiries by a late letter writer have been branded with the little epithet of mushroom policy; and he insinuates that for the colonies to pretend to claim any privileges will draw down the resentment of the Parliament on them. Is the defense of liberty become so contemptible, and pleading for just rights so dangerous? Can the guardians of liberty be thus ludicrous? Can the patrons of freedom be so jealous and so severe ? If the British House of Commons are rightfully possessed of a power to tax the colonies in America, this power must be vested in them by the British constitution, as they are one branch of the great legislative body of the nation. As they are the representatives of all the people in Britain, they have beyond doubt all the power such a representation can possibly give; yet great as this power is, surely it cannot exceed that of their constituents. And can it possibly be shown that the people in Britain have a sovereign authority over their fellow subjects in America ? Yet such is the authority that must be exercised in taking people's estates from them by taxes, or otherwise without their consent. In all aids granted to the crown by the Parliament, it is said with the greatest propriety, "We freely give unto Your Majesty"; for they give their own money and the money of those who have entrusted them with a proper power for that purpose. But can they with the same propriety give away the money of the Americans, who have never given any such power? Before a thing can be justly given away, the giver must certainly have acquired a property in it; and have the people in Britain justly acquired such a property in the goods and estates of the people in these colonies that they may give them away at pleasure?

In an imperial state, which consists of many separate governments each of which hath peculiar privileges and of which kind it is evident the empire of Great Britain is, no single part, though greater than another part, is by that superiority entitled to make laws for or to tax such lesser part; but all laws and all taxations which bind the whole must be made by the whole. This may be fully verified by the empire of Germany, which consists of many states, some powerful and others weak, yet the powerful never make laws to govern or to tax the little and weak ones, neither is it done by the emperor, but only by the diet, consisting of the representatives of the whole body. Indeed, it must be absurd to suppose that the common people of Great Britain have a sovereign and absolute authority over their fellow subjects in America, or even any sort of power whatsoever over them; but it will be still more absurd to suppose they can give a power to their representatives which they have not themselves. If the House of Commons do not receive this authority from their constituents it will be difficult to tell by what means they obtained it, except it be vested in them by mere superiority and power.

Should it be urged that the money expended by the mother country for the defense and protection of America, and especially during the late war, must justly entitle her to some retaliation from the colonies, and that the stamp duties and taxes intended to be raised in them are only designed for that equitable purpose; if we are permitted to examine how far this may rightfully vest the Parliament with the power of taxing the colonies we shall find this claim to have no sort of equitable foundation. In many of the colonies, especially those in New England, who were planted, as before observed, not at the charge of the crown or kingdom of England, but at the expense of the planters themselves, and were not only planted but also defended against the savages and other enemies in long and cruel wars which continued for an hundred years almost without intermission, solely at their own charge: and in the year 1746, when the Duke D'Anville came out from France with the most formidable French fleet that ever was in the American seas, enraged at these colonies for the loss of Louisbourg the year before and with orders to make an attack on them; even in this greatest exigence, these colonies were left to the protection of Heaven and their own efforts. These colonies having thus planted and defended themselves and removed all enemies from their borders, were in hopes to enjoy peace and recruit their state, much exhausted by these long struggles; but they were soon called upon to raise men and send out to the defense of other colonies, and to make conquests for the crown. They dutifully obeyed the requisition, and with ardor entered into those services and continued in them until all encroachments were removed, and all Canada, and even the Havana, conquered. They most cheerfully complied with every call of the crown; they rejoiced, yea even exulted, in the prosperity and exaltation of the British empire. But these colonies, whose bounds were fixed and whose borders were before cleared from enemies by their own fortitude and at their own expense, reaped no sort of advantage by these conquests: they are not enlarged, have not gained a single acre of land, have no part in the Indian or interior trade. The immense tracts of land subdued and no less immense and profitable commerce acquired all belong to Great Britain, and not the least share or portion to these colonies, though thousands of their men have lost their lives and millions of their money have been expended in the purchase of them, for great part of which we are yet in debt, and from which we shall . . . not in many years be able to extricate ourselves. Hard will be the fate, yea cruel the destiny, of these unhappy colonies if the reward they are to receive for all this is the loss of their freedom; better for them Canada still remained French, yea far more eligible that it ever should remain so than that the price of its reduction should be their slavery.

If the colonies are not taxed by Parliament, are they therefore exempted from bearing their proper share in the necessary burdens of government? This by no means follows. Do they not support a regular internal government in each colony as expensive to the people here as the internal government of Britain is to the people there? Have not, the colonies here, at all times when called upon by the crown, raised money for the public service, done it as cheerfully as the Parliament have done on like occasions? Is not this the most easy, the most natural, and most constitutional way of raising money in the colonies? What occasion then to distrust the colonies — what necessity to fall on an invidious and unconstitutional method to compel them to do what they have ever done freely? Are not the people in the colonies as loyal and dutiful subjects as any age or nation ever produced; and are they not as useful to the kingdom, in this remote quarter of the world, as their fellow subjects are who dwell in Britain? The Parliament, it is confessed, have power to regulate the trade of the whole empire; and hath it not full power, by this means, to draw all the money and all the wealth of the colonies into the mother country at pleasure? What motive, after all this, can remain to induce the Parliament to abridge the privileges and lessen the rights of the most loyal and dutiful subjects, subjects justly entitled to ample freedom, who have long enjoyed and not abused or forfeited their liberties, who have used them to their own advantage in dutiful subserviency to the orders and interests of Great Britain? Why should the gentle current of tranquillity that has so long run with peace through all the British states, and flowed with joy and happiness in all her countries, be at last obstructed, be turned out of its true course into unusual and winding channels by which many of those states must be ruined, but none of them can possibly be made more rich or more happy?

Before we conclude, it may be necessary to take notice of the vast difference there is between the raising money in a country by duties, taxes, or otherwise, and employing and laying out the money again in the same country, and raising the like sums of money by the like means and sending it away quite out of the country where it is raised. Where the former of these is the case, although the sums raised may be very great, yet that country may support itself under them; for as fast as the money is collected together, it is again scattered abroad, to be used in commerce and every kind of business; and money is not made scarcer by this means, but rather the contrary, as this continual circulation must have a tendency to prevent, in some degree, its being hoarded. But where the latter method is pursued, the effect will be extremely different; for here, as fast as the money can be collected, 'tis immediately sent out of the country, never to return but by a tedious round of commerce, which at best must take up much time. Here all trade, and every kind of business depending on it, will grow dull, and must languish more and more until it comes to a final stop at last. If the money raised in Great Britain in the three last years of the late war, and which exceeded forty millions sterling, had been sent out of the kingdom, would not this have nearly ruined the trade of the nation in three years only? Think, then, what must be the condition of these miserable colonies when all the money proposed to be raised in them by high duties on the importation of divers kinds of goods, by the post office, by stamp duties, and other taxes, is sent quite away, as fast as it can be collected, and this to be repeated continually and last forever! Is it possible for colonies under these circumstances to support themselves, to have any money, any trade, or other business, carried on in them? Certainly it is not; nor is there at present, or ever was, any country under Heaven that did, or possibly could, support itself under such burdens.

We finally beg leave to assert that the first planters of these colonies were pious Christians, were faithful subjects who, with a fortitude and perseverance little known and less considered, settled these wild countries, by God's goodness and their own amazing labors, thereby added a most valuable dependence to the crown of Great Britain; were ever dutifully subservient to her interests; so taught their children that not one has been disaffected to this day, but all have honestly obeyed every royal command and cheerfully submitted to every constitutional law; have as little inclination as they have ability to throw off their dependency; have carefully avoided every offensive measure and every interdicted manufacture; have risked their lives as they have been ordered, and furnished their money when it has been called for; have never been troublesome or expensive to the mother country; have kept due order and supported a regular government; have maintained peace and practiced Christianity; and in all conditions, and in every relation, have demeaned themselves as loyal, as dutiful, and as faithful subjects ought; and that no kingdom or state hath, or ever had, colonies more quiet, more obedient, or more profitable than these have ever been.

May the same divine goodness that guided the first planters, protected the settlements, inspired Kings to be gracious, Parliaments to be tender, ever preserve, ever support our present gracious King; give great wisdom to his ministers and much understanding to his Parliaments; perpetuate the sovereignty of the British constitution, and the filial dependency and happiness of all the colonies.

 P ———.

Providence, in New England
November 30, 1764.

# BENJAMIN RUSH

# AN EARLY ARGUMENT AGAINST SLAVERY, THE PECULIAR INSTITUTION IN AMERICA

## On Slave-Keeping

So much hath been said upon the subject of Slave-keeping, that an apology may be required for this paper. The only one I shall offer is, that the evil still continues. This may in part be owing to the great attachment we have to our own interest, and in part to the subject not being fully exhausted. The design of the following paper is to sum up the leading arguments against it, several of which have not been urged by any of those authors who have written upon it.

Without entering into the history of the facts which relate to the slave-trade, I shall proceed immediately to combat the principal arguments which are used to support it.

And here I need hardly say any thing in favor of the Intellects of the Negroes, or of their capacities for virtue and happiness, although these have been supposed by some to be inferior to those of the inhabitants of Europe. The accounts which travellers give us of their ingenuity, humanity, and strong attachment to their parents, relations, friends and country, show us that they are equal to the Europeans, when we allow for the diversity of temper and genius which is occasioned by climate. We have many well attested anecdotes of as sublime and disinterested virtue among them as ever adorned a Roman or a Christian character.[1] But we are to distinguish between an African in

From Dagobert D. Reeves, *The Selected Writings of Benjamin Rush* (Philosophical Library, 1947)

[1] See SPECTATOR, Vol. I. No. 11.

There is now in the town of Boston a Free Negro Girl, about 18 years of age, who has been but 9 years in the country, whose singular genius and accomplishments are such as not only do honor to her sex, but to human nature. Several of her poems have been printed, and read with pleasure by the public. [Author's footnote] his own country, and an African in a state of slavery in America. Slavery is so foreign to the human mind, that the moral faculties, as well as those of the understanding are debased, and rendered torpid by it. All the vices which are charged upon the Negroes in the southern colonies and the West-Indies, such as Idleness, Treachery, Theft, and the like, are the genuine offspring of slavery, and serve as an argument to prove that they were not intended, by Providence for it.

Nor let it be said, in the present Age, that their black color (as it is commonly called), either subjects them to, or qualifies them for slavery.[1] The vulgar notion of their being descended from Cain, who was supposed to have been marked with this color, is too absurd to need a refutation. Without enquiring into the Cause of this blackness, I shall only add upon this subject, that so far from being a curse, it subjects the Negroes to no inconveniencies, but on the contrary qualifies them for that part of the Globe in which providence has placed them. The ravages of heat, diseases and time, appear less in their faces than in a white one; and when we exclude variety of color from our ideas of Beauty, they may be said to possess every thing necessary to constitute it in common with the white people.[2]

It has been urged by the inhabitants of the Sugar Islands and South Carolina, that it would be impossible to carry on the manufactories of Sugar, Rice, and Indigo, without Negro slaves. No manufactory can ever be of consequence enough to society, to admit the least violation of the laws of justice or humanity. But I am far from thinking the arguments used in favor of employing Negroes for the cultivation of these articles, should have any weight. M. Le Poivre, late envoy from the king of France, to the king of Cochin-China, and now intendant of the isles of Bourbon and Mauritius, in his observations upon the manners and arts of the various nations in Africa and Asia, speaking of

---

[1] Montesquieu, in his Spirit of Laws, treats this argument with the ridicule it deserves.

"Were I to vindicate our right to make slaves of the Negroes, these should be my arguments.

The Europeans having extirpated the American Indians, were obliged to make slaves of the Africans, for clearing such vast tracts of land.

Sugar.would be too dear, if the plants which produce it were cultivated by any other than slaves.

These creatures are all over black, and with such a flat nose, that they can scarcely be pitied.

It is hardly to be believed that God, who is a wise being, should place a soul, especially a good soul, in such a black ugly body.

The Negroes prefer a glass necklace to that gold, which polite nations so highly value: can there be a greater proof of their wanting common sense.

It is impossible for us to suppose these creatures to be men, because, allowing them to be men, a suspicion would follow, that we ourselves are not Christians."

Book XV. Chap. v.

[2] "I am black, but *comely*."          —SONG OF SOLOMON.
[Author's footnotes]

the culture of sugar in Cochin-China, has the following remarks — "It is worthy observation too, that the sugar cane is there cultivated by freemen, and all the process of preparation and refining, the work of free hands. Compare then the price of the Cochin-Chinese production with the same commodity which is cultivated and prepared by the wretched slaves of our European colonies, and judge if, to procure sugar from our colonies, it was necessary to authorize by law the slavery of the unhappy Africans transported to America. From what I have observed at Cochin-China, I cannot entertain a doubt, but that our West-India colonies, had they been distributed without reservation amongst a free people, would have produced double the quantity that it now procured from the labor of the unfortunate Negroes.

What advantage, then, has accrued to Europe, civilized as it is, and thoroughly versed in the laws of nature, and the rights of mankind, by legally authorizing in our colonies, the daily outrages against human nature, permitting them to debase man almost below the level of the beasts of the field? These slavish laws have proved as opposite to its interest, as they are to its honor, and to the laws of humanity. This remark I have often made.

Liberty and property form the basis of abundance, and good agriculture: I never observed it to flourish where those rights of mankind were not firmly established. The earth which multiplies her productions with a kind of profusion, under the hands of the free-born laborer seems to shrink into barrenness under the sweat of the slave. Such is the will of the great Author of our Nature, who has created man free, and assigned to him the earth, that he might cultivate his possession with the sweat of his brow; but still should enjoy his Liberty.

Now if the plantations in the islands and the southern colonies were more limited, and freemen only employed in working them, the general product would be greater, although the profits to individuals would be less, — a circumstance this, which by diminishing opulence in a few, would suppress luxury and vice, and promote that equal distribution of property, which appears best calculated to promote the welfare of society.—[1] I know it has been said by some, that none but

[1]From this account of Le Poivre's, we may learn the futility of the argument, that the number of vessels in the sugar trade, serve as a nursery for seamen, and that the Negroes consume a large quantity of the manufactures of Great Britain. If freemen only were employed in the islands, a double quantity of sugar would be made, and of course twice the number of vessels and seamen would be made use of in the trade. One freeman consumes yearly four times the quantity of British goods that a Negro does. Slaves multiply in all countries slowly. Freemen multiply in proportion as slavery is discouraged. It is to be hoped therefore that motives of policy will at last induce Britons to give up a trade, which those of justice and humanity cannot prevail upon them to relinquish. [Author's footnote]

the natives of warm climates could undergo the excessive heat and labor of the West India islands. But this argument is founded upon an error; for the reverse of this is true. I have been informed by good authority, that one European who escapes the first or second year, will do twice the work, and live twice the number of years that an ordinary Negro will do: nor need we be surprised at this, when we hear that such is the natural fertility of the soil, and so numerous the spontaneous fruits of the earth in the interior parts of Africa, that the natives live in plenty at the expence of little or no labor, which, in warm climates, has ever been found to be incompatible with long life and happiness. Future ages, therefore, when they read the accounts of the Slave Trade (— if they do not regard them as fabulous) — will be at a loss which to condemn most, our folly or our guilt, in abetting this direct violation of the laws of nature and religion.

But there are some who have gone so far as to say that slavery is not repugnant to the genius of Christianity, and that it is not forbidden in any part of the Scriptures. Natural and revealed Religion always speak the same things, although the latter delivers its precepts with a louder, and more distinct voice than the former. If it could be proved that no testimony was to be found in the Bible against a practice so pregnant with evils of the most destructive tendency to society, it would be sufficient to overthrow its divine original. We read it is true of Abraham's having slaves born in his house; and we have reason to believe, that part of the riches of the patriarchs consisted in them: but we can no more infer the lawfulness of the practice, from the short account which the Jewish historian gives us of these facts, than we can vindicate telling a lie, because Rahab is not condemned for it in the account which is given of her deceiving the king of Jericho.[1] We read that some of the same men indulged themselves in a plurality of wives, without any strictures being made upon their conduct for it; and yet no one will pretend to say, that this is not forbidden in many parts of the Old Testament.[2] But we are told the Jews kept the heathens, in perpetual

---

[1] 3 And the king of Jericho sent unto Rahab, saying, Bring forth the men that are come to thee, which are entered into thine house: for they be come to search out all the country.

4 And the woman took the two men, and hid them, and said thus, There came men unto me, but I wist not whence they *were*.

5 And it came to pass *about the time* of shutting of the gate, when it was dark, that the men went out: whither the men went, I wot not: pursue after them quickly, for ye shall overtake them.

6 But she brought them up to the roof of the house, and hid them with the stalks of flax, which she had laid in order upon the roof. [Author's footnote]

JOSHUA, Chap. II.

[2] Prov. v. 18, 19, 20.

bondage.[1] The design of providence in permitting this evil, was probably to prevent the Jews from marrying among strangers, to which their intercourse with them upon any other footing than that of slaves, would naturally have inclined them.[2] Had this taken place — their Natural Religion would have been corrupted — they would have contracted all their vices,[3] and the intention of providence in keeping them a distinct people, in order to accomplish the promise made to Abraham, that "in his Seed all the Nations of the earth should be blessed," would have been defeated; so that the descent of the MESSIAH from ABRAHAM, could not have been traced, and the divine commission of the Son of God, would have wanted one of its most powerful arguments to support it. But with regard to their own countrymen, it is plain, perpetual slavery was not tolerated. Hence, at the end of seven years or in the year of the jubilee, all the Hebrew slaves were set at liberty,[4] and it was held unlawful to detain them in servitude longer than that time, except by their own consent. But if, in the partial revelation which GOD made, of his will to the Jews, we find such testimonies against slavery, what may we not expect from the Gospel, the design of which was to abolish all distinctions of name and country. While the Jews thought they complied with the precepts of the law, in confining the love of their neighbour "to the children of their own people," Christ commands us to look upon all mankind even our enemies[5] as our neighbours and brethren, and "in all things, to do unto them whatever we would wish they should do unto us." He tells us further that his "Kingdom is not of this World," and therefore constantly avoids saying any thing that might interfere directly with the Roman or Jewish governments: so that altho' he does not call upon masters to emancipate their slaves, or upon slaves to assert that liberty

[1]Levit. xxv. 44, 45, 46.

[2]That marriage with strangers was looked upon as a crime among the Jews, we learn from Ezra ix. 1 to 6, also from the whole of Chapter x.

[3]May not this be the reason why swine's flesh was forbidden to the Jews, lest they should be tempted to eat with their heathen neighbours, who used it in diet? This appears more probable than the opinion of Doctor MEAD, who supposes that it has a physical tendency to produce the leprosy; or that of VOLTAIRE, who asserts that the Jews learned to abstain from this flesh from the Egyptians, who valued the Hog almost to a degree of idolatry for its great usefulness in rooting up the Ground. What makes this conjecture the more probable is, that the Jews abstained from several other kinds of flesh used by their heathen neighbours, which have never been accused of bringing on diseases of the skin, and which were used constantly in diet by the Egyptians.

[4] Deuteronomy xxiv. 7.

[5] This is strongly inculcated in the story of the good Samaritan, Luke x. [Author's footnotes]

wherewith God and nature had made them free, yet there is scarcely a parable or a sermon in the whole history of his life, but what contains the strongest arguments against slavery. Every prohibition of covetousness — intemperance — pride — uncleanness — theft — and murder, which he delivered, — every lesson of meekness, humility, forbearance, charity, self-denial, and brotherly-love which he taught, are levelled against this evil; — for slavery, while it includes all the former vices, necessarily excludes the practice of all the latter virtues, both from the master and the slave. — Let such, therefore, who vindicate the traffic of buying and selling souls, seek some modern system of religion to support it, and not presume to sanctify their crimes by attempting to reconcile it to the sublime and perfect Religion of the Great Author of Christianity.

There are some amongst us who cannot help allowing the force of our last argument, but plead as a motive for importing and keeping slaves, that they become acquainted with the principles of the religion of our country.— This is like justifying a highway robbery because part of the money acquired in this manner was appropriated to some religious use.— Christianity will never be propagated by any other methods than those employed by Christ and his apostles. Slavery is an engine as little fitted for that purpose as fire or the sword. A Christian slave is a contradiction in terms. But if we enquire into the methods employed for converting the Negroes to Christianity, we shall find the means suited to the end proposed. In many places Sunday is appropriated to work for themselves. Reading and writing are discouraged among them. A belief is even inculcated among some, that they have no souls. In a word,—Every attempt to instruct or convert them, has been constantly opposed by their masters. Nor has the example of their Christian masters any tendency to prejudice them in favor of our religion. How often do they betray, in their sudden transports of anger and resentment (against which there is no restraint provided towards their Negroes) the most violent degrees of passion and fury!— What luxury — what ingratitude to the supreme being — what impiety in their ordinary conversation do some of them discover in the presence of their slaves; I say nothing of the dissolution of marriage vows, or the entire abolition of matrimony, which the frequent sale of them introduces, and which are directly contrary to the law of nature and the principles of Christianity Would to heaven I could here conceal the shocking violations of chastity, which some of them are obliged to undergo without daring to complain. Husbands have been forced to prostitute their wives, and mothers their daughters, to gratify the brutal lust of a master. This — all — this is practised — blush — ye impure and hardened monsters, while I repeat it — by men who call themselves Christians!

But further — It has been said that we do a kindness to the Negroes by bringing them to America, as we thereby save their lives, which had been forfeited by their being conquered in war.[1]

Let such as prefer or inflict slavery rather than death, disown their being descended from or connected with our mother countries. — But it will be found, upon enquiry, that many are stolen or seduced from their friends, who have never been conquered; and it is plain, from the testimony of historians and travellers, that wars were uncommon among them, until the Christians who began the slave trade, stirred up the different nations to fight against each other. Sooner let them imbrue their hands in each others blood, or condemn one another to perpetual slavery, than the name of one Christian, or one American be stained by the perpetuation of such enormous crimes. Nor let it be urged that by treating slaves well, we render their situation happier in this country than it was in their own.— slavery and vice are connected together, and the latter is always a source of misery. Besides, by the greatest humanity we can show them, we only lessen, but do not remove the crime, for the injustice of it continues the same. The laws of retribution are so strongly inculcated by the moral governor of the world, that even the ox is entitled to his reward for "treading the corn." How great then must be the amount of that injustice which deprives so many of our fellow creatures of the just reward of their labor![2]

But it will be asked here, What steps shall we take to remedy

this evil, and what shall we do with those slaves we have already in this country? This is indeed a most difficult question. But let every

---

[1] "From the right of killing in case of conquest, politicians have drawn that of reducing to slavery; a consequence as ill grounded as the principle.

There is no such thing as a right of reducing people to slavery, but when it becomes necessary for the preservation of the conquest. Preservation, but not servitude, is the end of conquest; though servitude may happen sometimes to be a necessary means of preservation.

Even in that case it is contrary to the nature of things, that the slavery should be perpetual. The people enslaved ought to be rendered capable of becoming subjects."

Montesquieu's Spirit of Laws, Book x. Chap. 3

[2] The debt of a master to a Negro man whose work is valued at ten pounds sterling a year, deducting forty shillings a year, which is the most that is laid out for their clothing in the West-Indies, amounts, in the course of 20 years, to L. 160 sterling. The victuals are included in the above wages. These consist chiefly of vegetables, and are very cheap. [Author's footnotes]

man contrivc to answer it for himself. If you possessed an estate which was bequeathed to you by your ancestors, and were afterwards convinced that it was the just property of another man, would you think it right to continue in the possession of it? Would you not give it up immediately to the lawful owner? The voice of all mankind would mark him for a villain who would refuse to comply with this demand of justice. And is not keeping a slave after you are convinced of the unlawfulness of it — a crime of the same nature? All the money you save, or acquire by their labor is stolen from them; and however plausible the excuse may be that you form to reconcile it to your consciences, yet be assured that your crime stands registered in the court of Heaven as a breach of the eighth commandment.

The first step to be taken to put a stop to slavery in this country, is to leave off importing slaves. For this purpose let our assemblies unite in petitioning the King and Parliament to dissolve the African Company.[1] It is by this incorporated band of robbers that the trade has been chiefly carried on to Armerica. We have the more reason to expect relief from an application at this juncture, as, by a late decision in favor of a Virginia slave, at Westminster-Hall, the clamors of the whole nation are raised against them. Let such of our countrymen as engage in the slave trade, be shunned as the greatest enemies to our country, and, let the vessels which bring the slaves to us, be avoided as if they bore in them the seeds of that forbidden fruit, whose baneful taste destroyed both the natural and moral world. — As for the Negroes among us, who, from having acquired all the low vices of slavery, or who, from age or infirmities are unfit to be set at liberty, I would propose, for the good of society, that they should continue the property of those with whom they grew old, or from whom they contracted those vices and infirmities. But let the young Negroes be educated in the principles of virtue and religion — let them be taught to read and write and afterwards instructed in some business, whereby they may be able to maintain themselves. Let laws be made to limit the time of their servitude, and to entitle them to all the privileges of free-born British subjects. At any rate let retribution be done to God and to society.

And now my countrymen, What shall I add more to rouse up your indignation against slave-keeping. Consider the many complicated

---

[1] The Virginia Assembly, which had the honor of being first on the continent in opposing the American Stamp Act by their Resolves, have lately set another laudable example to the colonies in being the first in petitioning for a redress of this grievance. [Author's footnote]

crimes it involves in it. Think of the bloody wars which are fomented by it, among the African nations, or if these are too common to affect you, think of the pangs which attend the dissolution of the ties of nature in those who are stolen from their relations. Think of the many thousands who perish by sickness, melancholy and suicide, in their voyages to America. Pursue the poor devoted victims to one of the West India islands, and see them exposed there to public sale. Hear their cries, and see their looks of tenderness at each other upon being separated. — Mothers are torn from their daughters, and brothers from brothers, without the liberty of a parting embrace. Their master's name is now marked upon their breasts with a red hot iron. But let us pursue them into a sugar field, and behold a scene still more affecting than this — See! the poor wretches with what reluctance they take their instruments of labor into their hands.— Some of them, overcome with heat and sickness, seek to refresh themselves by a little rest, — But, behold an overseer approaches them. — In vain they sue for pity.— He lifts up his whip, while streams of blood follow every stroke. Neither age nor sex are spared. — Methinks one of them is a woman far advanced in her pregnancy. — At a little distance from these behold a man, who from his countenance and deportment appears as if he was descended from illustrious ancestors. — Yes. — He is the son of a prince, and was torn, by a stratagem, from an amiable wife and two young children— Mark his sullen looks! — now he bids defiance to the tyranny of his master, and in an instant plunges a knife into his heart. — But, let us return from this Scene, and see the various modes of arbitrary punishments inflicted upon them by their masters. Behold one covered with stripes, into which melted wax is poured — another tied down to a block or a stake — a third suspended in the air by his thumbs — a fourth obliged to set or stand upon red hot iron — a fifth, — I cannot relate it. — Where now is law or justice? Let us fly to them to step in for their relief. — Alas! — The one is silent, and the other denounces more terrible punishments upon them. Let us attend the place appointed for inflicting the penalties of the law. See here one without a limb, whose only crime was an attempt to regain his liberty — another led to a gallows for eating a morsel of bread, to which his labor gave him a better title than his master — a third famishing on a gibbet — a fourth, in a flame of fire! — his shrieks pierce the heavens. — O! God! Where is thy vengeance! — O! humanity — justice — liberty — religion! — Where, — where are ye fled. —

This is no exaggerated picture. It is taken from real life. Before I conclude I shall take the liberty of addressing several classes of my countrymen in behalf of our brethren (for by that name may we now call them) who are in a state of slavery among us.

In the first place let MAGISTRATES both supreme and inferior, exert the authority they are invested with, in suppressing this evil. Let them discountenance it by their example, and show a readiness to concur in every measure proposed to remedy it.

Let LEGISLATORS, reflect upon the trust reposed in them. Let their laws be made after the spirit of religion — liberty — and our most excellent English Constitution. You cannot show your attachment to your King or your love to your country better than by suppressing an evil which endangers the dominions of the former, and will in time destroy the liberty of the latter.[1] Population, and the accession of strangers, in which the riches of all countries consist, can only flourish in proportion as slavery is discouraged. Extend the privileges we enjoy, to every human creature born among us, and let not the journals of our assemblies be disgraced with the records of laws, which allow exclusive privileges to men of one color in preference to another.[2]

Ye men of sense and virtue — Ye advocates for American liberty, rouse up and espouse the cause of humanity and general liberty. Bear a testimony against a vice which degrades human nature, and dissolves that universal tie of benevolence which should connect all the children of men together in one great family. — The plant of liberty is of so tender a nature, that it cannot thrive long in the neighbourhood of slavery. Remember the eyes of all Europe are fixed upon you, to

---

[1]By a late calculation, it appears that there are eight hundred and fifty thousand Negro slaves in the British colonies and islands. From the number and burden of ships which are sent from England to Africa for slaves, we can with a good deal of certainty, conclude, that there are not less than one hundred thousand of them imported into America every year. By particular enquiry it was found, that one hundred aud four thousand were imported in the year 1768.    "In moderate governments, it is a point of the highest importance, that there should not be a great number of slaves. The political liberty of those states adds to the value of civil liberty; and he who is deprived of the latter, is also deprived of the former. He sees the happiness of a society, of which he is not so much as a member; he sees the security of others fenced by laws, himself without so much protection. He sees his master has a soul, that can enlarge itself; while his own is constrained to submit to almost continual depression. Nothing more assimilates a man to a beast, than living among freemen, himself a slave. Such people as these are the natural enemies of a society, and their number must be dangerous."
Spirit of Laws, Book xv. Chap. 12.

[2]The alterations in the laws in favour of Negroes, should be gradual, — 'till the evil habits they have acquired by slavery, are eradicated. There are several privileges, however, which might be extended to them immediately, without the least risk to society, in particular that inestimable one of trial by juries. [Author's footnotes]

preserve an asylum for freedom in this country, after the last pillars of it are fallen in every other quarter of the globe.

But chiefly — ye ministers of the gospel, whose dominion over the principles and actions of men is so universally acknowledged and felt, — Ye who estimate the worth of your fellow creatures by their immortality, and therefore must look upon all mankind as equal; — let your zeal keep pace with your opportunities to put a stop to slavery. While you inforce the duties of "tithe and cummin," neglect not the weightier laws of justice and humanity. Slavery is an Hydra sin, and includes in it every violation of the precepts of the Law and the Gospel. In vain will you command your flocks to offer up the incense of faith and charity, while they continue to mingle the sweat and blood of Negro slaves with their sacrifices. — If the blood of Abel cried aloud for vengeance; — If, under the Jewish dispensation, cities of refuge could not screen the deliberate murderer — if even manslaughter required sacrifices to expiate it, — and if a single murder so seldom escapes with impunity in any civilized country, what may you not say against that trade, or those manufactures — or laws,[1] which destroy the lives of so many thousands of our fellow-creatures every year? If in the Old Testament "God swears by his holiness, and by the excellency of Jacob, that the earth shall tremble, and every one mourn that dwelleth therein for the iniquity of those who oppress the poor and crush the needy," "who buy the poor with silver, and the needy with a pair of shoes,[2] what judgments may you not denounce upon those who continue to perpetrate these crimes, after the more full discovery which God has made of the law of equity in the New Testament. Put them in mind of the rod which was held over them a few years ago in the Stamp and Revenue Acts. remember that national crimes require national punishments, and without declaring what punishment awaits this evil, you may venture to assure them, that it cannot pass with impunity, unless God shall cease to be just or merciful.

---

[1]"If any Negro or other slave under punishment by his master, or his order for running away, or any other crimes or misdemeanors towards his said master, unfortunately shall suffer in life or member, no person whatever shall be liable to any fine; But if any man shall of wantonness, or only of bloody mindedness, or cruel intention, wilfully kill a Negro, or other slave of his own, he shall deliver into the public treasury fifteen pounds sterling, and not be liable to any other punishment, or forfeiture or the same."

Laws of Barbadoes, Act 329.

[2] Amos iv. 1,2. — viii. 6, 7. [Author's footnotes]

# ALEXANDER HAMILTON

# FUNDAMENTAL RIGHTS AND NATURAL LAW

The first thing that presents itself is a wish, that "I had, explicitly, declared to the public my ideas of the natural rights of mankind. Man, in a state of nature (you say) may be considered, as perfectly free from all restraints of law and government, and, then, the weak must submit to the strong."[1]

I shall, henceforth, begin to make some allowance for that enmity, you have discovered to the natural rights of mankind. For, though ignorance of them in this enlightened age cannot be admitted, as a sufficient excuse for you; yet, it ought, in some measure, to extenuate your guilt. If you will follow my advice, there still may be hopes of your reformation. Apply yourself, without delay, to the study of the law of nature. I would recommend to your perusal, Grotius Puffendorf, Locke, Montesquieu, and Burlemaqui.[2] I might mention other excellent writers on this subject; but if you attend, diligently, to these, you will not require any others.

There is so strong a similitude between your political principles and those maintained by Mr. Hobbs,[3] that, in judging from them, a person might very easily *mistake* you for a disciple of his. His opinion was, exactly, coincident with yours, relative to man in a state of nature. He held, as you do, that he was, then, perfectly free from all restraint of *law* and *government*. Moral obligation, according to him, is derived from the introduction of civil society; and there is no virtue, but what

---

[1]From Harold C. Syrett and Jacob E. Cooke, *The Papers of Alexander Hamilton*, Vol. 1 (Columbia University Press, 1961). This selection appeared as Hamilton's response to the "Farmer."

[2]"Burlamoqui," in "Errata."

[3]"Hobbes," in "Errata." [Hobbes was author of *Leviathan* and a strong proponent of central government.— Editor]

is purely artificial, the mere contrivance of politicians, for the maintenance of social intercourse. But the reason he run this absurd and impious doctrine, was, that he disbelieved the existence of an intelligent superintending principle, who is the governor, and will be the final judge of the universe . . .

To grant, that there is a supreme intelligence, who rules the world, and has established laws to regulate the actions of his creatures; and, still, to assert, that man, in a state of nature, may be considered as perfectly free from all restraints of *law* and *government*, appear to a common understanding, altogether irreconcileable.

Good and wise men, in all ages, have embraced a very dissimilar theory. They have supposed, that the deity, from the relations, we stand in, to himself and to each other, has constituted an eternal and immutable law, which is, indispensibly, obligatory upon all mankind, prior to any human institution whatever.

This is what is called the law of nature, "which, being coeval with mankind, and dictated by God himself, is, of course, superior in obligation to any other. It is binding over all the globe, in all countries, and at all times. No human laws are of any validity, if contrary to this; and such of them as are valid, derive all their authority, mediately, or immediately, from this original." BLACKSTONE.[1]

Upon this law, depend the natural rights of mankind, the supreme being gave existence to man, together with the means of preserving and beautifying that existence. He endowed him with rational faculties, by the help of which, to discern and pursue such things, as were consistent with his duty and interest, and invested him with an inviolable right to personal liberty, and personal safety.

Hence, in a state of nature, no man had any mo*ral* power to deprive another of his life, limbs, property or liberty; nor the least authority to command, or exact obedience from him; except that which arose from the ties of consanguinity.

Hence also, the origin of all civil government, justly established, must be a voluntary compact, between the rulers and the ruled; and must be liable to such limitations, as are necessary for the security of the *absolute rights* of the latter; for what original title can any man or set of men have, to govern others, except their own consent? To usurp dominion over a people, in their own despite, or to grasp at a more

[1] The quotation is from Blackstone's *Commentaries*, "Introduction," Section II ("Of *the* Nature of Laws *in general*"), p. 41.

extensive power than they are willing to entrust, is to violate that law of nature, which gives every man a right to his personal liberty; and can, therefore, confer no obligation to obedience.

"The principal aim of society is to protect individuals, in the enjoyment of those absolute rights, which were vested in them by the immutable laws of nature; but which could not be preserved, in peace, without that mutual assistance, and intercourse, which is gained by the institution of friendly and social communities. Hence it follows, that the first and primary end of human laws, is to maintain and regulate these *absolute rights* of individuals." BLACKSTONE.[1]

If we examine the pretensions of parliament, by this criterion, which is evidently, a good one, we shall, presently detect their injustice. First, they are subversive of our natural liberty, because an authority is assumed over us, which we by no means assent to. And secondly, they divest us of that moral security, for our lives and properties, which we are intitled to, and which it is the primary end of society to bestow. For such security can never exist, while we have no part in making the laws, that are to bind us; and while it may be the interest of our uncontroled legislators to oppress us as much as possible.

To deny these principles will be not less absurd, than to deny the plainest axioms: I shall not, therefore, attempt any further illustration of them.

You say, "when I assert, that since Americans have not, by any act of theirs, impowered the British parliament to make laws for them, it follows they can have no just authority to do it, I advance a position subversive of that dependence, which all colonies must, from their very nature, have on the mother country." The premises from which I drew this conclusion, are indisputable. You have not detected any fallacy in them; but endeavor to overthrow them by deducing a false and imaginary consequence. My principles admit the only dependence which can subsist, consistent with any idea of civil liberty, or with the future welfare of the British empire, as will appear hereafter.

"The dependence of the colonies, on the mother country," (you assert) "has ever been acknowledged. It is an impropriety of speech, to talk of an independent colony: The words independent and colony, convey contradictory ideas, much like ki*lling* and *sparing*. As soon as a colony becomes independent on the parent state, it ceases to be any

---

[1] The quotation is from Blackstone's *Commentaries*, Book I *("Of the* Rights *of* Persons"), Ch. I ("Of *the absolute* Rights *of* Individuals"), *p.* 124.

longer a colony, just as when you kill a sheep, you cease to spare him."

... The fundamental source of all your errors, sophisms and false reasonings is a total ignorance of the natural rights of mankind. Were you once to become acquainted with these, you could never entertain a thought, that all men are not, by nature, entitled to a parity of privileges. You would be convinced, that natural liberty is a gift of the beneficent Creator to the whole human race, and that civil liberty is founded in that; and cannot be wrested from any people, without the most manifest violation of justice. *Civil liberty, is only natural liberty, modified and secured by the sanctions of civil society.* It is not a thing, in its own nature, precarious and dependent on human will and caprice; but is conformable to the constitution of man, as well as necessary to the *well-being* of society.

Upon this principle, colonists as well as other men, have a right to civil liberty: For, if it be conducive to the happiness of society (and reason and experience testify that it is) it is evident, that every society, of whatsoever kind, has an absolute and perfect right to it, which can never be with-held without cruelty and injustice. The practice[1] of Rome, towards her colonies, cannot afford the shadow of an argument against this. That mistress of the world was often unjust. And the treatment of her dependent provinces is one of the greatest blemishes in her history. Through the want of that civil liberty, for which we are now so warmly contending, they groaned under every species of wanton oppression. If we are wise, we shall take warning from thence; and consider a like state of dependence, as more to be dreaded, than pestilence and famine.

The right of colonists, therefore, to exercise a legislative power, is an inherent right. It is founded upon the right of all men to freedom and happiness. For civil liberty cannot possibly have any existence, where the society, for whom laws are made, have no share in making them; and where the interest of their legislators is not inseparably interwoven with theirs. Before you asserted, that the right of legislation was derived "from the indulgence or grant of the parent state," you should have proved two things, that all men have not a natural right to freedom, and that civil liberty is not advantageous to society.

---

[1] If her practice proves any thing, it equally proves, that she had a right to plunder them, as much as possible. This doctrine, I presume, will not be disagreeable to some ears. There are many who would rejoice to see America plundered, in a like manner, provided they could be appointed the instruments. [Hamilton's footnote]

"The position, (you say) that we are bound by no laws, but those, to which we have assented, either by ourselves, or by our representatives, is a novel position, unsupported by any authoritative record of the British constitution, ancient or modern. It is republican, in its very nature; and tends to the utter subversion of the English monarchy. "This position has arisen from an artful change of terms. To say that an Englishman is not bound by any laws, but those to which the representatives of the nation have given their consent, is to say what is true. But to say, that an Englishman is bound by no laws but those to which he hath consented, in person, or by his representative, is saying what never was true, and never can be true. A great part of the people have no vote in the choice of representatives, and, therefore, are governed by laws, to which, they never consented, either by themselves, or by *their* representatives."

The foundation of the English constitution rests upon this principle, that no laws have any validity, or binding force, without the consent and approbation of the *people*, given in the persons of *their* representatives, periodically elected by *themselves*. This constitutes the democratical part of the government . . .

# THOMAS JEFFERSON

# A BILL FOR ESTABLISHING RELIGIOUS FREEDOM

12 June 1779

Well aware that the opinions and belief of men depend not on their own will, but follow involuntarily the evidence proposed to their minds, that Almighty God hath created the mind free, and manifested his Supreme will that free it shall remain, by making it altogether insusceptible of restraint: That all attempts to influence it by temporal punishments or burthens, or by civil incapacitations, tend only to beget habits of hypocrisy and meanness, and are a departure from the plan of the holy author of our religion, who being Lord both of body and mind, yet chose not to propagate it by coercions on either, as was in his Almighty power to do, but to extend it by its influence on reason alone: That the impious presumption of legislators and rulers, civil as well as ecclesiastical, who, being themselves but fallible and uninspired men, have assumed dominion over the faith of others, setting up their own opinions and modes of thinking, as the only true and infallible, and as such, endeavouring to impose them on others, hath established and maintained false religions over the greatest part of the world, and through all time: That to compel a man to furnish contributions of money for the propagation of opinions which he disbelieves and abhors, is sinful and tyrannical: That even the forcing him to support this or that teacher of his own religious persuasion, is depriving him of the comfortable liberty of giving his contributions to the particular pastor whose morals he would make his pattern, and whose powers he feels most persuasive to righteousness, and is withdrawing from the Ministry those temporal rewards which, proceeding from an approbation of their personal conduct, are an additional incitement to earnest and unremitting labour for the instruction of mankind: That our civil rights have no dependance on our religious opinions, any more than on our opinions in physicks or geometry: That therefore the proscribing any citizen as unworthy the publick confidence by laying upon him an incapacity of being called to offices of trust and emolument, unless he profess or renounce this or that religious opinion, is depriving him injuriously of those privileges and advantages to which, in common with his fellow citizens he has a natural right: That it tends also to corrupt the principles of that very religion it is meant to encourage, by bribing with a monopoly of worldly honours and emoluments, those who will externally profess and conform to it: That though indeed these are criminal who do not withstand such temptation, yet neither are those innocent who lay the bait in their way: That the opinions of men are not the object of civil government, nor under its jurisdiction: That to suffer the civil Magistrate to intrude his powers into the field of opinion, and to restrain the profession or propagation of principles on supposition of their ill tendency, is a dangerous fallacy, which at once destroys all religious liberty; because he being of course Judge of that tendency will make his own opinions the rule of judgment, and approve or condemn the sentiments of others only as they shall square with, or differ from his own: That it is time enough for the rightful purposes of civil government for its officers to interfere when principles break out into overt acts against peace and good order: And finally, that truth is great and will prevail if left to herself; that she is the proper and sufficient antagonist to errour, and has nothing to fear from the conflict, unless by human interposition, disarmed of her natural weapons, free argument and debate; errours ceasing to be dangerous when it is permitted freely to contract them

We the General Assembly of *Virginia* do enact, that no man shall be compelled to frequent or support any relig[i]ous Worship place or Ministry whatsoever, nor shall be enforced. restrained, molested, or burthened in his body or goods, nor shall otherwise suffer on account of his religious opinions or belief, but that all men shall be free to profess, and by argument to maintain their opinions in matters of religion, and that the same shall in no wise diminish, enlarge, or affect their civil capacities.

And though we know that this Assembly, elected by the people for the ordinary purposes of legislation only, have no power to restrain the acts of succeeding Assemblies, constituted with powers equal to our own, and that therefore to declare this act irrevocable would be of no effect in law; yet we are free to declare, and do declare, that the rights hereby asserted are of the natural rights of mankind, and that if any act shall be hereafter passed to repeal the present, or to narrow its operation, such act will be an infringement of natural right.

# THOMAS PAINE

# ON THE NATURE OF GOVERNMENT

The cause of America is in a great measure the cause of all mankind. Many circumstances have, and will arise, which are not local, but universal, and through which the principles of all lovers of mankind are affected, and in the event of which their affections are interested. The laying a country desolate with fire and sword, declaring war against the natural rights of all mankind, and extirpating the defenders thereof from the face of the earth, is the concern of every man to whom nature hath given the power of feeling; . . .

Some writers have so confounded society with government, as to leave little or no distinction between them; whereas they are not only different, but have different origins. Society is produced by our wants, and government by our wickedness; the former promotes our happiness *positively* by uniting our affections, the latter *negatively* by restraining our vices. The one encourages intercourse, the other creates distinctions. The first is a patron, the last a punisher.

Society in every state is a blessing, but Government, even in its best state, is but a necessary evil; in its worst state an intolerable one; for when we suffer, or are exposed to the same miseries *by a Government* which we might expect in a country *without Government*, our calamity is heightened by reflecting that we furnish the means by which we suffer. Government, like dress, is the badge of lost innocence; the palaces of kings are built upon the ruins of the bowers of paradise. For were the impulses of conscience clear, uniform and irresistibly obeyed,

From Thomas Paine's *Common Sense*, *"On the Origin and Design of Government in General, with Concise Remarks on the English Constitution."*

man would need no other lawgiver; but that not being the case, he finds it neccssary to surrender up a part of his property to furnish means for the protection of the rest; and this he is induced to do by the same prudence which in every other case advises him, out ot two evils to choose the least. Wherefore, security being the true design and end of government, it unanswerably follows that whatever from thereof appears most likely to ensure it to us, with the least expence and greatest benefit, is preferable to all others.

In order to gain a clear and just idea of the design and end of government, let us suppose a small number of persons settled in some sequestered part of the earth, unconnected with the rest ; they will then represent the first peopling of any country, or of the world. In this state of natural liberty, society will be their first thought. A thousand motives will excite them thereto; the strength of one man is so unequal to his wants, and his mind so unfitted for perpetual solitude, that he is soon obliged to seek assistance and relief of another, who in his turn requires the same. Four or five united would be able to raise a tolerable dwelling in the midst of a wilderness, but one man might labour out the common period of life without accomplishing any thing; when he had felled his timber he could not remove it, nor erect it after it was removed; hunger in the mean time would urge him to quit his work, and every different want would call him a different way. Disease, nay even misfortune, would be death; for though neither might be mortal, yet either would disable him from living, and reduce him to a state in which he might rather be said to perish than to die.

Thus necessity, like a gravitating power, would soon form our newly arrived emigrants into society, the reciprocal blessings of which would supercede, and render the obligations of law and government unnecessary while they remained perfectly just to each other; but as nothing but Heaven is impregnable to vice, it will unavoidably happen that in proportion as they surmount the first difficulties of emigration, which bound them together in a common cause, they will begin to relax in their duty and attachment to each other: and this remissness will point out the necessity of establishing some form of government to supply the defect of moral virtue.

Some convenient tree will afford them a State House, under the branches of which the whole Colony may assemble to deliberate on public matters. It is more than probable that their first laws will have the title only of Regulations and be enforced by no other penalty than public disesteem. In this first parliament every man by natural right will have a seat.

But as the Colony encreases, the public concerns will increase likewise, and the distance at which the members may be separated, will render it too inconvenient for all of them to meet on every occasion as at first, when their number was small, their habitations near, and the public concerns few and trifling. This will point out the convenience of their consenting to leave the legislative part to be managed by a select number chosen from the whole body, who are supposed to have the same concerns at stake which those have who appointed them, and who will act in the same manner as the whole body would act were they present. If the colony continue encreasing, it will become necessary to augment the number of representatives, and that the interest of every part of the colony may be attended to, it will be found best to divide the whole into convenient parts, each part sending its proper number: and that the *elected* might never form to themselves an interest separate from the *electors,* prudence will point out the propriety of having elections often: because as the *elected* might by that means return and mix again with the general body of the *electors* in a few months, their fidelity to the public will be secured by the prudent reflection of not making a rod for themselves. And as this frequent interchange will establish a common interest with every part of the community, they will mutually and naturally support each other, and on this, (not on the unmeaning name of king,) depends the *strength of government, and the happiness of the governed.*

Here then is the origin and rise of government; namely, a mode rendered necessary by the inability of moral virtue to govern the world; here too is the design and end of government, viz. Freedom and security. And however our eyes may be dazzled with show, or our ears deceived by sound; however prejudice may warp our wills, or interest darken our understanding, the simple voice of nature and reason will say, 'tis right.

I draw my idea of the form of government from a principle in nature which no art can overturn, viz. that the more simple any thing is, the less liable it is to be disordered, and the easier repaired when disordered; and with this maxim in view I offer a few remarks on the so much boasted constitution of England. That it was noble for the dark and slavish times in which it was erected, is granted. When the world was overrun with tyranny the least remove therefrom was a glorious rescue. But that it is imperfect, subject to convulsions, and incapable of producing what it seems to promise, is easily demonstrated.

Absolute governments, (tho' the disgrace of human nature) have this advantage with them, they are simple; if the people suffer, they know the head from which their suffering springs; know likewise the remedy; and are not bewildered by a variety of causes and cures. But the constitution of England is so exceedingly complex, that the nation may suffer for years together without being able to discover in which part the fault lies; some will say in one and some in another, and every political physician will advise a different medicine.

I know it is difficult to get over local or long standing prejudices, yet if we will suffer ourselves to examine the component parts of the English constitution, we shall find them to be the base remains of two ancient tyrannies, compounded with some new Republican materials.

*First.* — The remains of Monarchical tyranny in the person of the King.

*Secondly* — The remains of Aristocratical tyranny in the persons of the Peers.

*Thirdly.* — The new Republican materials, in the persons of the Commons, on whose virtue depends the freedom of England .

The two first, by being hereditary, are independant of the People; wherefore in a *constitutional sense* they contribute nothing towards the freedom of the State. To say that the constitution of England is an *union* of three powers, reciprocally *checking* each other, is farcical; either the words have no meaning, or they are flat contradictions. To say that the Commons is a check upon the King, presupposes two things.

*First.* — That the King is not to be trusted without being looked after; or in other words, that a thirst for absolute power is the natural diseasc of monarchy.

*Secondly.* — That the Commons, by being appointed for that purpose, are either wiser or more worthy of confidence than the Crown.

But as the same constitution which gives the Commons a power to check the King by withholding the supplies, gives afterwards the King a power to check the Commons, by empowering him to reject their other bills; it again supposes that the King is wiser than those whom it has already supposed to be wiser than him. A mere absurdity!

There is something exceedingly ridiculous in the composition of Monarchy; it first excludes a man from the means of information, yet empowers him to act in cases where the highest judgment is required.

The state of a king shuts him from the World, yet the business of a king requires him to know it thoroughly; wherefore the different parts, by unnaturally opposing and destroying each other, prove the whole character to be absurd and useless.

Some writers have explained the English constitution thus: the King, say they, is one, the people another; the Peers are a house in behalf of the King, the commons in behalf of the people; but this hath all the distinctions of a house divided against itself; and though the expressions be pleasantly arranged, yet when examined they appear idle and ambiguous; and it will always happen, that the nicest construction that words are capable of, when applied to the description of something, which either cannot exist, or is too incomprehensible to be within the compass of description, will be words of sound only, and though they may amuse the ear, they cannot inform the mind: for this explanation includes a previous question, vis. h*ow came the king by a power which the people are afraid to trust, and always obliged to check?* Such a power could not be the gift of a wise people, neither can any power, *which needs checking* be from God; yet the provision which the constitution makes supposes such a power to exist.

But the provision is unequal to the task; the means either cannot or will not accomplish the end, and the whole affair is a *Felo de se:* for as the greater weight will always carry up the less, and as all the wheels of a machine are put in motion by one, it only remains to know which power in the constitution has the most weight, for that will govern: and tho' the others, or a part of them, may clog, or, as the phrase is, check the rapidity of its motion, yet so long as they cannot stop it, their endeavours will be ineffectual: The first moving power will at last have its way, and what it wants in speed is supplied by time.

That the crown is this overbearing part in the English constitution needs not be mentioned, and that it derives its whole consequence merely from being the giver of places and pensions is self-evident; wherefore, though we have been wise enough to shut and lock a door against absolute Monarchy, we at the same time have been foolish enough to put the Crown in possession of the key.

The prejudice of Englishmen, in favour of their own government, by King, Lords and Commons, arises as much or more from national pride than reason. Individuals are undoubtedly safer in England than in some other countries: but the will of the king is as much the law of the land in Britain as in France, with this difference, that instead of proceeding directly from his mouth, it is handed to the people under the formidable shape of an act of parliament. For the fate of Charles the First hath only made kings more subtle — not more just.

Wherefore, laying aside all national pride and prejudice in favour of modes and forms, the plain truth is that *it is wholly owing to the constitution of the people, and not to the constitution of the government* that the crown is not as oppressive in England as in Turkey. An inquiry into the *constitutional errors* in the English form of government, is at this time highly necessary; for as we are never in a proper condition of doing justice to others, while we continue under the influence of some leading partiality, so neither are we capable of doing it to ourselves while we remain fettered by any obstinate prejudice. And as a man who is attached to a prostitute is unfitted to choose or judge of a wife, so any prepossession in favour of a rotten constitution of government will disable us from discerning a good one.

### Of Monarchy and Hereditary Succession.

Mankind being originally equals in the order of creation, the equality could only be destroyed by some subsequent circumstance: the distinctions of rich and poor may in a great measure be accounted for, and that without having recourse to the harsh sounding names of oppression and avarice. Oppression is often the *consequence*, but seldom or never the *means* of riches; and tho' avarice will preserve a man from being necessitously poor, it generally makes him too timorous to be wealthy.

But there is another and greater distinction for which no truly natural or religious reason can be assigned, and that is the distinction of men into KINGS and SUBJECTS. Male and female are the distinctions of nature, good and bad the distinctions of heaven; but how a race of men came into the world so exalted above the rest, and distinguished like some new species, is worth inquiring into, and whether they are the means of happiness or of misery to mankind.

In the early ages of the world, according to the scripture chronology there were no kings; the consequence of which was, there were no wars; it is the pride of kings which throws mankind into confusion. Holland, without a king hath enjoyed more peace for this last century than any of the monarchical governments in Europe. Antiquity favours the same remark; for the quiet and rural lives of the first Patriarchs have a happy something in them, which vanishes when we come to the history of Jewish royalty.

Government by kings was first introduced into the world by the Heathens, from whom the children of Israel copied the custom. It was the most prosperous invention the Devil ever set on foot for the promotion of idolatry. The Heathens paid divine honours to their deceased kings, and the Christian World hath improved on the plan by doing the same to their living ones. How impious is the title of sacred Majesty applied to a worm, who in the midst of his splendor is crumbling into dust!

As the exalting one man so greatly above the rest cannot be justified on the equal rights of nature, so neither can it be defended on the authority of scripture; for the will of the Almighty as declared by Gideon, and the prophet Samuel, expressly disapproves of government by Kings. All anti-monarchical parts of scripture, have been very smoothly glossed over in monarchical governments, but they undoubtedly merit the attention of countries which have their governments yet to form. Render u*nto Cesar the things which are Cesar's*, is the scripture doctrine of courts, yet it is no support of monarchical government, for the Jews at that time were without a king, and in a state of vassalage to the Romans.

Near three thousand years passed away, from the Mosaic account of the creation, till the Jews under a national delusion requested a king. Till then their form of government (except in extraordinary cases where the Almighty interposed) was a kind of Republic, administered by a judge and the elders of the tribes. Kings they had none, and it was held sinful to acknowledge any being under that title but the Lord of Hosts. And when a man seriously reflects on the idolatrous homage which is paid to the persons of kings, he need not wonder that the Almighty, ever jealous of his honour, should disapprove a form of government which so impiously invades the prerogative of Heaven.... But where, say some, is the King of America? I'll tell you, friend, he reigns above, and doth not make havoc of mankind like the Royal Brute of Great Britain. Yet that we may not appear to be defective even in earthly honours, let a day be solemnly set apart for proclaiming the Charter; let it be brought forth placed on the Divine Law, the Word of God; let a crown be placed thereon, by which the world may know, that so far as we approve of monarchy, that in America the law is king. For as in absolute governments the King is law, so in free countries the law ought to be king; and there ought to be no other. But lest any ill use should afterwards arise, let the Crown at the conclusion of the ceremony be demolished, and scattered among the people whose right it is.

A government of our own is our natural right: and when a man seriously reflects on the precariousness of human affairs, he will become convinced, that it is infinitely wiser and safer, to form a constitution of our own in a cool deliberate manner, while we have it in our power, than to trust such an interesting event to time and chance. If we omit it now, some Massanello* may hereafter arise, who, laying hold of popular disquietudes, may collect together the desperate and the discontented, and by assuming to themselves the powers of government, finally sweep away the liberties of the Continent like a deluge. Should the government of America return again into the hands of Britain, the tottering situation of things will be a temptation for some desperate adventurer to try his fortune; and in such a case, what relief can Britain give? Ere she could hear the news, the fatal business might be done; and ourselves suffering like the wretched Britons under the oppression of the Conqueror. Ye that oppose independance now, ye know not what ye do: ye are opening a door to eternal tyranny, by keeping vacant the seat of government. There are thousands and tens of thousands, who would think it glorious to expel from the Continent, that barbarous and hellish power, which hath stirred up the Indians and the Negroes to destroy us; the cruelty hath a double guilt, it is dealing brutally by us, and treacherously by them.

To talk of friendship with those in whom our reason forbids us to have faith, and our affections wounded thro' a thousand pores instruct us to detest, is madness and folly. Every day wears out the little remains of kindred between us and them; and can there be any reason to hope, that as the relationship expires, the affection will encrease, or that we shall agree better when we have ten times more and greater concerns to quarrel over than ever?

Ye that tell us of harmony and reconciliation, can ye restore to us the time that is past? Can ye give to prostitution its former innocence? neither can ye reconcile Britain and America. The last cord now is broken, the people of England are presenting addresses against us.

---

*Thomas Anello, otherwise Massanello. a fisherman of Naples, who after spiriting up his countrymen in the public market place, against the oppression of the Spaniards, to whom the place was then subject, prompted them to revolt, and in the space of a day became King. ———— Author.

There are injuries which nature cannot forgive; she would cease to be nature if she did. As well can the lover forgive the ravisher of his mistress, as the Continent forgive the murders of Britain. The Almighty hath implanted in us these unextinguishable feelings for good and wise purposes. They are the Guardians of his Image in our hearts. They distinguish us from the herd of common animals. The social compact would dissolve, and justicc be extirpated from the earth, or have only a casual existence were we callous to the touches of affection. The robber and the murderer would often escape unpunished, did not the injuries which our tempers sustain, provoke us into justice.

O! ye that love mankind! Ye that dare oppose not only the tyranny but the tyrant, stand forth! Every spot of the old world is overrun with oppression. Freedom hath been hunted round the Globe. Asia and Africa have long expelled her. Europe regards her like a stranger, and England hath given her warning to depart. O! receive the fugitive, and prepare in time an asylum for mankind.

# PART III

*In Europe, charters of liberty have been granted by power. America has set the example and France has followed it, of charters of power granted by liberty. This revolution in the practice of the world may, with honest praise, be pronounced the most triumphant epoch of its history and the most consoling presage of its happiness.*

— John Adams to Thomas Jefferson in 1815

# THE CONSTITUTIONAL DEBATE

Having won their independence in the Revolution, the early Americans now faced the challenge of forming a nation, a government and a constitution worthy of their cherished liberties. In the course of the "great national discussion" that followed, issues unique to the formation of union and ordered government rose to the fore. The loosely knit confederation of states proved inadequate to the imperative needs of a free and sovereign people. The task of establishing one nation under law, of ordaining a new written constitution, now lay ahead.

Amid all the challenges that followed in the wake of war, however, none was so paramount as the protection of their newly-won rights and liberties. In the task of forging a new nation, the preservation of their ancient rights was paramount to those on both sides of the constitutional debate. The need for a formal Bill of Rights was debated at the Constitutional Convention in Philadelphia in 1787. A significant number of states ratified the proposed Constitution only upon the condition that the first federal congress would consider a proposal to add a series of amendments to the newly ratified document. Thus was the ratification process itself marked by a substantial division over the issue of individual rights retained by the people. It is worthy of note to us today that the passion for individual rights and liberties has rarely, if ever, been greater in our history than in the aftermath of the American Revolution. The civil rights movement of the 1960s notwithstanding, Americans living since the revolutionary generations have had a tough match to prove themselves equal in their passion to preserve their individual rights and liberties as against the encroaching powers of government.

In the first of the pieces to follow, John Dickenson speaks to the fundamental right to a jury trial. It is difficult to over-stress the vital importance attached to this right by early Americans. The common law right to a jury trial was held to be of the highest and most fundamental order in both England and America. It was made variously explicit as such in the several state constitutions after the Revolution. The right to a jury of one's peers as part of Due Process of law, when facing the loss of one's life, liberty or property, was expressly declared even before King John signed the Magna Carta in 1215. The rights declared by Magna Carta at Runnymede in that year have endured to this day, and the vital right to a jury trial has proved its longevity from its ancient and glorious origins in the words of that document. Dickenson argues the necessity for an explicit and universal right to a jury trial in civil cases, no less than in criminal prosecutions. Despite a variety of statements of this common law right in the state constitutions, the framers agreed to an explicit declaration of the right at two points in the Constitution, including the right to a civil jury in the Seventh Amendment itself.

It is also worthy of note to point out one risk widely known to and debated among the framers themselves concerning the inclusion of an express Bill of Rights. To declare some rights expressly, while denying to others explicit mention in the Constitution, could well be interpreted as a relinquishment of those rights not so expressly stated. It was indeed Hamilton's view that too much specificity in the statement of certain rights would be taken as a waiver of other, equally or more fundamental rights not expressly declared in the text of the Constitution or Bill of Rights itself. This thoughtful concern is further evidenced in George Mason's view, that to secure such rights it was necessary to add a clause reserving for the people those rights and powers not expressly granted to the government. Our Ninth and Tenth Amendments attest to this early concern for the safeguarding of those fundamental individual rights not explicitly enumerated in the Constitution.

In *The Federalist* paper number 10 we see a famous piece touching on several aspects of the proposed Constitution. The concern is chiefly with the effects of faction or party, majority or minority interests motivated by religious, economic or other special interest adverse to those of other citizens. The reality of faction and party in politics appeared to Madison as a political cancer that could destroy the numerous advantages of a federal union. He suggests some alternatives to counter the effects of faction and the dangers he perceived as flowing

from them: 1) Destroying or curtailing the liberty that gives rise to such interest groups, and 2) Attempting to produce in all citizens the same opinions, passions and interests of a uniform nature. Even assuming the possibility of the second alternative, however, either remedy would be far worse than the disease itself. Indeed, asserts Madison, "Liberty is to faction what air is to fire, an ailment without which it instantly expires." We would not wish the annihilation of air, reasons Madison, "because it imparts to fire its destructive agency".

In Madison's analysis, property is the most single, influential cause of factions. It operates as a powerful and an impressive tool in the hands of either majority or minority. This might strike us as indeed a somewhat harsh verdict for a right we so widely consider to be fundamental, the very right to our possession, to our homes and our goods. It was Madison's concern, however, to secure the protection of the *public's* good and the rights of society no less than those of private persons and their interests. The safeguard of individual rights, the rights to life, to liberty and property, while preserving the public's interest and the viability of popular government was the greatest puzzle to be solved by our ingenious forefathers.

The objection that the proposed Constitution lacked a Bill of Rights is indeed addressed by Hamilton in the *Federalist Paper No. 84*. Addressing this alleged defect in the proposed written Constitution, Hamilton points to the fact that several of the existing state constitutions were themselves lacking in a Bill of Rights. These included that of New York, Hamilton's own state. Hamilton argued that several of the basic rights contended for by the anti-federalists and others are contained in the body of the proposed federal Constitution itself. Thus included are the right to a jury trial for crimes [including that of treason], Habeas Corpus [the right to challenge one's imprisonment on constitutional grounds], Bills of Attainder and ex post facto laws. A Bill of Rights, thus argued Hamilton, has no place in a republic, which is founded on the ultimate power and authority of the people, and the laws of God. They would have no *need* to declare their rights, which are theirs from the start. It was thus the sovereign people themselves, and *not* the authority of government, much less that of a king, contended Hamilton, that grants to each and all those fundamental rights so deeply cherished by all Americans.

We see also in Madison the same concern for the risks inherent in any list of particulars that would specify individual rights as against the government. The fear was that the central government could simply arrogate to itself any rights and powers not specifically spelled out in the text of a Bill of Rights. The soundness of the proposed federal Constitution notwithstanding, we should note again the refusal of several states to ratify the new frame of government except on condition that just such a bill of particulars would attach, i.e., a Bill of Rights that would make explicit those fundamental rights and liberties retained by the people.

George Mason addresses the contrary concern that the proposed Constitution *lacked* a Bill of Rights. He also echoes the fear that a power-hungry government might in fact imply to itself all power and authority *not* expressly reserved to the states or the people.

Mason's fear for the lack of a Bill of Rights is in turn echoed through the writings of Thomas Jefferson. We can see, in the eloquence of Jefferson's words in a letter to Madison, a strong sense of urgency regarding the inclusion of a Bill of Rights in our Constitution. Jefferson did believe the proposed plan of government basically sound. Author of the Declaration of Independence, and a bill for establishing religious freedom, Jefferson expressed eloquently his view of the need for a formal Bill of Rights in our federal Constitution. It was to be the essential touch, a vital element to an otherwise excellent frame of government, a major document as yet lacking in some important particulars. Jefferson worked successfully in his own state of Virginia for religious freedom and other liberties that we today know as our First Amendment rights to freedom of speech, religion and conscience.

Thus were the passions and the concerns of our framers, who set about the business of forming a fair and adequate government for a sovereign people. Having won the Revolution and the peace to follow, they emerged from the Anglo-American struggle with all of their rights intact. The great challenge that remained was now that of nationhood, of self-government and a Constitution which, with hope, would preserve their ancient and cherished rights.

To forge a nation conceived in liberty, to write the Constitution that would meld together a loose confederation of sovereign states, this was the task that loomed on the horizon. To thus protect and preserve the birthrights of liberty and of mankind for all under the law, while forging a strong federal union, was the destined task of the first generation of sovereign America.

# RICHARD HENRY LEE

# FEDERAL FARMER NO. 16

The trial by jury in criminal as well as in civil causes, has long been considered as one of our fundamental rights, and has been repeatedly recognized and confirmed by most of the state conventions. But the constitution expressly establishes this trial in criminal, and wholly omits it in civil causes. The jury trial in criminal causes, and the benefit of the writ of habeas corpus, are already as effectually established as any of the fundamental or essential rights of the people in the United States. This being the case, why in adopting a federal constitution do we now establish these, and omit all others, or all others, at least with a few exceptions, such as again agreeing there shall be no ex post facto laws, no titles of nobility, &c. We must consider this constitution, when adopted, as the supreme act of the people, and in construing it hereafter, we and our posterity must strictly adhere to the letter and spirit of it, and in no instance depart from them: in construing the federal constitution, it will be not only impracticable, but improper to refer to the state constitutions. They are entirely distinct instruments and inferior acts: besides, by the people's now establishing certain fundamental rights, it is strongly implied, that they are of opinion, that they would not otherwise be secured as a part of the federal system, or be regarded in the federal administration as fundamental. Further, these same rights, being established by the state constitutions, and secured to the people, our recognizing them now, implies, that the people thought them insecure by the state establishments, and extinguished or put afloat by the new arrangement of the social system, unless re-established. — Further, the people, thus establishing some few rights, and remaining totally silent about others similarly circumstanced, the implication indubitably is, that they mean to relinquish the latter, or at least feel indifferent about them. Rights, therefore, inferred from general principles of reason, being precarious and hardly ascertainable in the common affairs of society, and the people, in forming a federal constitution, explicitly showing they conceive these rights to be thus circumstanced, and accordingly proceed to enumerate and establish some of them, the conclusion will be, that they have established all which they esteem valuable and sacred. On every principle, then, the people especially having began, ought to go through enumerating, and establish particularly all the rights of individuals, which can by any possibility come in question in making and executing federal laws. I have already observed upon the excellency and importance of the jury trial in civil as well as in criminal causes, instead of establishing it in criminal causes only: we ought to establish it generally: — instead of the clause of forty or fifty words relative to this subject, why not use the language that has always been used in this country, and say, "the people of the United States shall always be entitled to the trial by jury." This would shew the people still hold the right sacred, and enjoin it upon congress substantially to preserve the jury trial in all cases, according to the usage and custom of the country. I have observed before, that it is the *jury trial* we want; the little different appendages and modifications tacked to it in the different states, are no more than a drop in the ocean: the jury trial is a solid uniform feature in a free Government; it is the substance we would save, not the little articles of form.

---

While the authorship of this piece is uncertain, it speaks forcefully to the common law right to a jury trial in both criminal and civil cases. It is thus included here.

# HAMILTON, MADISON AND JAY

# THE FEDERALIST ON THE DANGERS OF FACTION AND PARTIES

### The Federalist, Number 10

To the People of the State of New York:

AMONG the numerous advantages promised by a well-constructed Union, none deserves to be more accurately developed than its tendency to break and control the violence of faction. The friend of popular governments never finds himself so much alarmed for their character and fate, as when he contemplates their propensity to this dangerous vice. He will not fail, therefore, to set a due value on any plan which, without violating the principles to which he is attached, provides a proper cure for it. The instability, injustice, and confusion introduced into the public councils, have, in truth, been the mortal diseases under which popular governments have everywhere perished; as they continue to be the favorite and fruitful topics from which the adversaries to liberty derive their most specious declamations. The valuable improvements made by the American constitutions on the popular models, both ancient and modern, cannot certainly be too much admired; but it would be an unwarrantable partiality, to contend that they have as effectually obviated the danger on this side as was wished and expected. Complaints are everywhere heard from our most considerate and virtuous citizens, equally the friends of public and private faith, and of public and personal liberty; that our governments are too unstable; that the public good is disregarded in the conflicts of rival parties; and that measures are too often decided, not according to the rules of justice and the rights of the minor party, but by the superior force of an interested and overbearing majority. However anxiously we

From *The Federalist: a Collection of Essays written in favour of the New Constitution,* by Alexander Hamilton, James Madison and John Jay. [Originally published in New York by McLean, 1788]

may wish that these complaints had no foundation, the evidence of known facts will not permit us to deny that they are in some degree true. It will be found, indeed, on a candid review of our situation, that some of the distresses under which we labor have been erroneously charged on the operation of our governments; but it will be found, at the same time, that other causes will not alone account for many of our heaviest misfortunes; and, particularly, for that prevailing and increasing distrust of public engagements, *and alarm for private rights,* which are echoed from one end of the continent to the other. These must be chiefly, if not wholly, effects of the unsteadiness and injustice with which a factious spirit has tainted our public administrations.

By a faction, I understand a number of citizens, whether amounting to a majority or minority of the whole, who are united and actuated by some common impulse of passion, or of interest, adverse to the rights of other citizens, or to the permanent and aggregate interests of the community.

There are two methods of curing the mischiefs of faction: the one, by removing its cause; the other, by controlling its effects.

There are again two methods of removing the causes of faction: the one, by destroying the liberty which is essential to its existence; the other, by giving to every citizen the same opinions, the same passions, and the same interests.

It could never be more truly said than of the first remedy, that it was worse than the disease. Liberty is to faction what air is to fire, an aliment without which it instantly expires. But it could not be less folly to abolish liberty, which is essential to political life, because it nourishes faction, than it would be to wish the annihilation of air, which is essential to animal life, because it imparts to fire its destructive agency.

The second expedient is as impracticable as the first would be unwise. As long as the reason of man continues fallible, and he is at liberty to exercise it, different opinions will be formed. As long as the connection subsists between his reason and his self-love, his opinions and his passions will have a reciprocal influence on each other; and the former will be objects to which the latter will attach themselves. The diversity in the faculties of men, from which the rights of property originate, is not less an insuperable obstacle to a uniformity of interests.

The protection of these faculties is the first object of government. From the protection of different and unequal faculties of acquiring property, the possession of different degrees and kinds of property immediately results; and from the influence of these on the sentiments and views of the respective proprietors, ensues a division of the society into different interests and parties.

The latent causes of faction are thus sown in the nature of man; and we see them everywhere brought into different degrees of activity, according to the different circumstances of civil society. A zeal for different opinions concerning religion, concerning government, and many other points, as well of speculation as of practice; an attachment to different leaders ambitiously contending for pre-eminence and power; or to persons of other descriptions whose fortunes have been interesting to the human passions, have, in turn, divided mankind into parties, inflamed them with mutual animosity, and rendered them much more disposed to vex and oppress each other than to co-operate for their common good. So strong is this propensity of mankind to fall into mutual animosities, that where no substantial occasion presents itself, the most frivolous and fanciful distinctions have been sufficient to kindle their unfriendly passions and excite their most violent conflicts. But the most common and durable source of factions has been the various and unequal distribution of property. Those who hold and those who are without property have ever formed distinct interests in society. Those who are creditors, and those who are debtors, fall under a like discrimination. A landed interest, a manufacturing interest, a mercantile interest, a moneyed interest, with many lesser interests, grow up of necessity in civilized nations, and divide them into different classes, actuated by different sentiments and views. The regulation of these various and interfering interests forms the principal task of modern legislation, and involves the spirit of party and faction in the necessary and ordinary operations of the government.

No man is allowed to be a judge in his own cause, because his interest would certainly bias his judgment, and, not improbably, corrupt his integrity. With equal, nay with greater reason, a body of men are unfit to be both judges and parties at the same time; yet what are many of the most important acts of legislation, but so many judicial determinations, not indeed concerning the rights of single persons, but concerning the rights of large bodies of citizens? and what are the different classes of legislators but advocates and parties to the causes which they determine? Is a law proposed concerning private debts? it is a question to which the creditors are parties on one side and the debtors on the other. Justice ought to hold the balance between them. Yet the parties are, and must be, themselves the judges; and the most numerous party, or, in other words, the most powerful faction must be expected to prevail. Shall domestic manufactures be encouraged, and in what degree, by restrictions on foreign manufactures? are questions which would be differently decided by the landed and the manufacturing classes, and probably by neither with a sole regard to justice and the public good. The apportionment of taxes on the various descriptions of property is an act which seems to require the most exact impartiality; yet there is, perhaps, no legislative act in which greater opportunity and temptation are given to a predominant party, to trample on the rules of justice. Every shilling with which they overburden the inferior number, is a shilling saved to their own pockets.

It is in vain to say that enlightened statesmen will be able to adjust these clashing interests, and render them all subservient to the public good. Enlightened statesmen will not always be at the helm. Nor, in many cases, can such an adjustment be made at all without taking into view indirect and remote considerations, which will rarely prevail over the immediate interest which one party may find in disregarding the rights of another or the good of the whole.

The inference to which we are brought is, that the causes of faction cannot be removed, and that relief is only to be sought in the means of controlling its effects.

If a faction consists of less than a majority, relief is supplied by the republican principle, which enables the majority to defeat its sinister views by regular vote. It may clog the administration, it may convulse the society; but it will be unable to execute and mask its violence under the forms of the Constitution. When a majority is included in a faction, the form of popular government, on the other hand, enables it to sacrifice to its ruling passion or interest both the public good and the rights of other citizens. To secure the public good, and private rights, against the danger of such a faction, and at the same time to preserve the spirit and the form of popular government, is then the great object to which our inquiries are directed. Let me add that it is the great *desideratum*, by which this form of government can be rescued from the opprobrium under which it has so long labored, and be recommended to the esteem and adoption of mankind.

By what means is this object attainable? Evidently by one of two only. Either the existence of the same passion or interest in a majority at the same time, must be prevented; or the majority, having such coexistent passion or interest, must be rendered, by their number and local situation, unable to concert and carry into effect schemes of oppression. If the impulse and the opportunity be suffered to coincide, we well know that neither moral nor religious motives can be relied on as an adequate control. They are not found to be such on the injustice and violence of individuals, and lose their efficacy in proportion to the number combined together, that is, in proportion as their efficacy becomes needful.

From this view of the subject it may be concluded that a pure democracy, by which I mean a society consisting of a small number of citizens, who assemble and administer the government in person, can admit of no cure for the mischiefs of faction. A common passion or interest will, in almost every case, be felt by a majority of the whole; a communication and concert results from the form of government itself; and there is nothing to check the inducements to sacrifice the weaker party or an obnoxious individual. Hence it is that such democracies have ever been spectacles of turbulence and contention; have ever been found incompatible with personal security, or the rights of property, and have in general been as short in their lives as they have been violent in their deaths. Theoretic politicians, who have patronized this species of government, have erroneously supposed that by reducing mankind to a perfect equality in their political rights, they would, at the same time, be perfectly equalized and assimilated in their possessions, their opinions, and their passions.

A republic, by which I mean a government in which the theme of representation takes place, opens a different prospect, and promises the cure for which we are seeking. Let us examine the points in which it varies from pure democracy, and we shall comprehend both the nature of the cure and the efficacy which it must derive from the union.

The two great points of difference between a democracy and a republic are: First, the delegation of the government, in the latter, to a small number of citizens elected by the rest; secondly, the greater number of citizens, and greater sphere of country, over which the latter may be extended.

The effect of the first difference is, on the one hand, to refine and enlarge the public views, by passing them through the medium of a chosen body of citizens, whose wisdom may best discern the true interest of their country, and whose patriotism and love of justice will be least likely to sacrifice it to temporary or partial considerations. Under such a regulation, it may well happen that the public voice, pronounced by the representatives of the people, will be more consonant to the public good than if pronounced by the people themselves, convened for the purpose. On the other hand, the effect may be inverted. Men of factious tempers, of local prejudices, or of sinister designs, may, by intrigue, by corruption, or by other means, first obtain the suffrages, and then betray the interests, of the people. The question resulting is, whether small or extensive republics are more favorable to the election of proper guardians of the public weal; and it is clearly decided in favor of the latter by two obvious considerations.

In the first place, it is to be remarked that, however small the republic may be, the representatives must be raised to a certain number, in order to guard against the cabals of a few; and that, however large it may be, they must be limited to a certain number, in order to guard against the confusion of a multitude. Hence, the number of representatives in the two cases not being in proportion to that of the constituents, and being proportionally greatest in the small republic, it follows that, if the proportion of fit characters be not less in the large than in the small republic, the former will present a greater option, and consequently a greater probability of a fit choice.

In the next place, as each representative will be chosen by a greater number of citizens in the large than in the small republic, it will be more difficult for unworthy candidates to practise with success the vicious arts, by which elections are too often carried; and the suffrages of the people, being more free, will be more likely to centre in men who possess the most attractive merit and the most diffusive and established characters.

It must be confessed that in this as in most other cases, there is a mean, on both sides of which inconveniences will be found to lie. By enlarging too much the number of electors, you render the representative too little acquainted with all their local circumstances and lesser interests; as by reducing it too much, you render him unduly attached to these, and too little fit to comprehend and pursue great and national objects. The federal Constitution forms a happy combination in this respect; the great and aggregate interests being referred to the national, the local and particular to the State legislatures.

The other point of difference is, the greater number of citizens and extent of territory which may be brought within the compass of republican than of democratic government; and it is this circumstance principally which renders factious combinations less to be dreaded in the former than in the latter. The smaller the society, the fewer probably will be the distinct parties and interests composing it; the fewer the distinct parties and interests, the more frequently will a majority be found of the same party; and the smaller the number of individuals composing a majority, and the smaller the compass within which they are placed, the more easily will they concert and execute their plans of oppression. Extend the sphere and you take in a greater variety of parties and interests; you make it less probable that a majority of the whole will have a common motive to invade the rights of other citizens; or if such a common motive exists, it will be more difficult for all who feel it to discover their own strength, and to act in unison with each other. Besides other impediments, it may be remarked that, where there is a consciousness of unjust or dishonorable purposes, communication is always checked by distrust in proportion to the number whose concurrence is necessary.Hence, it clearly appears, that the same advantage which a republic has over a democracy, in controlling the effects of faction, is enjoyed by a large over a small republic,—is enjoyed by the Union over the States composing it. Does the advantage consist in the substitution of representatives whose enlightened views and virtuous sentiments render them superior to local prejudices and to schemes of injustice? It will not be denied that the representation of the Union will be most likely to possess these requisite endowments. Does it consist in the greater security afforded by a greater variety of parties, against the event of any one party being able to outnumber and oppress the rest? In an equal degree does the increased variety of parties comprised within the Union, increase this security. Does it, in fine, consist in the greater obstacles opposed to the concert and accomplishment of the secret wishes of an unjust and interested majority? Here, again, the extent of the Union gives it the most palpable advantage.

The influence of factious leaders may kindle a flame within their particular States, but will be unable to spread a general conflagration through the other States. A religious sect may degenerate into a political faction in a part of the confederacy; but the variety of sects dispersed over the entire face of it must secure the national councils against any danger from that source. A rage for paper money, for an abolition of debts, for an equal division of property, or for any other improper or wicked project, will be less apt to pervade the whole body of the Union than a particular member of it; in the same proportion as such a malady is more likely to taint a particular county or district, than an entire State.

In the extent and proper structure of the Union, therefore, we behold a republican remedy for the diseases most incident to republican government. And according to the degree of pleasure and pride we feel in being republicans, ought to be our zeal in cherishing the spirit and supporting the character of federalists.

PUBLIUS.

## The Federalist, Number 84
*On Alleged Defects in the Constitution*

To the People of the State of New York:

IN THE course of the foregoing review of the Constitution I have taken notice of and endeavored to answer most of the objections which have appeared against it. There, however, remain a few which either did not fall naturally under any particular head or were forgotten in their proper places. These shall now be discussed; but as the subject has been drawn into great length, I shall so far consult brevity as to compromise all my observations on these miscellaneous points in a single paper.

The most considerable of the remaining objections is that the plan of the Convention contains no bill of rights. Among other answers given to this, it has been upon different occasions remarked that the constitutions of several of the States are in a similar predicament. I add that New York is of the number; and yet the opposers of the new system, in this State who profess an unlimited admiration for its Constitution, are among the most intemperate partisans of a bill of rights. To justify their zeal in this matter, they allege two things: one is that though the constitution of New York has no bill of rights prefixed to it, yet it contains in the body of it various provisions in favor of particular privileges and rights, which, substance, amount to the same thing; the other is that the Constitution adopts, in their full extent, the common and statute law of Great Britain, by which many other rights, not expressed in it, are equally secured.

From *The Federalist,* op.cit.

To the first I answer that the Constitution proposed by the Convention contains, as well as the Constitution of this State, a number of such provisions.

Independent of those which relate to the structure of the government, we find the following: Article I, section 3, clause 7, "Judgment in cases of impeachment shall not extend further than to removal from office, and disqualification to hold and enjoy any office of honor, trust, or profit under the United States; but the party convicted shall, nevertheless, be liable and subject to indictment, trial, judgment, and punishment according to law"; section 9, of the same article, clause 2, "The privilege of the writ of habeas corpus shall not be suspended, unless when in cases of rebellion or invasion the public safety may require it"; clause 3, "No bill of attainder or *ex-post-facto* law shall be passed"; clause 7, "No title of nobility shall be granted by the United States; and no person holding any office of profit or trust under them, shall, without the consent of the Congress, accept of any present, emolument, office, or title of any kind whatever, from any king, prince, or foreign State"; article 3, section 2, clause 3,"The trial of all crimes, except in cases of impeachment, shall be by jury; and such trial shall be held in the State where the said crimes shall have been committed; but when not committed within any State, the trial shall be at such place or places as the Congress may by law have directed"; section 3 of the same article,"Treason against the United States shall consist only in levying war against them, or in adhering to their enemies, giving them aid and comfort. No person shall be convicted of treason, unless on the testimony of two witnesses to the same overt act, or of confession in open court"; and clause 3, of the same section, "'The Congress shall have power to declare the punishment of treason; but no attainder of treason shall work corruption of blood, or forfeiture, except during the life of the person attainted."

It may well be a question whether these are not, upon the whole, of equal importance with any which are to be found in the Constitution of this State. The establishment of the writ of habeas corpus, the prohibition of *ex-post-facto* laws and of titles of nobility, to which we have no corresponding provision in our Constitution, are perhaps greater securities to liberty and republicanism than any it contains. The creation of crimes after the commission of the fact, or, in other words, the subjecting of men to punishment for things which, when they were done, were breaches of no law, and the practice of arbitrary imprisonment, have been in all ages the favorite and most formidable instruments of tyranny. The observations of the judicious Blackstone,[1] in reference to the latter are well worthy of recital: "To bereave a man of life," says he, "or by violence to confiscate his estate without accusation or trial, would be so gross and notorious an act of despotism, as must at once convey the alarm of tyranny throughout the whole nation; but confinement of the person, by secretly hurrying him to jail, where his sufferings are unknown or forgotten, is a less public, a less striking, and therefore a more dangerous engine of arbitrary government." And as a remedy for this fatal evil he is everywhere peculiarly emphatical in his encomiums on the *Habeas Corpus* act, which in one place he calls "the bulwark of the British Constitution."[2]

Nothing need be said to illustrate the importance of the prohibition of titles of nobility. This may truly be denominated the corner-stone of republican government; for so long as they are excluded, there can never be serious danger that the government will be any other than that of the people.

To the second, that is, to the pretended establishment of the common and statute law by the Constitution, I answer that they are expressly made subject "to such alterations and provisions as the legislature shall from time to time make concerning the same." They are, therefore, at any moment liable to repeal by the ordinary legislative power, and, of course, have no constitutional sanction. The only use of the declaration was to recognize the ancient law, and to remove doubts which might have been occasioned by the Revolution. This consequently can be considered as no part of a declaration of rights; which under our constitutions must be intended as *limitations of the power of the government itself* [editor's emphasis].

It has been several times truly remarked that bills of rights are, in their origin, stipulations between kings and their subjects, abridgments of prerogative in favor of privilege, reservations of rights not surrendered to the prince. Such was Magna Charta, obtained by the barons, sword in hand, from King John. Such were the subsequent confirmations of that charter by succeeding princes. Such was the Petition of Right assented to by Charles I, in the beginning of his reign. Such, also, was the Declaration of Right presented by the Lords and Commons to

---

[1]Vide Blackstone's "Commentaries," vol. I, p. 136. [Authors]

[2]Vide Blackstone's "Commentaries," vol. 4, p. 438. [Authors]

the Prince of Orange in 1688, and afterwards thrown into the form of an act of parliament called the Bill of Rights. It is evident, therefore, that, according to their primitive signification, they have no application to constitutions, professedly founded upon the power of the people, and executed by their immediate representatives and servants. Here, in strictness, the people surrender nothing; and, as they retain everything, they have no need of particular reservations. "We, the people of the United States, to secure the blessings of liberty to ourselves and our posterity, do ordain and establish this Constitution for the United States of America." Here is a better recognition of popular rights than volumes of those aphorisms which make the principal figure in several of our State bills of rights, and which would sound much better in a treatise of ethics than in a constitution of government.

But a minute detail of particular rights is certainly far less applicable to a Constitution like that under consideration, which is merely intended to regulate the general political interests of the nation, than to a constitution which has the regulation of every species of personal and private concerns. If, therefore, the loud clamors against the plan of the Convention on this score are well founded, no epithets of reprobation will be too strong for the Constitution of this State; but the truth is that both of them contain all which, in relation to their objects, is reasonably to be desired.

I go further, and affirm that bills of rights, in the sense and to the extent in which they are contended for, are not only unnecessary in the proposed Constitution, but would even be dangerous. They would contain various exceptions to powers not granted, and, on this very account would afford a colorable pretext to claim more than were granted; for why declare that things shall not be done which there is no power to do? Why, for instance, should it be said that the liberty of the press shall not be restrained, when no power is given by which restrictions may be imposed? I will not contend that such a provision would confer a regulating power, but it is evident that it would furnish, to men disposed to usurp, a plausible pretence for claiming that power. They might urge with a semblance of reason that the Constitution ought not to be charged with the absurdity of providing against the abuse of an authority which was not given, and that the provision against restraining the liberty of the press afforded a clear implication that a power to prescribe proper regulations concerning it was intended to be vested in the national government. This may serve as a specimen of the numerous handles which would be given to the doctrine of constructive powers, by the indulgence of an injudicious zeal for bills of rights.

On the subject of the liberty of the press, as much as has been said, I cannot forbear adding a remark or two: in the first place I observe, that there is not a syllable concerning it in the Constitution of this State; in the next, I contend that whatever has been said about it in that of any other State amounts to nothing. What signifies a declaration, that "the property of the press shall be inviolably preserved"? What is the liberty of the press? Who can give it any definition which would not leave the utmost latitude for evasion? I hold it to be impracticable; and from this, I infer that its security, whatever fine declarations may be inserted in any constitution respecting it, must altogether depend on public opinion, on the general spirit of the people and of the government.* And here, after all, as is intimated upon another occasion, must we seek for the only solid basis of all our rights.

There remains but one other view of this matter to conclude the point. The truth is, after all the declamation we have heard, that the Constitution is itself, in every rational sense, and to every useful purpose, a bill of rights. The several bills of rights in Great Britain form its Constitution, and, conversely, the constitution of each State is its bill of rights; and the proposed Constitution, if adopted, will be the bill of rights of the Union. Is it one object of a bill of rights to declare and specify the political priveleges of the citizens in the structure and administration of the government? This is done in the most ample and precise manner in the plan of the Convention; comprehending various precautions for the public security, which are not to be found in any of the State constitutions. Is another object of a bill of rights to define certain immunities and modes of proceeding, which are relative to

*To show that there is a power in the Constitution by which the liberty of the press may be affected, recourse has been had to the power of taxation. It is said that duties may be laid upon the publications so high as to amount to a prohibition. I know not by what logic it could be maintained that the declarations in the State constitutions, in favor of freedom of the press, would be a constitutional impediment to the imposition of duties upon publications by the State legislatures. It cannot certainly be pretended that any degree of duties, however low, would be an abridgment of the liberty of the press. We know that newspapers are taxed in Great Britain, and yet it is notorious that the press nowhere enjoys greater liberty than in that country. And if duties of any kind may be laid without a violation of that liberty, it is evident that the extent must depend on legislative discretion, regulated by public opinion; so that, after all, general declarations respecting the property of the press, will give it no greater security than it will have without them. The same invasions of it may be effected under the State constitutions which contain those declarations through the means of taxation, as under the proposed Constitution, which has nothing of the kind. It would be quite as significant to declare that government ought to be free, that taxes ought not to be excessive, etc., as that the liberty the press ought not to be restrained.—PUBLIUS

personal and private concerns? This we have seen has also been attended to, in a variety of cases, in the same plan. Adverting, therefore, to the substantial meaning of a bill of rights, it is absurd to allege that it is not to be found in the work of the Convention. It may be said that it does not go far enough, though it will not be easy to make this appear; but it can with no propriety be contended that there is no such thing. It certainly must be immaterial what mode is observed as to the order of declaring the rights of the citizens, if they are to be found in any part of the instrument which establishes the government; and, hence, it must be apparent that much of what has been said on this subject rests merely on verbal and nominal distinctions, entirely foreign from the substance of the thing.

Another objection which has been made, and which, from the frequency of its repetition, it is to be presumed is relied on, is of this nature. "It is improper," say the objectors, "to confer such large powers as are proposed, upon the national government; because the seat of that government must of necessity be too remote from many of the States to admit a proper knowledge, on the part of the constituent, of the conduct of the representative body." This argument, if it proves anything, proves that there ought to be no general government whatever, for the powers which, it seems to be agreed on all hands, ought to be vested in the Union, cannot be safely intrusted to a body which is not under every requisite control. But there are satisfactory reasons to show that the objection is, in reality, not well founded. There is in most of the arguments which relate to distance a palpable illusion of the imagination. What are the sources of information by which the people in Montgomery County must regulate their judgment of the conduct of their representatives in the State Legislature? Of personal observation they can have no benefit. This is confined to the citizens on the spot. They must, therefore, depend on the information of intelligent men, in whom they confide; and how must these men obtain their information? Evidently from the complexion of public measures, from the public prints, from correspondences with their representatives, and with other persons who reside at the place of their deliberation. This does not apply to Montgomery County only, but to all the counties at any considerable distance from the seat of government.

It is equally evident that the same sources of information would be open to the people, in relation to the conduct of their representatives in the general government; and the impediments to a prompt communication which distance may be supposed to create will be overbalanced by the effects of the vigilance of the State governments. The executive and legislative bodies of each State will be so many sentinels over the persons employed in every department of the national administration; and, as it will be in their power to adopt and pursue a regular and effectual system of intelligence, they can never be at a loss to know the behavior of those who represent their constituents in the national councils, and can readily communicate the same knowledge to the people. Their disposition to apprise the community of whatever may prejudice its interests from another quarter may be relied upon, if it were only from the rivalship of power; and we may conclude with the fullest assurance that the people, through that channel, will be better informed of the conduct of their national representatives than they can be by any means they now possess of that of their State representatives.

It ought also to be remembered that the citizens who inhabit the country at and near the seat of government will, in all questions that affect the general liberty and prosperity, have the same interest with those who are at a distance; and that they will stand ready to sound the alarm when necessary, and to point out the actors in any pernicious project. The public papers will be expeditious messengers of intelligence to the most remote inhabitants of the Union.

Among the many curious objections which have appeared against the proposed Constitution, the most extraordinary and the least colorable is derived from the want of some provision respecting the debts due to the United States. This has been represented as a tacit relinquishment of those debts, and as a wicked contrivance to screen public defaulters. The newspapers have teemed with the most inflammatory railings on this head; yet there is nothing clearer than that the suggestion is entirely void of foundation, the offspring of extreme ignorance or extreme dishonesty. In addition to the remarks I have made upon the subject in another place, I shall only observe that, as it is a plain dictate of common-sense, so it is also an established doctrine of political law that "States neither lose any of their rights, nor are discharged from any of their obligations, by a change in the form of their civil government."*

---

*Vide Rutherford's "Institutes," vol. 2, book II, chap. x., sects. xiv and xv. Vide also Grotius, book II, chap. ix., sects. viii. and ix —PUBLIUS

# JAMES MADISON

# FUNDAMENTAL RIGHTS IN THE PROPOSED CONSTITUTION— EXPLICIT OR IMPLICIT?

*Against Objections to a Bill of Rights*

It has been objected also against a bill of rights, that, by enumerating particular exceptions to the grant of power, it would disparage those rights which were not placed in that enumeration; and it might follow by implication, that those rights which were not singled out, were intended to be assigned into the hands of the General Government, and were consequently insecure. This is one of the most plausible arguments I have ever heard urged against the admission of a bill of rights into this system; but, I conceive, that it may be guarded against. I have attempted it, as gentlemen may see by turning to the last clause of the fourth resolution [the Ninth Amendment].

From Annals 1:439 (June 8, 1789).

# GEORGE MASON

# DID WE REALLY NEED A BILL OF RIGHTS?

MR. GEORGE MASON, still thought that there ought to be some express declaration in the constitution, asserting that rights not given to the general government, were retained by the states. He apprehended that unless this was done, many valuable and important rights would be concluded to be given up by implication. All governments were drawn from the people, though many were perverted to their oppression. The government of Virginia, he remarked, was drawn from the people; yet there were certain great and important rights, which the people by their bill *of* rights declared to be paramount to the power of the legislature. He asked, why should it not be so in this constitution? Was it because we were more substantially represented in it, than in the state government? If in the state government, where the people were substantially and fully presented, it was necessary that the great rights of human nature should be secure from the enc[r]oachments of the legislature; he asked, if it was not more necessary in his government, where they were but inadequately represented? He declared, that artful sophistry and evasions could not satisfy him. He could see no clear distinction between rights relinquished by a positive grant, and lost by implication. Unless there were a bill of rights, implication might swallow up all our rights.

From Papers 3:1084-85 (June 16, 1788).

# THOMAS JEFFERSON
# TO JAMES MADISON

# FREE-SPEECH, FREE PRESS AND
# THE RIGHT TO A JURY TRIAL

I sincerely rejoice at the acceptance of our new constitution by nine states. It is a good canvas, on which some strokes only want retouching. What these are, I think are sufficiently manifested by the general voice from North to South, which calls for a bill of rights. It seems pretty generally understood that this should go to Juries, Habeas corpus, Standing armies, Printing, Religion and Monopolies. I conceive there may be difficulty in finding general modification of these suited to the habits of all the states. But if such cannot be found then it is better to establish trials by jury, the right of Habeas corpus, freedom of the press and freedom of religion in all cases, and to abolish standing armies in time of peace, and Monopolies, in all cases, than not to do it in any. The few cases wherein these things may do evil, cannot be weighed against the multitude wherein the want of them will do evil. In disputes between a foreigner and a native, a trial by jury may be improper. But if this exception cannot be agreed to, the remedy will be to model the jury by giving the medietas linguae in civil as well as Criminal cases. Why suspend the Habeus corpus in insurrections and rebellions? The parties, who may be arrested may be charged instantly with a well defined crime. Of course the judge will remand them. If the publick safety requires that the government should have a man imprisoned on less probable testimony in those than in other emergencies; let him be taken and tried, retaken and retried, while the necessity continues, only giving him redress against the government for damages. Examine the history of England: see how few of the cases of the suspension of the Habeas corpus law have been worthy of that suspension. They have been either real treasons wherein the parties might as well have been charged at once, or sham-plots where it was shameful they should ever have been suspected. Yet for the few cases wherein the suspension of the hab. corp. has done real good, that operation is now become habitual, and the minds of the nation almost prepared to live under it's constant suspension. A declaration that the federal government will never restrain the presses from printing any thing they please, will not take away the liability of the printers for false facts printed. The declaration that religious faith shall be unpunished, does not give impunity to criminal acts dictated by religious error. The saying there shall be no monopolies lessens the incitements to ingenuity, which is spurred on by the hope of a monopoly for a limited time, as of 14. years; but the benefit even of limited monopolies is too doubtful to be opposed to that of their general suppression. If no check can be found to keep the number of standing troops within safe bounds, while they are tolerated as far as necessary, abandon them altogether, discipline well the militia, and guard the magazines with them. More than magazine-guards will be useless if few, and dangerous if many. No European nation can ever send against us such a regular army as we need fear, and it is hard if our militia are not equal to those of Canada or Florida. My idea then is, that tho' proper exceptions to these general rules are desirable and probably practicable, yet if the exceptions cannot be agreed on, the establishment of the rules in all cases will do ill in very few. I hope therefore a bill of rights will be formed to guard the people against the federal government, as they are already guarded against their state governments in most instances.[1]

---

[1] From the *Papers of Thomas Jefferson (1788)*

# PART IV

*The sacred rights of mankind are not to be rummaged for among old parchments, or musty records. They are written, as with a sunbeam, in the whole volume of human nature by the hands of divinity itself; and can never be erased or obscured by mortal power.*

—from the Papers of Alexander Hamilton

# TOWARD NATIONHOOD: EARLY INTERPRETATIONS OF OUR BASIC FREEDOMS

Having written a federal constitution and a Bill of Rights, the framers and founders now faced the challenges of nationhood in full. The new union, yet to be forged and melded together into one nation, presented a challenge evoking the deepest issues of our heritage. The task was now that of forging a new nation under those principles of law and liberty set forth in the written Constitution, the blueprint for a new order in a new world.

Mere "parchment barriers" of liberty were, however, yet to be put to the test. The vaguaries of interpretation still lay ahead; there must be a body of law, a jurisprudence to interpret, to define and apply the fine and majestic principles of liberty set forth in the Bill of Rights. That the fundamental rights of all mankind should have been declared in a new charter of liberty was indeed accomplished in the ratification of the Bill of Rights in 1791. It became the first order of the day to effectively interpret and to apply its resonant words and principles to the business of a new government. The mood was one of high political passion. The spirit of liberty prevailed wide and deep on this side of the Atlantic, as did the American determination to preserve their strong — yet somewhat fragile — freedoms within the context of a strong federal union.

For Thomas Jefferson, one of the major functions of government is to determine that degree of punishment appropriate to the offense against society. It was its function, more specifically, to reform, to rehabilitate the perpetrators of crime, to rectify their ways in conformity to the requirements of law. Punishment, in Jefferson's view, was not the mere exaction of society's revenge upon an outrageous wrongdoer. Jefferson took the more positive view of reforming the convicted perpetrator of crime into a productive member of society. He was himself opposed to the death penalty (except as a last resort) and reasoned that capital punishment only eliminates the offender while failing to eradicate the crime or to reform the convicted criminal. Government must, in its vital service of rendering justice, act always in a way consistent with the value of life, liberty, property and the potential well-being of all. The principle that punishment must fit the offense is reflected clearly in the language of our Eighth Amendment. We can see in its words a clear echo of Jefferson's concern that cruel and unusual punishment, disproportionate to the crime committed, defeats the very purpose of criminal laws — that of the reform of criminals and the prevention of crime.

We see in the writings of Connecticut's Zephaniah Swift yet another strong focus on the rights accorded to the criminally accused. Swift speaks in affirmation of the fundamental rights afforded to all criminal defendants under the Constitution. These include, as Swift mentions, the right to the full and effective assistance of counsel in one's defense when facing a criminal prosecution. This "right to counsel", to the assistance of an attorney when confronting the full force of the state in a criminal prosecution, is protected under our Sixth Amendment. It is, indeed, one of the most vital in that cluster of rights accorded to the criminally accused in the Fourth, Fifth and Sixth Amendments of the federal constitution. Along with the right to a jury trial itself, the "right to counsel" found its way into the Sixth Amendment as one of the paramount rights accorded to all criminal defendants facing felony charges or imprisonment. Also touched upon by Swift and explicit in the Sixth Amendment itself is the right of a criminal defendant to face her accusers directly, to confront, to cross-examine and produce witnesses on her own behalf at trial.

The final piece, that of an early U.S. Supreme Court decision, embodies yet another fundamental right afforded to those facing criminal prosecution. It is one originally deemed vital enough to have been written into the body of the Constitution itself. This is the prohibition against state legislatures regarding ex post facto laws. An ex post facto law is one, enacted by a state legislature, that would make a crime of an innocent act lawful at the time it was performed. While not among the first ten Amendments, the prohibition against ex post facto is made explicit in Article I, Section 9 of the Constitution itself.

In *Calder vs Bull* (1798), the U.S. Supreme Court, in an early opinion, considered the constitutionality of a Connecticut law. The legislature passed a statute that would overturn the decree of a probate court in favor of Mr. Calder and his wife. Calder had successfully contested a will, resulting in the enforcement of his wife's right to inherit real estate as the heir of a deceased physician. The Connecticut legislature then enacted a statute allowing for several rights of appeal in cases of contested wills. Calder challenged the new law, contending that it was in violation of his constitutional protection under the ex post facto clause of Article I. The Court upheld the Connecticut statute.

The Court determined here, in its Chase-Iredell opinions, that the boundary and limits of any natural or "fundamental" right must be found in the federal constitution itself. thus affording due respect to the states in the wisdom of their own legislatures to pass laws appropriate to their own welfare. It was nonetheless established, in the renown opinion of Justice Chase, that no legislature can enact a law that would punish an act originally innocent when performed. Such retrospective laws that could punish an innocent act "after the fact" were viewed by the Court as manifestly unjust and oppressive, not to be countenanced under the Constitution.

There are a number of refinements today in the 200 years of jurisprudence, regarding ex post facto, which have passed since the *Calder* case. These include a prohibition against the lowering of standards of evidence for the purpose of easier conviction and the increasing of punishment prescribed for the crime after the fact of its commission. Still, *Calder* remains good law today in its essential limitation to criminal cases. The right against ex post facto laws remains an essential bulwark of liberty in the rights of the criminally accused.

Still other protections, incorporated into the body of the Constitution itself, serve to protect individual rights against the encroachments of power. These include the prohibition, as against state governments, from impairing obligations of contracts, against the enactment of bills of attainder and titles of nobility. These are all contained in Article I, Section 10. The ancient common law right of Habeas Corpus, challenging one's imprisonment on constitutional grounds, is expressly preserved in Article I, Section 9. The reader is referred to other excellent works and to the U.S. Supreme Court reports themselves for a constitutional history of these and other fundamental rights. Over two hundred years of jurisprudence in the courts have wrought many significant changes and extensions in the interpretations of our basic freedoms.

# THOMAS JEFFERSON
# A BILL FOR PROPORTIONING
# CRIMES AND PUNISHMENTS
# (1778)

Whereas it frequently happens that wicked and dissolute men resigning themselves to the dominion of inordinate passions, commit violations on the lives, liberties and property of others, and, the secure enjoyment of these having principally induced men to enter into society, government would be defective in it's principal purpose were it not to restrain such criminal acts, by inflicting due punishments on those who perpetrate them; but it appears at the same time equally deducible from the purposes of society that a member thereof, committing an inferior injury, does not wholly forfiet the protection of his fellow citizens, but, after suffering a punishment in proportion to his offence is entitled to their protection from all greater pain, so that it becomes a duty in the legislature to arrange in a proper scale the crimes which it may be necessary for them to repress, and to adjust thereto a corresponding gradation of punishments.

And whereas the reformation of offenders, tho' an object worthy the attention of the laws, is not effected at all by capital punishments, which exterminate instead of reforming, and should be the last melancholy resource against those whose existence is become inconsistent with the safety of their fellow citizens, which also weaken the state by cutting off so many who, if reformed, might be restored sound members to society, who, even under a course of correction, might be rendered useful in various labors for the public, and would be living and long continued spectacles to deter others from committing the like offences.

And forasmuch the experience of all ages and countries hath shewn that cruel and sanguinary laws defeat their own purpose by engaging the benevolence of mankind to withold prosecutions, to smother testimony, or to listen to it with bias, when, if the punishment were only proportioned to the injury, men would feel it their inclination as well as their duty to see the laws observed.

For rendering crimes and punishments therefore more proportionate to each other: Be it enacted by the General assembly that no crime shall be henceforth punished by deprivation of life or limb except those hereinafter ordained to be so punished.

If a man do levy war against the Commonwealth or be adherent to the enemies of the commonwealth giving to them aid or comfort in the commonwealth, or elsewhere, and thereof be convicted of open deed, by the evidence of two sufficient witnesses, or his own voluntary confession, the said cases, and no others, shall be adjudged treasons which extend to the commonwealth, and the person so convicted shall suffer death by hanging, and shall forfiet his lands and goods to the Commonwealth.

If any person commit Petty treason, or a husband murder his wife, a parent his child, or a child his parent, he shall suffer death by hanging, and his body be delivered to Anatomists to be dissected.

Whosoever committeth murder by poisoning shall suffer death by poison.

Whosoever committeth murder by way of duel, shall suffer death by hanging; and if he were the challenger, his body, after death, shall be gibbeted. He who removeth it from the gibbet shall be guilty of a misdemeanor: and the officer shall see that it be replaced.

Whosoever shall commit murder in any other way shall suffer death by hanging....

# ZEPHANIAH SWIFT

# A SYSTEM OF LAWS OF THE STATE OF CONNECTICUT (1796)

The attorney for the state then proceeds to lay before the jury, all the evidence against the prisoner, without any remarks or arguments. The prisoner by himself or counsel, is then allowed to produce witnesses to counteract and obviate the testimony against him; and to exculpate himself with the same freedom as in civil cases. We have never admitted that cruel and illiberal principle of the common law of England that when a man is on trial for his life, he shall be refused counsel, and denied those means of defence, which are allowed, when the most trifling pittance of property is in question. The flimsy pretence, that the court are to be counsel for the prisoner will only highten our indignation at the practice: for it is apparent to the least consideration, that a court can never furnish a person accused of a crime with the advice, and assistance necessary to make his defence. This doctrine might with propriety have been advanced, at the time when by the common law of England, no witnesses could be adduced on the part of the prisoner, to manifest his innocence, for he could then make no preparation for his defense. One cannot read without horror and astonishment, the abominable maxims of law, which deprived persons accused, and on trial for crimes, of the assistance of counsel, except as to points of law, and the advantage of witnesses to exculpate themselves from the charge. It seems by the ancient practice, that whenever a person was accused of a crime, every expedient was adopted to convict him and every privilege denied him, to prove his innocence. In England, however, as the law now stands, prisoners are allowed the full advantage of witnesses, but excepting in a few cases, the common law is enforced, in denying them counsel, except as to points of law.

Our ancestors, when they first enacted their laws respecting crimes, influenced by the illiberal principles which they had imbibed in their native country, denied counsel to prisoners to plead for them to anything but points of law. It is manifest that there is as much necessity for counsel to investigate matters of fact, as points of law, if truth is to be discovered.

The legislature has become so thoroughly convinced of the impropriety and injustice of shackling and restricting a prisoner with respect to his defence, that they have abolished all those odious laws, and every person when he is accused of a crime, is entitled to every possible privilege in making his defence. and manifesting his innocence, by the instrumentality of counsel, and the testimony of witnesses.

# CALDER VS. BULL

# THE RIGHT OF EX POST FACTO

An *ex post facto* law, within the meaning of the U.S. Constitution, is one which makes an action done before the passing of the law which was innocent when done, criminal: or makes a crime greater than it was before committed; or inflicts a greater punishment than the law annexed to the crime when commited, or alters the legal rules of evidence, and receives less, or different testimony, than the law required at the commission of the offence, in order to convict the offender.

*Ex post facto* laws extend to criminal, and not to civil, cases; they are restricted to the creation. and perhaps enhancement, of crimes, pains, and penalties . . .

The counsel for the plaintiffs in error, contend, that the said resolution or law of the Legislature of Connecticut, granting a new hearing, in the above case, is an *ex post facto* law, prohibited by the Constitution of the United States; that any law of the federal government, or of any of the state governments, contrary to the constitution of the United States, is void; and that this court possesses the power to declare such law void.

It appears to me a self-evident proposition, that the several state legislatures retain all the powers of legislation, delegated to them by the state constitutions; which are not expressly taken away by the constitution of the United States. The establishing courts of justice, the appointment of judges, and the making regulations for the administration of justice, within each state, according to its laws, on all subjects

From an early U.S. Supreme Court opinion, *Calder vs. Bull.* [3 Dallas 386 (1798)]

not entrusted to the federal government, appears to me to be the peculiar and exclusive province, and duty of the state Legislatures. All the powers delegated by the people of the United States to the Federal government are defined, and no constructive powers can be exercised by it, and all the powers that remain in the state governments are indefinite; except only in the constitution of Massachusetts....

Whether the Legislature of any of the states can revise and correct by law, a decision of any of its courts of justice, although not prohibited by the constitution of the state, is a question of very great importance, and not necessary now to be determined; because the resolution or law in question does not go so far. I cannot subscribe to the omnipotence of a state Legislature, or that it is absolute and without control; although its authority should not be expressly restrained by the constitution, or fundamental law, of the state. The people of the United States erected their constitutions, or forms of government, to establish justice, to promote the general welfare, to secure the blessings of liberty, and to protect their persons and property from violence. The purposes for which men enter into society will determine the nature and terms of the social compact; and as they are the foundation of the legislative power, they will decide what are the proper objects of it: The nature, and ends of legislative power will limit the exercise of it. This fundamental principle flows from the very nature of our free Republican governments, that no man should be compelled to do what the laws do not require; nor to refrain from acts which the laws permit. There are acts which the federal, or state, Legislature cannot do, without exceeding their authority. There are certain vital principles in our free Republican governments, which will determine and overrule an apparent and flagrant abuse of legislative power; as to authorize manifest injustice by positive law; or to take away that security for personal liberty, or private property, for the protection whereof the government was established. An act of the Legislature (for I cannot call it a law) contrary to the great first principles of the social compact, cannot be considered a rightful exercise of legislative authority. The obligation of a law in governments established on express compact, and on republican principles, must be determined by the nature of the power, on which it is founded. A few instances will suffice to explain what I mean. A law that punished a citizen for an innocent action, or, in other words, for an act, which, when done, was in violation of no existing law; a law that destroys, or impairs, the lawful private contracts of citizens; a law that makes a man a judge in his own cause; or a law that takes property from A. and gives it to B. It is against all reason and justice, for a people to entrust a Legislature with such powers; and, therefore, it cannot be presumed that they have done it. The genius, the nature, and the spirit, of our state governments, amount to a prohibition of such acts of legislation; and the general principles of law and reason forbid them. The Legislature may enjoin, permit, forbid, and punish innocence as a crime, or violate the right of an antecedent lawful private contract; or the right of private property. To maintain that our federal, or state, Legislature possesses such powers, if they had not been expressly restrained, would, in my opinion, be a political heresy, altogether inadmissible in our free republican governments.

All the restrictions contained in the constitution of the United States on the power of the state Legislatures, were provided in favor of the authority of the federal government. The prohibition against their making any *ex post facto* laws was introduced for greater caution, and very probably arose from the knowledge, that the Parliament of Great Britain claimed and exercised a power to pass such laws, under the denomination of bills of attainder, of bills of pains and penalties; the first inflicting capital, and the other less, punishment. These acts were legislative judgments; and an exercise of judicial power. Sometimes they respected the crime, by declaring acts to be treason, which were not treason, when committed; at other times, they violated the rules of evidence ( to supply a deficiency of legal proof) by admitting one witness, when the existing law required two; by receiving evidence without oath; or the oath of the wife against the husband; or other testimony, which the courts of justice would not admit; at other times they inflicted punishments, where the party was not, by law, liable to any punishment, than the law annexed to the offense. — The ground for the exercise of such legislative power was this, that the safety of the kingdom depended on the death, or other punishment, of the offender; as if traitors, when discovered, could be so formidable, or the government so insecure! With very few exceptions, the advocates of such laws were stimulated by ambition, or personal resentment, and vindictive malice. To prevent such, and similar, acts of violence and injustice, I believe, the Federal and State Legislatures, were prohibited from passing any bill of attainder; or any *ex post facto* law.

The constitution of the United States, article 1, section 9 prohibits the Legislature of the United States from passing any *ex post facto* law;

and, in section 10, lays several restrictions on the authority of the Legislatures of the several states; and, among them, "that no state shall pass any *ex post facto* law."

It may be remembered, that the legislatures of several of the states, to wit, Massachusetts, Pennsylvania, Delaware, Maryland, and North and South Carolina, are expressly prohibited, by their state constitutions, from passing any *ex post facto* law.

I shall endeavor to show what law is to be considered an *ex post facto* law, within the words and meaning of the prohibition in the Federal constitution. The prohibition, "that no state shall pass any *ex post facto* law," necessarily requires some explanation; for naked and without explanation, it is unintelligible, and means nothing. Literally, it is only that a law shall not be passed concerning, and after the fact, or thing done, or action committed. I would ask, what fact; of what nature, or kind; and by whom done? That Charles 1st king of England, was beheaded; that Oliver Cromwell was Protector of England, that Louis 16th, late king of France, was guillotined; are all facts, that have happened; but it would be nonsense to suppose, that the states were prohibited from making any law after either of these events, and with reference thereto. The prohibition, in the letter, is not to pass any law concerning and after the fact; but the plain and obvious meaning and intention of the prohibition is this; *that the Legislatures of the several states shall not pass laws, after a fact done by a subject or citizen, which shall have relation to such fact, and shall punish him for having done it [editor's emphasis]*. The prohibition considered in this light, is an additional bulwark in favor of the personal security of the subject, or protect his person from punishment by legislative acts, having a retrospective operation. I do not think it was inserted to secure the citizen in his private rights, of either property, or contracts. The prohibition not to make anything but gold and silver coin a tender in payment of debts, and not to pass any law impairing the obligation of contracts, were inserted to secure private rights; but the restriction not to pass any *ex post facto* law, was to secure the person of the subject from injury, or punishment, in consequence of such law. If the prohibition against making *ex post facto* laws was intended to secure personal rights from being affected, or injured, by such laws, and the prohibition is sufficiently extensive for that objects, the other restraints, I have enumerated, were unnecessary, and therefore improper; for both of them are retrospective.

I will state what laws I consider *ex post facto* laws, within the words and the intent of the prohibition. 1st. Every law that makes an action done before the passing of the law; and which was innocent when done, criminal; and punishes such action. 2d. Every law that aggravates a crime, or makes it greater than it was, when committed. 3d. Every law that changes the punishment, and inflicts a greater punishment, and inflicts a greater punishment, than the law annexed to the crime, when committed. 4th. Every law that alters the legal rules of evidence, and receives less, or different, tetimony, than the law required at the time of the commission of the offense, in order to convict the offender. [These laws] are manifestly unjust and oppressive. In my opinion, the true distinction is between ex post facto laws, and retrospective laws. Every *ex post facto* law must necessarily be retrospective; but every retrospective law is not an *ex post facto* law: The former, only, are prohibited. Every law that takes away, or impairs, rights vested, agreeably to existing laws, is retrospective, and is generally unjust, and may be oppressive; and it is a good general rule, that a law should have no retrospect: but there are cases in which laws may justly, and for the benefit of the community, and also of individuals, relate to a time antecedent to their commencement; as statutes of oblivion, or of pardon. They are certainly retrospective, and literally both concerning, and after, the facts committed. But I do not consider any law *ex post facto*, within the prohibition, that mollifies the rigor of the criminal law; but only those that create, or aggravate, the crime; or increase the punishment, or change the rules of evidence, for the purpose of conviction. Every law that is to have an operation before the making thereof, as to commence at an antecedent time; or to save time from the statute of limitations; or to excuse acts which were unlawful, and before committed, and the like; is retrospective. But such laws may be proper or necessary, as the case may be. There is a great and apparent difference between making an unlawful act lawful; and the making an innocent action criminal, and punishing it as a crime. The expressions "*ex post facto* laws," are technical, they had been in use long before the Revolution, and had acquired an appropriate meaning, by legislators, lawyers, and authors. The celebrated and judicious Sir William Blackstone in his commentaries, considers an *ex post facto* law precisely in the same light I have done. His opinion is confirmed by his successor, Mr. Wooddeson; and by the author of the Federalist, who I esteem superior to both, for his extensive and accurate knowledge of the true principles of government . . .

It is not to be presumed, that the federal or state legislatures will pass laws to deprive citizens of rights vested in them by existing laws: unless for the benefit of the whole community; and on making full satisfaction. The restraint against making any ex post facto laws was not considered, by the framers of the constitutuion, as extended to prohibit the depriving a citizen even of a vested right to property [with just compensation] . . .

It seems to me, that the right of property, in its origin, could only arise from compact express or implied, and I think it the better opinion, that the right as well as the mode, or manner, of acquiring property, and of alienating or transferring, inheriting, or transmitting it, is conferred by society; it is regulated by civil institution, and is always subject to the rules prescribed by positive law. When I say that a right is vested in a citizen, I mean, that he has the power to do certain actions; or to possess certain things, according to the law of the land.

If any one has a right to property such right is a perfect and exclusive right; but no one can have such right before he has acquired a better right to the property, than any other person in the world, a right, therefore only to recover property cannot be called a perfect and exclusive right . . .

The resolution (or law) alone had no manner of effect on any right whatever vested in Calder and wife. The resolution (or law) combined with the new hearing, and the decision, in virtue of it, took away their right to recover the property in question. But when combined they took away no right of property vested in Calder and wife; because the decree against the will (21 March, 1783) did not vest in or transfer any property to them.

I am under a necessity to give a construction, or explanation of the words "ex post facto laws," because they have not any certain meaning attached to them. But I will not go farther than I feel myself bound to to; and if I ever exercise the jurisdiction I will not decide any law to be void, but in a very clear case.

I am of opinion, that the decree of the supreme court of errors of Connecticut be affirmed, with costs.

The question then which arises on the pleadings in this cause is, whether the resolution of the legislature of Connecticut, be an ex post facto law, within the meaning of the constitution of the United States?

I am of opinion, that it is not. The words, ex post facto, when applied to a law, have a technical meaning, and, in legal phraseology, refer to crimes, pains and penalties. Judge Blackstone's description of the terms is clear and accurate. "There is, says he, a still more unreasonable method than this, which is called making of laws ex post facto, when after an action, indifferent in itself, is committed, the legislators, then, for the first time, declares it to have been a crime, and inflicts a punishment upon the person who has committed it. Here it is impossible, that the party could forsee that an action, innocent when it was done, should be afterwards converted to guilt by a subsequent law; he had, therefore, no cause to abstain from it; and all punishment for not abstaining, must of consequence be cruel and unjust." 1 Bl. Com. 46. Here the meaning annexed to the terms, ex post facto laws, unquestionably refers to crimes, and nothing else. The historic page abundantly evinces, that the power of passing such laws should be withheld from legislators; as it is a dangerous instrument in the hands of bold, unprincipled, aspiring and party men, and has been too often used to effect the most detestable purposes.

On inspecting such of our state constitutions, as take notice of laws made *ex post facto*, we shall find, that they are understood in the same sense . . .

*Iredell, Justice:*—Though I concur in the general result of the opinions, which have delivered, I cannot entirely adopt the reasons that are assigned upon the occasion . . .

But, let us, for a moment, suppose, that the resolution, granting a new trial, was a legislative act, it will by no means follow, that it is an act affected by the constitutional prohibition, that "no state shall pass any ex post facto law." I will endeavor to state the general principles, which influence me, on this point, succinctly and clearly, though I have not had an opportunity to reduce my opinion to writing.

If, then, a government, composed of legislative, executive and judicial departments, were established, by a Constitution, which imposed no limits on legislative power, the consequence would inevitably be, that whatever the legislative power chose to enact, would be lawfully enacted, and the judicial power, could never interpose to pronounce it void. It is true, that some speculative jurists have held, that a legislative act against natural justice must, in itself, be void; but I cannot think that, under such a government, any court of justice would possess a power to declare it so. Sir William Blackstone, having put the strong case of an act of parliament, which should authorize a man to try his own cause, explicitly adds, that even in that case, "there is no court that has power to defeat the intent of the legislature, when couched in such evident and express words as leave no doubt whether it was the intent of the legislature, or no." 1Bl. Com. 91.

In order, therefore, to guard against so great an evil, it has been the policy of all the American states, which have, individually, framed their state constitutions since the revolution, and of the people of the United States, when they framed the federal constitution, to define with precision the objects of the legislative power, and to restrain its exercise within marked and settled boundaries. If any act of Congress, or of the legislature of a state, violates those constitutional provisions, it is unquestionably void; though, I admit, that as the authority to declare it void is of a delicate and awful nature, the court will never resort to that authority, but in a clear and urgent case. If on the other hand, the legislature of the union, or the legislature of any member of the union, shall pass a law, within the general scope of their constitutional power, the court cannot pronounce it to be void, merely because it is, in their judgment, contrary to the principles of natural justice. The ideas of natural justice are regulated by no fixed standard; the ablest and the purest men have differed upon the subject; and all that the court could properly say, in such an event, would be, that the legislature (possessed of an equal right of opinion) had passed an act which, in the opinion of the judges, was inconsistent with the abstract principles of natural justice. There are then but two lights, in which the subject can be viewed. 1st. If the legislature pursue the authority, their acts are invalid. In the former case, they exercise the discretion vested in them by the people, to whom alone they are responsible for the faithful discharge of their trust; but in the latter case, they violate a fundamental law, which must be our guide, whenever we are called upon as judges to determine the validity of a legislative act.

Still, however, in the present instance, the act or resolution of the legislature of Connecticut, cannot be regarded as an ex post *facto* law; for, the true construction of the prohibition extends to criminal, not to civil, cases. It is only in criminal cases, indeed, in which the danger to be guarded against, is greatly to be apprehended. The history of every country in Europe will furnish flagrant instances of tyranny exercised under the pretext of penal dispensations. Rival factions, in their efforts to crush each other, have superseded all the forms, and suppressed all the sentiments of justice; while attainders, on the principle of retaliation and proscription, have marked all the vicissitudes of party triumph. The temptation to such abuses of power is unfortunately too alluring for human virtue; and, therefore, the framers of the American constitutions have wisely denied to the respective legislatures, federal as well as state, the possession of the power itself. They shall not pass any *ex post facto* law; or, in other words, they shall not inflict a punishment for any act, which was innocent at the time it was committed; nor increase the decree of punishment previously denounced for any specific offense.

The policy, the reason and humanity of the prohibition, do not, I repeat, extend to civil cases, to cases that merely affect the private property of citizens. Some of the most necessary and important acts of legislation are, on the contrary, founded upon the principle, that private rights must yield to public exigences. Highways are run through private grounds. Fortifications, light-houses, and other public edifices, are necessarily sometimes built upon the soil owned by individuals. In such, and similar cases, if the owners should refuse voluntarily to accommodate the public, they must be constrained, as far as the public necessities require; and justice is done, by allowing them a reasonable equivalent. Without the possession of this power the operations of government would often be obstructed, and society itself would be endangered. It is not sufficient to urge, that the power may be abused, for, such is the nature of all power, — such is the tendency of every human institution; and, it might as fairly be said, that the power of taxation, which is only circumscribed by the discretion of the body, in which it is vested, ought not to be granted, because the legislature, disregarding its true objects, might, for visionary and useless projects, impose a tax to the amount of nineteen shillings in the pound. We must be content to limit power where we can, and where we cannot, consistently with its use, we must be content to repose a salutary confidence. It is our consolation that there never existed a government, in ancient or modern times, more free from danger in this respect, than the governments of America.

Upon the whole, though there cannot be a case, in which an *ex post facto* law in criminal matters is requisite, or justifiable (for providence never can intend to promote the prosperity of any country by bad means) yet, in the present instance the objection does not arise. Because, 1st, if the act of the legislature of Connecticut was a judicial act, it is not within the words of the constitution; and 2d. even if it was a legislative act, it is not within the meaning of the prohibition.

# POSTSCRIPT

It is my hope that the reader has gained some insight into the original sense and concept of liberty held by the early Americans and their British precursers. This work was conceived and has proceeded on the conviction that we have a good deal to learn from our Anglo-American ancestors about the roots of freedom within our tradition. We are indeed behooved, in contemporary America and after 200 years of nationhood, to look back to those vital roots that gave birth to the fundamental rights that we enjoy and often take for granted. The drive and impetus behind the declaration of our most cherished rights and liberties arose out of a world impassioned with the spirit of liberty. If its political culture was a messy one, if its politics was dubious at times, it was also one supremely dedicated to the principles of civil and political freedoms for all.

It is worth noting also that our Bill of Rights was framed by practical thinkers, by statesmen possessing an extraordinarily clear grasp of the evils of government. They often mistrusted it, fought its ever-encroaching domain of power and authority, its tendency to shackle the vital freedoms of citizens and subjects. Our framers knew well that their American brethren were not immune from the temptations of power and tyranny. It was within this critical, yet impassioned and informed, context that they set forth some of the most eloquent and enduring words ever struck by the pen of mankind. It is, indeed, not surprising that the Bill of Rights, a document inspired by the urgent plight of embattled liberty in America, should have the blessings of longevity in its survival for two hundred years.

It is also fair to say, however, that Madison and his likes might today express some surprise in the fact that their cherished charter of liberty, the Bill of Rights, has survived as long as it has. That any charter of liberty or constitution should endure for two centuries and more, that it would continue to grow in glory, to expand in its urgency and application to the life of a free people, bespeaks something of a miracle. The mere fact of the longevity of the Bill of Rights, throughout two centuries of American history frought with civil, political and economic strife, suggests great amenability to the vicissitudes of time and chance.

It is also well to note the very late-blooming reality of our Bill of Rights in its national application. For nearly a century and a half, the force and effect of its words remained but a slumbering potential, an eloquent proclamation in a nation preoccupied with economic expansion. It was at first little more that a resolution of the first federal congress, and then one without the force of law to effectuate its hallowed proclamations of liberty and right. Not taken seriously as a truly national charter of liberty until well into the twentieth century, the Bill of Rights began to awaken from its slumbers only in our own era. It has indeed taken the crucible of war and civil strife, of dissent and persistent litigation in the courts, to establish its force and effect as the law of the land. Several of its safeguards, in the first ten amendments to our federal constitution, remain to be applied or "incorporated" through the Fourteenth Amendment.

As the original amendments to our federal constitution, the Bill of Rights was originally intended as a check upon the encroaching powers of the *federal* government. The several states jealously guarded their own sovereignty in an era when the greatest fears were those regarding an over-intrusive central government. Only by way of the long and rocky road of dispute, of constitutional interpretation and litigation, had the Bill of Rights even begun to see its application to the authority of state governments. The long process of its nationalization, known in the law as "incorporation" through the Due Process Clause of the Fourteenth Amendment, is one of deeply historical interest in our history.

Yet the historical battle for liberty continues to this day. Regarding the Bill of Rights alone, several of its clauses have yet to be "incorporated" and made applicable to the states. These include the Fifth Amendment's right to indictment in criminal prosecutions and the right to a bail in criminal prosecutions. Even more important, perhaps, is the fact that many of our fundamental rights under the Constitution remain to be truly nationalized in their application and practice at every level of federal, state and local government.

The long road to incorporation of the Bill of Rights, via the Fourteenth Amendment, is indeed an intriguing story in itself and beyond the immediate scope of this work. It is worth noting, however, that this most valuable amendment came into being shortly following the conclusion of our civil war in 1865. Originally enacted with the intent to protect newly emancipated negro slaves against further oppressions by the states, the Fourteenth Amendment has since become the chief means of effectuating most of our civil rights legislation at the federal level. Its enabling clauses allow Congress to make good on the Fourteenth Amendment itself, its promise of Equal Protection and Due Process of Law. Its clauses are explicitly binding upon the state legislatures. Its declarations of equal protection and due process of law give constitutional grounds to victims of discrimination in the vindication of their fundamental rights as American citizens.

The Bill of Rights today has become a fateful pivot of contention surrounding many current questions of civil and political liberty. Its grand phrases pervade the halls of Congress, of state legislatures, of state and federal courts everywhere in the land..

Its enduring legacy of liberty continues as a vital touchstone in recognition of the all too fragile nature of our fundamental rights — indeed of human rights the world over. Its growing success as the force of law has turned most often upon the fate of its unpopular exponents: those eccentrics, protesters, dissidents, "outlaws" and other "not very nice people" in the words of former Supreme Court Justice Felix Frankfurter. These champions of liberty have insisted upon their rights against all odds and intense public disfavor of their activities. We are the better today for their struggles.

There is surely a fundamental and delicate balance to be maintained here. It is that precarious balance of power as between the state, the rights of society on the one hand, and the rights and liberties of individuals, on the other. The success of our whole experiment in constitutional self-government has turned and will continue to turn upon the fulcrum of this delicate balance. This means nothing less, perhaps, than the challenge of maintaining liberty under law, of keeping the civil peace and well-being of all while affording the safeguards of liberty for each. From the Magna Carta of King John's day to the Bill of Rights in our own day, the struggle for the rights of man has continued onward. A struggle fought not without the sword crossing the flesh, it must remain forever cognizant of that delicate balance between order and right.

That the challenge of maintaining the balance between power and right persists to this day needs but little effort to prove. The evidence of that challenge is forever with us; it is manifest throughout our society today. It is manifest in the public debates regarding the prevention and prosecution of violent crime, of the increasing traffic in drugs and the resulting need for more effective control. The challenge is clearly evident in current issues and debates surrounding the rights of criminal defendants, their access to the courts and the full panoply of their fundamental rights. Our concern for proper balance is further evidenced in discussions surrounding the proper role of the courts themselves. Ought they to be judicially active or not, in a system supposedly marked by a constitutional separation of powers?

The liberal and active Supreme Court of the Warren era of the 1960s has given way to a far more conservative and cautious court today. We may legitimately ask ourselves at this time, whether the U.S. Supreme Court is today adequately protects the safeguards of the Bill of Rights. Results of late indicate a high court somewhat less solicitous of the fundamental rights of individuals and, in particular, those facing criminal prosecution. Will the balance be reset? Will we see only a vascillating change from one extreme to the other in the interpretation of our fundamental rights from one era to the next? Of a narrowing vision of right in the land of liberty? The choice, of course, is ours. But time will tell.

But what of our people and of society itself? Is the vision of our sacred liberties now narrowing in the eyes of high public officials? Are we now less acutely aware of, less concerned about the rights of man today? Of the freedom of expression? Of the free exercise of religious faith and the traditional separation between church and state that have made these shores the land of liberty and tolerance? Have we somehow grown less sensible of the rights of the criminally accused among us? And have we also, in our concern for safe streets, for a safer and more wholesome society, not lost sight of those haunting words of liberty set forth in the writings of the first American statesmen and their compatriots on both sides of the Atlantic? They have truly bequeathed to us a charter of liberty in the Bill of Rights. To paraphrase Benjamin Franklin, let us keep it if we can.

We are indeed a rights oriented society. Prick an American and he reaches for his constitutional rights. We are a people only too eager to sue, to challenge in the courts the slightest perceived infringement of our fundamental rights. Behold only the decades-long work of the American Civil Liberties Union, the efforts of the civil rights movement of the recent past, the continuing protests of feminists and other libertarians of all stripes and colors. In a society perhaps more libertarian than any that have ever existed thus far in the world, everyone clamors for the assertion of his or her rights under law. In such a socially contentious and litigious atmosphere, is it too much to ask for a self-education, for a lesson in returning our attention to the very roots of our cherished rights? To the sources and origins of freedom itself within our heritage?

Two hundred years of jurisprudence now lie behind the Constitution and Bill of Rights. Having here explored the intellectual origins of our fundamental rights, what indeed lies in store for their future? The Bill of Rights is not merely a document, not merely a declaration of legal rights as against the government. It is, in force and effect, a charter of liberty. It bespeaks a spirit of freedom louder and deeper than any mere enumeration of legal rights could. It is more than a "parchment barrier" erected in defense of our fragile freedoms. Should we not thus read it according to its spirit, the broad conceptions of liberty shared by its framers?

We talk glibly today about the "right of privacy", rights to abortion, to jobs, housing and welfare assistance. Some of us even enshrine our concepts of right and liberty in the language of "natural law", as evidenced in recent Senate confirmation hearings concerning one Supreme Court appointment. If indeed we can make our case at all for such claims to rights, "natural" or otherwise, it must be the hallowed authority of our Bill of Rights that will allow us to do so—in spirit if not always in letter.

Yet, is the Bill of Rights not but a dead letter for too many? For over a century it remained a largely slumbering document, awash in its eloquence and without the force of law. While, at most, a check against the encroaching power of our federal government, it was in many respects deemed inapplicable at all to the state and local legislatures. It has become of truly national force and effect only in our own time, largely in the second half of the twentieth century. It continues to grow, to evolve and adapt to the exigencies of life and the complexities of government, in the words of Mr. Justice Holmes, to the "felt necessities" of the times.

But what of its prognosis for the future, as we now head in but a few years into the twenty first century? Can we look forward to a new vitality, a new direction in the interpretation of our fundamental rights and freedoms? Or well we return, in the words of Sophocles, to an "eternal vigil of the grave-? Will we see the full splendor and eloquence of its intended meaning expand in force, in vitality and application? Or will be be left with a mere document of the liberty, a "parchment barrier" without the power to light the darkness of a growing erosion of our rights?

This work has proceeded on the conviction that our ancestors bequeathed to us a most valuable inheritance in our charter of liberty. The British and American peoples have for long considered liberty to be their birthright, an inheritance of right uniquely theirs by tradition and law. We speak of its deeply constitutional and even contractual nature, as a set of rights and freedoms to which we are uniquely entitled. From the earliest colonial charters that first endowed freedom to our shores up to the liberation of an enslaved Europe on the beaches of Normandy in 1944 and beyond, it has been our mission to wage the defense of freedom in almost every corner of the globe. It has been and, with hope, will continue to be the unique Anglo-American challenge to maintain and defend our rich heritage of freedom on both sides of the Atlantic and, indeed, for freedom-loving peoples everywhere.

# APPENDIX

# PETITION OF RIGHT

**7 June 1628**
*To the King's most excellent majesty.*

HUMBLY shew unto our sovereign lord the King, the lords spiritual and temporal, and commons in parliament assembled, That whereas it is declared and enacted by a statute made in the time of the reign of King Edward the First commonly called *Statutum de tallagio non concedendo,* That no tallage or aid shall be laid or levied by the King or his heirs in this realm, without the good will and assent of the archbishops, bishops, earls, barons, knights, burgesses, and other the freemen of the commonalty of this realm; (2) and by authority by parliament holden in the five and twentieth year of the reign of King Edward the Third, it is declared and enacted, That from thenceforth no person should be compelled to make any loans to the King against his will, because such loans were against reason and the franchise of the land; (3) and by other laws of this realm it is provided, That none should be charged by any charge or imposition called a benevolence, nor by such like charge: (4) by which the statutes before mentioned, and other the good laws and statutes of this realm, your subjects have inherited this freedom, That they should not be compelled to contribute to any tax, tallage, aid or other like charge not set by common consent in parliament.

II. Yet nevertheless, of late divers commissions directed to sundry commissioners in several counties, with instructions, have issued; by means whereof your people have been in divers places assembled, and required to lend certain sums of money unto your Majesty, and many of them, upon their refusal so to do, have had an oath administred unto them not warrantable by the laws of statutes of this realm, and have been constrained to become bound to make appearance and give attendance before your privy council and in other places, and others of them have been therefore imprisoned, confined, and sundry other ways molested and disquieted; (2) and divers other charges have been laid and levied upon your people in several counties by lord lieutenants, deputy lieutenants, commissioners for musters, justices of peace and others, by command or direction from your Majesty, or your privy council, against the laws and free customs of the realm.

III. And where also by the statute called *The great charter of the liberties of England,* it is declared and enacted, That no freeman may be taken  or imprisoned, or be disseised of his freehold or liberties, or his free customs, or be outlawed or exiled, or in manner destroyed, but by the lawful judgment of his peers, or by the law of the land.

IV. And in the eight and twentieth year of the reign of King Edward the Third, it was declared and enacted by authority of parliament, That no man of what estate or condition that he be, should be put out of his land or tenements, nor taken, nor imprisoned, nor disherited, nor put to death without being brought to answer by due process of law:

V. Nevertheless against the tenor of the said statutes, and other the good laws and statutes of your realm to that end provided, divers of your subjects have of late been imprisoned without any cause shewed; (2) and when for their deliverance they were brought before your justices by your Majesty's writs of habeas corpus, there to undergo and receive as the court should order, and their keepers commanded to certify the causes of their detainer, no cause was certified, but that they were detained by your Majesty's special command, signified by the lords of your privy council, and yet were returned back to several prisons, without being charged with any thing to which they might make answer according to the law:

VI. And whereas of late great companies of soldiers and mariners have been dispersed into divers counties of the realm, and the inhabitants against their wills have been compelled to receive them into their houses, and there to suffer them to sojourn, against the laws and customs of this realm, and to the great grievance and vexation of the people:

VII. And whereas also by authority of parliament, in the five and twentieth year of the reign of King Edward the Third, it is declared and enacted, That no man should be forejudged of life or limb against the form of the great charter and the law of the land; (2) and by the said great charter and other the laws and statutes of this your realm, no man ought to be adjudged to death but by the laws established in this your realm, either by the customs of the same realm, or by acts of parliament: (3) and whereas no offender of what kind soever is exempted from the proceedings to be used, and punishments to be inflicted by the laws and statutes of this your realm: nevertheless of late time divers commissions under your Majesty's great seal have issued forth, by which certain persons have been assigned and appointed commissioners with power and authority to proceed within the land, according to the justice of martial law, against such soldiers or mariners, or other dissolute persons joining with them, as should commit any murder, robbery, felony, mutiny or other outrage or misdemeanor whatsoever, and by such summary course and order as is agreeable to martial law, and as is used in armies in time of war, to proceed to the trial and condemnation of such offenders, and them to cause to be executed and put to death according to the law martial:

VIII. By pretext whereof some of your Majesty's subjects have been by some of the said commissioners put to death, when and where, if by the laws and statutes of the land they had deserved death, by the same laws and statutes also they might, and by no other ought to have been judged and executed:

IX. And also sundry grievous offenders, by colour thereof claiming an exemption, have escaped the punishments due to them by the laws and statutes of this your realm, by reason that divers of your officers and ministers of justice have unjustly refused or forborn to proceed against such offenders according to the same laws and statutes, upon pretence that the said offenders were punishable only by martial law, and by authority of such commissions as aforesaid: (2) which commissions, and all other of like nature, are wholly and directly contrary to the said laws and statutes of this your realm.

X. They do therefore humbly pray your most excellent Majesty, That no man hereafter be compelled to make or yield any gift, loan, benevolence, tax, or such-like charge, without common consent by act of parliament; (2) and that none be called to make answer, or take such oath, or to give attendance, or be confined, or otherwise molested or disquieted concerning the same, or for refusal thereof; (3) and that no freeman, in any such manner as is before-mentioned, be imprisoned or detained; (4) and that your Majesty would be pleased to remove the said soldiers and mariners, and that your people may not be so burthened in time to come; (5) and that the aforesaid commissions, for proceeding by martial law, may be revoked and annulled; and that hereafter no commissions of like nature may issue forth to any person or persons whatsoever to be executed as aforesaid, lest by colour of them any of your Majesty's subjects to destroyed, or put to death contrary to the laws and franchise of the land.

XI. All which they most humbly pray of your most excellent Majesty as their rights and liberties, according to the laws and statutes of this realm; and that your Majesty would also vouchsafe to declare, that the awards, doings and proceedings, to the prejudice of your people in any of the premisses, shall not be drawn hereafter into consequence or example; (2) and that your Majesty would be also graciously pleased, for the further comfort and safety of your people, to declare your royal will and pleasure, That in the things aforesaid all your officers and ministers shall serve you according to the laws and statutes of this realm, as they tender the honour of your Majesty, and the prosperity of this kingdom.

# VIRGINIA DECLARATION OF RIGHTS

**12 June 1776**

A DECLARATION OF RIGHTS made by the Representatives of the good people of VIRGINIA, assembled in full and free Convention, which rights do pertain to them and their posterity, as the basis and foundation of Government.

1. That all men are by nature equally free and independent, and have certain inherent rights, of which, when they enter into a state of society, they cannot, by any compact, deprive or divest their posterity; namely, the enjoyment of life and liberty, with the means of acquiring and possessing property, and pursuing and obtaining happiness and safety.

2. That all power is vested in, and consequently derived from, the People; that magistrates are their trustees and servants, and at all times amenable lo them.

3. That Government is, or ought to be, instituted for the common benefit. protection, and security of the people, nation, or community; of all the various modes and forms of Government that is best which is capable of producing the greatest degree of happiness and safety, and is most effectually secured against the danger of mal-administration; — and that, whenever any Government shall be found inadequate or contrary to these purposes, a majority of the community hath an

indubitable, unalienable, and indefeasible right, to reform, alter, or abolish it, in such manner as shall be judged most conducive to the public weal.

4. That no man, or set of men, are entitled to exclusive or separate emoluments and privileges from the community, but in consideration of publick services; which, not being descendible, neither ought the offices of Magistrate, Legislator, or Judge, to be hereditary.

5. That the Legislative and Executive powers of the State should be separate and distinct from the Judicative; and, that the members of the two first may be restrained from oppression, by feeling and participating the burdens of the people, they should, at fixed periods, be reduced to a private station, return into that body from which they were originally taken, and the vacancies be supplied by frequent, certain, and regular elections, in which all, or any part of the former members, to be again eligible, or ineligible, as the law shall direct.

6. That elections of members to serve as Representatives of the people, in Assembly, ought to be free; and that all men, having sufficient evidence of permanent common interest with, and attachment to, the community, have the right of suffrage, and cannot be taxed or deprived of their property for publick uses without their own consent or that of their Representative so elected, nor bound by any law to which they have not, in like manner, assented, for the publick good.

7. That all power of suspending laws, or the execution of laws, by any authority, without consent of the Representatives of the people, is injurious to their rights, and ought not to be exercised.

8. That in all capital or criminal prosecutions a man hath a right to demand the cause and nature of his accusation, to be confronted with the accusers and witnesses, to call for evidence in his favour, and to a speedy trial by an impartial jury of his vicinage without whose unanimous consent he cannot be found guilty, nor can he be compelled to give evidence against himself; that no man be deprived of his liberty except by the law of the land, or the judgment of his peers.

9. That excessive bail ought not to be required, nor excessive fines imposed, nor cruel and unusual punishments inflicted.

10. That general warrants, whereby any officer or messenger may be commanded to search suspected places without evidence of a fact committed, or to seize any person or persons not named, or whose offence is not particularly described and supported by evidence, are grievous and oppressive, and ought not to be granted.

11. That in controversies respecting property, and in suits between man and man, the ancient trial by Jury is preferable to any other, and ought to be held sacred.

12. That the freedom of the Press is one of the greatest bulwarks of liberty, and can never be restrained but by despotick Governments.

13. That a well-regulated Militia, composed of the body of the people, rained to arms, is the proper, natural, and safe defence of a free State; that Standing Armies, in time of peace, should be avoided as dangerous to liberty; and that, in all cases, the military should be under strict subordination to, and governed by, the civil power.

14. That the people have a right to uniform Government; and, therefore, that no Government separate from, or independent of, the Government of *Virginia,* ought to be erected or established within the limits thereof.

15. That no free Government, or the blessing of liberty, can be preserved to any people but by a firm adherence to justice, moderation, temperance, frugality, and virtue, and by frequent recurrence to fundamental principles.

16. That Religion, or the duty which we owe to our *Creator,* and the manner of discharging it, can be directed only by reason and conviction, not by force or violence; and, therefore, all men are equally entitled to the free exercise of religion, according to the dictates of conscience; and that it is the mutual duty of all to practise Christian forbearance, love, and charity, towards each other.

# DECLARATION OF INDEPENDENCE

**4 July 1776**
*In Congress, July 4, 1776*
*The unanimous Declaration of the thirteen united States of America*

When in the Course of human events, it becomes necessary for one people to dissolve the political bands which have connected them with another, and to assume among the powers of the earth, the separate and equal station to which the Laws of Nature and of Nature's God entitle them, a decent respect to the opinions of mankind requires that they should declare the causes which impel them to the separation.

—We hold these truths to be self evident, that all men are created equal, that they are endowed by their Creator with certain unalienable Rights, that among these are Life, Liberty and the pursuit of Happiness.

— That to secure these rights, Governments are instituted among Men, deriving their just powers from the consent of the governed,

—That whenever any Form of Government becomes destructive of these ends, it is the Right of the People to alter or to abolish it, and to institute new Government, laying its foundation on such principles and organizing its powers in such form, as to them shall seem most likely to effect their Safety and Happiness. Prudence, indeed, will dictate that Governments long established should not be changed for light and transient causes; and accordingly all experience hath shown, that mankind are more disposed to suffer, while evils are sufferable, than to right themselves by abolishing the forms to which they are accustomed. But when a long train of abuses and usurpations, pursuing invariably the same Object evinces a design to reduce them under absolute Despotism, it is their right, it is their duty, to throw off such Government, and to provide new Guards for their future security.

— Such has been the patient sufferance of these Colonies; and such is now the necessity which constrains them to alter their former Systems of Government. The history of the present King of Great Britain is a history of repeated injuries and usurpations, all having in direct object the establishment of an absolute Tyranny over these States. To prove this, let Facts be submitted to a candid world.

—He has refused his Assent to Laws, the most wholesome and necessary for the public good.

—He has forbidden his Governors to pass Laws of immediate and pressing importance, unless suspended in their operation till his Assent should be obtained; and when so suspended, he has utterly neglected to attend to them.

— He has refused to pass other Laws for the accommodation of large districts of people, unless those people would relinquish the right of Representation in the Legislature, a right inestimable to them and formidable to tyrants only.

— He has called together legislative bodies at places unusual, uncomfortable, and distant from the depository of their public Records, for the sole purpose of fatiguing them into compliance with his measures.

— He has dissolved Representative Houses repeatedly, for opposing with manly firmness his invasions on the rights of the people.

— He has refused for a long time, after such dissolutions, to cause others to be elected; whereby the Legislative powers, incapable of Annihilation, have returned to the People at large for their exercise; the State remaining in the mean time exposed to all the dangers of invasion from without, and convulsions within.

— He has endeavoured to prevent the population of these States; for that purpose obstructing the Laws for Naturalization of Foreigners; refusing to pass others to encourage their migration hither, and raising the conditions of new Appropriations of Lands.

— He has obstructed the Administration of Justice, by refusing his Assent to Laws for establishing Judiciary powers.

— He has made Judges dependent on his Will alone, for the tenure of their offices, and the amount and payment of their salaries.

— He has erected a multitude of New Offices, and sent hither swarms of Officers to harrass our people, and eat out their substance.

— He has kept among us, in times of peace, Standing Armies, without the Consent of our legislatures.

— He has affected to render the Military independent of and superior to the Civil power.

— He has combined with others to subject us to a jurisdiction foreign to our constitution, and unacknowledged by our laws; giving his Assent to their Acts of pretended Legislation:

— For quartering large bodies of armed troops among us:

— For protecting them, by a mock Trial, from punishment for any Murders which they should commit on the inhabitants of these States:

— For cutting off our Trade with all parts of the world:

— For imposing Taxes on us without our Consent:

— For depriving us in many cases, of the benefits of Trial by Jury:

— For transporting us beyond Seas to be tried for pretended offences:

— For abolishing the free System of English laws in a neighbouring Province, establishing therein an Arbitrary government, and enlarging its Boundaries so as to render it at once an example and fit instrument for introducing the same absolute rule into these Colonies:

— For taking away our Charters, abolishing our most valuable Laws, and altering fundamentally the Forms of our Governments:

— For suspending our own Legislatures, and declaring themselves invested with power to legislate for us in all cases whatsoever.

— He has abdicated Government here, by declaring us out of his Protection and waging War against us.

— He has plundered our seas, ravaged our Coasts, burnt our towns, and destroyed the lives of our people.

— He is at this time transporting large Armies of foreign Mercenaries to compleat the works of death, desolation and tyranny. already begun with circumstances of Cruelty & perfidy scarcely paralleled in the most barbarous ages, and totally unworthy the Head of a civilized nation.

— He has constrained our fellow Citizens taken Captive on the high Seas to bear Arms against their Country, to become the executioners of their friends and Brethren, or to fall themselves by their Hands.

— He has excited domestic insurrections amongst us, and has endeavoured to bring on the inhabitants of our frontiers, the merciless Indian Savages, whose known rule of warfare, is an undistinguished destruction of all ages, sexes and conditions. In every stage of these

Oppressions We have Petitioned for Redress in the most humble terms: Our repeated Petitions have been answered only by repeated injury. A Prince, whose character is thus marked by every act which may define a Tyrant, is unfit to be the ruler of a free people. Nor have We been wanting in attentions to our Brittish brethren. We have warned them from time to time of attempts by their legislature to extend an unwarrantable jurisdiction over us. We have reminded them of the circumstances of our emigration and settlement here. We have appealed to their native justice and magnanimity, and we have conjured them by the ties of our common kindred to disavow these usurpations, which, would inevitably interrupt our connections and correspondence. They too have been deaf to the voice of justice and of consanguinity. We must, therefore, acquiesce in the necessity, which denounces our Separation, and hold them, as we hold the rest of mankind, Enemies in War, in Peace Friends.

WE, THEREFORE, the REPRESENTATIVES of the UNITED STATES OF AMERICA, in General Congress, Assembled, appealing to the Supreme Judge of the world for the rectitude of our intentions, do, in the Name, and by Authority of the good People of these Colonies, solemnly publish and declare, That these United Colonies are, and of Right ought to be FREE AND INDEPENDENT STATES; that they are Absolved from all Allegiance to the British Crown, and that all political connection between them and the State of Great Britain, is and ought to be totally dissolved; and that as Free and Independent States, they have full Power to levy War, conclude Peace, contract Alliances, establish Commerce, and to do all other Acts and Things which Independent States may of right do. — And for the support of this Declaration, with a firm reliance on the protection of Divine Providence, we mutually pledge to each other our Lives, our Fortunes and our sacred Honor.

[Some 56 signatures follow, representatives of the thirteen British colonies in America.]

# CONSTITUTION
# OF THE UNITED STATES

We the People of the United States, in Order to form a more perfect Union, establish Justice, insure domestic Tranquility, provide for the common defence, promote the general Welfare, and secure the Blessings of Liberty to ourselves and our Posterity, do ordain and establish this Constitution for the United States of America.

Article. I.

Section. 1. All legislative Powers herein granted shall be vested in a Congress of the United States, which shall consist of a Senate and House of Representatives.

Section. 2. The House of Representatives shall be composed of Members chosen every second Year by the People of the several States, and the Electors in each State shall have the Qualifications requisite for Electors of the most numerous Branch of the State Legislature.

No Person shall be a Representative who shall not have attained to the Age of twenty five Years, and been seven Years a Citizen of the United States, and who shall not, when elected, be an Inhabitant of that State in which he shall be chosen.

[Representatives and direct taxes shall be apportioned among the several States which may be included within this Union, according to their respective Numbers, which shall be determined by adding to the whole Number of free Persons, including those bound to Service for a Term of Years, and excluding Indians not taxed, three fifths of all other Persons][1]. The actual Enumeration shall be made within three Years after the first Meeting of the Congress of the United States, and within every subsequent Term of ten Years, in such Manner as they shall by Law direct. The number of Representatives shall not exceed one for every thirty Thousand, but each State shall have at Least one Representative; and until such enumeration shall be made, the State of New Hampshire shall be entitled to chose three, Massachusetts eight, Rhode-Island and Providence Plantations one, Connecticut five, New-York six, New Jersey four, Pennsylvania eight, Delaware one, Maryland six, Virginia ten, North Carolina five, South Carolina five, and Georgia three. When vacancies happen in the Representation from any State, the Executive Authority thereof shall issue Writs of Election to fill such Vacancies. The House of Representatives shall chose their Speaker and other Officers; and shall have the sole Power of Impeachment.

Section. 3. The Senate of the United States shall be composed of two Senators from each State, [chosen by the Legislature thereof][2] for six years; and each Senator shall have one Vote.

Immediately after they shall be assembled in Consequence of the first Election, they shall be divided as equally as may be into three Classes. The Seats of the Senators of the first Class shall be vacated at the Expiration of the second Year, of the second class at the Expiration of the fourth Year, and of the third class at the Expiration of the sixth Year, so that one third may be chosen every second Year; [and if Vacancies happen by Resignation, or otherwise, during the Recess of the Legislature of any State, the Executive thereof may make temporary Appointments until the next Meeting of the Legislature, which shall then find such Vacancies.][2]

No Person shall be a Senator who shall not have attained to the Age of thirty Years, and been nine Years a Citizen of the United States, and

---

[1]Changed by section 2 of the Fourteenth Amendment, but the "three fifths of all other Persons" refers to Negro slaves.

[2]Changed by the Seventeenth Amendment.

who shall not, when elected, be an Inhabitant of that State for which he shall be chosen.

The Vice President of the United States shall be President of the Senate, but shall have no vote unless they be equally divided.

The Senate shall choose their other Officers, and also a President pro tempore, in the Absence of the Vice President, or when he shall exercise the Office of President of the United States.

The Senate shall have the sole Power to try all Impeachments. When sitting for that Purpose, they shall be on Oath & or Affirmation. When the President of the United States is tried, the Chief Justice shall preside: And no Person shall be convicted without the Concurrence of two thirds of the Members present.

Judgment in Cases of Impeachment shall not extend further than to removal from Office, and disqualification to hold and enjoy any Office of honor, Trust or Profit under the United States but the Party convicted shall nevertheless be liable and subject to Indictment, Trial, Judgment and Punishment, according to Law.

Section. 4. The Times, Places and Manner of holding Elections for Senators and Representatives, shall be prescribed in each State by the Legislature thereof; but the Congress may at any time by Law make or alter such Regulations, except as to the Places of chusing Senators.

The Congress shall assemble at least once in every Year, and such Meeting shall be [on the first Monday in December,][1] unless they shall by Law appoint a different Day.

Section. 5. Each House shall be the Judge of the Elections, Returns and Qualifications of its own Members, and a Majority of each shall constitute a Quorum to do Business; but a smaller Number may adjourn from day to day, and may be authorized to compel the Attendance of

[1]Changed by the Seventeenth Amendment.

absent Members, in such Manner, and under such Penalties as each House may provide.

Each House may determine the Rules of its Proceedings, punish its Members for disorderly Behaviour, and, with the Concurrence of two thirds, expel a Member.

Each House shall keep a Journal of its Proceedings, and from time to time publish the same, excepting such Parts as may in their Judgment require Secrecy; and the Yeas and Nays of the Members of either House on any question shall, at the Desire of one fifth of those Present, be entered on the Journal.

Neither House, during the Session of Congress, shall, without the Consent of the other, adjourn for more than three days, nor to any other Place than that in which the two Houses shall be sitting.

Section. 6. The Senators and Representatives shall receive a Compensation for their Services, to be ascertained by Law, and paid out of the Treasury of the United States. They shall in all Cases, except Treason, Felony and Breach of the Peace, be privileged from Arrest during their Attendance at the Session of their respective Houses, and in going to and returning from the same; and for any Speech or Debate in either House, they shall not be questioned in any other Place.

No Senator or Representative shall, during the time for which he was elected, be appointed to any civil Office under the Authority of the United States, which shall have been created, or the Emoluments whereof shall have been encreased during such time; and no Person holding any Office under the United States, shall be a Member of either House during his Continuance in Office.

Section. 7. All Bills for raising Revenue shall originate in the House of Representatives; but the Senate may propose or concur with Amendments as on other Bills.

Every Bill which shall have passed the House of Representatives and the Senate, shall, before it becomes a Law, be presented to the President of the United States; If he approve he shall sign it, but if not he shall return it, with his Objections to that House in which it shall have originated, who shall enter the Objections at large on their Journal, and proceed to reconsider it. If after such Reconsideration two thirds of that House shall agree to pass the Bill, it shall be sent, together with the Objections, to the other House, by which it shall likewise be reconsidered, and if approved by two thirds of that House, it shall become a Law. But in all such Cases the Votes of both Houses shall be determined by yeas and Nays, and the Names of the Persons voting for and against the Bill shall be entered on the Journal of each House respectively. If any Bill shall not be returned by the President within ten Days (Sundays excepted) after it shall have been presented to him, the Same shall be a Law, in like Manner as if he had signed it, unless the Congress by their Adjournment prevent its Return, in which Case it shall not be a Law.

Every Order, Resolution, or Vote to which the Concurrence of the Senate and House of Representatives may be necessary (except on a question of Adjournment) shall be presented to the President of the United States, and before the Same shall take Effect, shall be approved by him, or being disapproved by him, shall be repassed by two thirds of the Senate and House of Representatives, according to the Rules and Limitations prescribed in the Case of a Bill.


Section. 8. The Congress shall have Power to lay and correct Taxes, Duties, Imposts and Excises, to pay the Debts and provide for the common Defence and general Welfare of the United States; but all Duties, Imposts and Excises shall be uniform throughout the United States;

To borrow Money on the credit of the United States; To regulate Commerce with foreign Nations, and among the several States, and with the Indian Tribes;

To establish an uniform Rule of Naturalization, and uniform Laws on the subject of Bankruptcies throughout the United States;

To coin Money, regulate the Value thereof, and of foreign Coin, and fix the Standard of Weights and Measures;

To provide for the Punishment of counterfeiting the Securities and current Coin of the United States;

To establish Post Offices and post Roads;

To promote the Progress of Science and useful Arts, by securing for limited Times to Authors and Inventors the exclusive Right to their respective Writings and Discoveries;

To constitute Tribunals inferior to the supreme Court;

To define and punish Piracies and Felonies committed on the high Seas, and Offenses against the Law of Nations;

To declare War, grant Letters of Marque and Reprisal, and make Rules concerning Captures on Land and Water;

To raise and support Armies, but no Appropriation of Money to that Use shall be for a longer Term than two Years;

To provide and maintain a Navy; To make Rules for the Government and Regulation of the land and naval Forces;

To provide for calling forth the Militia to execute the Laws of the Union, suppress Insurrections and repel Invasions;

To provide for organizing, arming, and disciplining, the Militia, and for governing such Part of them as my be employed in the Service of the United States, reserving to the States respectively, the Appointment of the Officers, and the Authority of training the Militia according to the discipline prescribed by Congress;

To exercise exclusive Legislation in all Cases whatsoever, over such District (not exceeding ten Miles square) as may, by Cession of particular States, and the Acceptance of Congress, become the Seat of the Government of the United States, and to exercise like Authority over all Places purchased by the Consent of the Legislature of the State in which the Same shall be, for the Erection of Forts, Magazines, Arsenals, dock-Yards and other needful Buildings;—And

To make all Laws which shall be necessary and proper for carrying into Execution the foregoing Powers, and all other Powers vested by this Constitution in the Government of the United States, or in any Department or Officer thereof.

Section 9. The Migration or Importion of such Persons as any of the States now existing shall think proper to admit, shall not be prohibited by the Congress prior to the Year one thousand eight hundred and eight, but a Tax or duty may be imposed on such Importion, not exceeding ten dollars for each Person.

The Privilege of the Writ of Habeas Corpus shall not be suspended, unless when in Cases of Rebellion or Invasion the public Safety may require it.

No Bill of Attainder or ex post facto Law shall be passed.

[No Capitation, or other direct, Tax shall be laid, unless in Proportion to the Census or Enumeration herein before directed to be taken.][1]

No Tax or Duty shall be laid on Articles exported from any State.

No Preference shall be given by any Regulation of Commerce or Revenue to the Ports of one State over those of another: nor shall Vessels bound to, or from, one State, be obliged to enter, clear, or pay Duties in another.

No Money shall be drawn from the Treasury, but in Consequence of Appropriations made by Law; and a regular Statement and Account of the Receipts and Expenditures of all public Money shall be published from time to time.

[1]Changed by the Sixth Amendment.

No Title of Nobility shall be granted by the United States: And no Person holding any Office of Profit or Trust under them, shall, without the Consent of the Congress, accept of any present, Emolument, Office, or Title, of any kind whatever, from any King, Prince, or foreign State.

Section. 10. No State shall enter into any Treaty, Alliance, or Confederation; grant Letters of Marque and Reprisal; coin Money; emit Bills of Credit; make any Thing but gold and silver Coin a Tender in Payment of Debts; pass any Bill of Attainder, ex post facto Law, or Law impairing the Obligation of Contracts, or grant any Title of Nobility.

No State shall, without the Consent of the Congress, lay any Imposts or Duties on Imports or Exports, except what may be absolutely necessary for executing it's inspection Laws: and the net Produce of all Duties and Imposts, laid by any State on Imports or Exports, shall be for the Use of the Treasury of the United States; and all such Laws shall be subject to the Revision and Controul of the Congress.

No State shall, without the Consent of Congress, lay any Duty of Tonnage, keep Troops, or Ships of War in time of Peace, enter into any Agreement or Compact with another State, or with a foreign Power, or engage in War, unless actually invaded, or in such imminent Danger as will not admit of delay.

Article. II.

Section. 1. The executive Power shall be vested in a President of the United States of America. He shall hold his Office during the Term of four Years, and, together with the Vice President, chosen for the same Term, be elected, as follows

Each State shall appoint, in such Manner as the Legislature thereof may direct, a Number of Electors, equal to the whole Number of Senators and Representatives to which the State may be entitled in the Congress: but no Senator or Representative, .or Person holding an

Office of Trust or Profit under the United States, shall be appointed an Elector.

[Section deleted regarding election of a President and Vice President, superseded by the Twelfth Amendment.]

The Congress may determine the Time of chusing the Electors, and the Day on which they shall give their Votes; which Day shall be the same throughout the United States.

No Person except a natural born Citizen, or a Citizen of the United States, at the time of the Adoption of this Constitution, shall be eligible to the Office of the President; neither shall any person be eligible to that Office who shall not have attained to the Age of thirty five Years, and been fourteen Years a Resident within the United States.

[Section deleted, superseded by the Twenty-fifth Amendment.]

The President shall, at stated Times, receive for his Services, a Compensation, which shall neither be increased nor diminished during the Period for which he shall have been elected, and he shall not receive within that Period any other Emolument from the United States, or any of them.

Before he enter on the Execution of his Office, he shall take the following Oath or Affirmation: "I do solemnly swear (or affirm) that I will faithfully execute the Office of President of the United States, and will to the best of my Ability, preserve, protect and defend the Constitution of the United States."

Section. 2. The President shall be Commander in Chief of the Army and Navy of the United States, and of the Militia of the several States, when called into the actual Service of the United States; he may require the Opinion, in writing, of the principal Officer of each of the executive Departments, upon any Subject relating to the Duties of their respective Offices, and he shall have Power to grant Reprieves and Pardons for Offenses against the United States, except in Cases of Impeachment.

He shall have Power, by and with the Advice and Consent of the Senate, to make Treaties, provided two thirds of the Senators present concur; and he shall nominate, and by and with the Advice and Consent of the Senate, shall appoint Ambassadors, other public Ministers and Consuls, Judges of the supreme Court, and all other Officers of the United States, whose Appointments are not herein otherwise provided for, and which shall be established by Law: but the Congress may by Law vest the Appointment of such inferior Officers, as they think proper, in the President alone, in the Courts of Law, or in the Heads of Departments.

The President shall have Power to fill up all Vacancies that may happen during the Recess of the Senate, by granting Commissions which shall expire at the End of their next Session.

Section. 3. He shall from time to time give to the Congress Information of the State of the Union, and recommend to their Consideration such Measures as he shall judge necessary and expedient; he may, on extraordinary Occasions, convene both Houses, or either of them, and in Case of Disagreement between them, with Respect to the Time of Adjournment, he may adjourn them to such Time as he shall think proper; he shall receive Ambassadors and other public Ministers; he shall take Care that the Laws be faithfully executed, and shall Commission all the Officers of the United States.

Section. 4. The President, Vice President and all civil Officers of the United States, shall be removed from Office on Impeachment for, and Conviction of, Treason, Bribery, or other high Crimes and Misdemeanors.

Article. III.

Section. 1. The judicial Power of the United States, shall be vested in one supreme Court, and in such inferior Courts as the Congress may from time to time ordain and establish. The Judges, both of the supreme and inferior Courts, shall hold their Offices during good Behaviour, and shall, at stated times, receive for their Services, a Compensation, which shall not be diminished during their Continuance in Office.

Section. 2. The judicial Power shall extend to all Cases, in Law and Equity, arising under this Constitution, the Laws of the United States; and Treaties made, or which shall be made, under their Authority; — to all Cases affecting Ambassadors, other public Ministers and Consuls; to all Cases of admiralty and maritime Jurisdiction; to Controversies to which the United States shall be a Party — to Controversies between two or more States, [between a State and Citizens of another State][1] between Citizens of different States; — between Citizens of the same State claiming Lands under Grants of different States, [and between a State, or the Citizens thereof, and foreign States, Citizens or Subjects.

In all Cases affecting Ambassadors, other public Ministers and Consuls, and those in which a State shall be Party, the supreme Court shall have original Jurisdiction. In all the other Cases before mentioned, the supreme Court shall have appellate Jurisdiction, both as to Law and Fact, with such Exceptions, and under such Regulations as the Congress shall make.

The Trial of all Crimes, except in Cases of Impeachment; shall be by Jury; and such Trial shall be held in the State where the said Crimes shall have been committed; but when not committed within any State, the Trial shall be at such Place or Places as the Congress may by Law have directed.

Section. 3. Treason against the United States, shall consist only in levying War against them, or in adhering to their Enemies, giving them Aid and Comfort. No Person shall be convicted of Treason unless on the Testimony of two Witnesses to the same overt Act, or on Confession in open Court.

The Congress shall have Power to declare the Punishment of Treason, but no Attainder of Treason shall work Corruption of Blood, or Forfeiture except during the Life of the Person attainted.

[1]Changed by the Eleventh Amendment.

Article. IV.

Section. 1. Full Faith and Credit shall be given in each State to the public Acts, Records, and judicial Proceedings of every other State; And the Congress may by general Laws prescribe the Manner in which such Acts, Records and Proceedings shall be proved, and the Effect thereof.

Section. 2. The Citizens of each State shall be entitled to all Privileges and Immunities of Citizens in the several States.

A Person charged in any State with Treason, Felony, or other Crime, who shall flee from Justice, and be found in another State, shall on Demand of the executive Authority of the State from which he fled, be delivered up, to be removed to the State having Jurisdiction of the Crime.

[No Person held to Service or Labour in one State, under the Laws thereof, escaping into another, shall, in Consequence of any Law or Regulation therein, be discharged from such Service or Labour, but shall be delivered up on aim of the Party to whom such Service or Labour may be due.][1]

Section. 3. New States may be admitted by the Congress into this Union; but no new State shall be formed or erected within the Jurisdiction of any other State; nor any State be formed by the Junction of two or more States, or Parts of States, without the Consent of the Legislatures of the States concerned as well as of the Congress.

The Congress shall have Power to dispose of and make all needful Rules and Regulations respecting the Territory or other Property belonging to the United States; and nothing in this Constitution shall be so construed as to Prejudice any Claims of the United States, or of any particular State.

[1]Changed by the Thirteenth Amendment.

Section. 4. The United States shall guarantee to every State in this Union a Republican Form of Government, and shall protect each of them against Invasion; and on Application of the Legislature, or of the Executive (when the Legislature cannot be convened) against domestic Violence.

## Article. V.

The Congress, whenever two thirds of both Houses shall deem it necessary, shall propose Amendments to this Constitution, or, on the Application of the Legislatures of two thirds of the several States, shall call a Convention for proposing Amendments, which in either Case, shall be valid to all Intents and Purposes, as Part of this Constitution, when ratified by the Legislatures of three fourths of the several States, or by Conventions in three fourths thereof as the one or the other Mode of Ratification maybe proposed by the Congress; Provided that no Amendment which may be made prior to the Year One thousand eight hundred and eight shall in any Manner affect the first and fourth Clauses in the Ninth Section of the first Article; and that no State, without its Consent, shall be deprived of it's equal Suffrage in the Senate.

## Article. VI.

All Debts contracted and Engagements entered into, before the Adoption of this Constitution, shall be as valid against the United States under this Constitution, as under the Confederation.

This Constitution, and the Laws of the United States which shall be made in Pursuance thereof; and all Treaties made, or which shall be made, under the Authority of the United States, shall be the supreme Law of the Land; and the Judges in every State shall be bound thereby, any Thing in the Constitution or Laws of any State to the Contrary notwithstanding. The Senators and Representatives before mentioned, and the Members of the several State Legislatures, and all executive and judicial Officers, both of the United States and of the several States, shall be bound by Oath or Affirmation, to support this Constitution; but no religious Test shall ever be required as a Qualification to any Office or public Trust under the United States.

Article. VII.

The Ratification of the Conventions of nine States, shall be sufficient for the Establishment of this Constitution between the States so ratifying the Same.

Done in Convention by the Unanimous Consent of the States present the Seventeenth Day of September in the Year of our Lord one thousand seven hundred and Eighty seven and of the Independence of the United States of America the Twelfth In Witness whereof We have hereunto subscribed our Names,

G.O Washington—President and deputy from Virginia
[Other names follow, representative of the thirteen states.]

# AMENDMENTS TO THE CONSTITUTION OF THE UNITED STATES OF AMERICA

Amendment I.

Congress shall make no law respecting an establishment of religion, or prohibiting the free exercise thereof; or abridging the freedom of speech, or of the press, or the right of the people peaceably to assemble, and to petition the Government for a redress of grievances.

Amendment II.

A well regulated Militia, being necessary to the security of a free State, the right of the people to keep and bear Arms, shall not be infringed.

Amendment Ill.

No Soldier shall, in time of peace be quartered in any house, without the consent of the Owner, nor in time of war, but in a manner to be prescribed by law.

Amendment IV.

The right of the people to be secure in their persons, houses, papers, and effects, against unreasonable searches and seizures, shall

The first ten Amendments (Bill of Rights) were ratified effective December 15, 1791.

not be violated, and no Warrants shall issue, but upon probable cause, supported by Oath or affirmation, and particularly describing the place to be searched, and the persons or things to be seized.

Amendment V.

No person shall be held to answer for a capital or otherwise infamous crime, unless on a presentment or indictment of a Grand Jury, except in cases arising in the land or naval forces, or in the Militia, when in actual service in time of War or public danger; nor shall any person be subject for the same offence to be twice put in jeopardy of life or limb, nor shall be compelled in any criminal case to be a witness against himself, nor be deprived of life, liberty, or property, without due process of law; nor shall private property be taken for public use without just compensation.

Amendment VI.

In all criminal prosecutions, the accused shall enjoy the right to a speedy and public trial, by an impartial jury of the State and district wherein the crime shall have been committed; which district shall have been previously ascertained by law, and to be informed of the nature and cause of the accusation; to be confronted with the witnesses against him; to have compulsory process for obtaining witnesses in his favor, and to have the assistance of counsel for his defence.

Amendment VII.

In Suits at common law, where the value in controversy shall exceed twenty dollars, the right of trial by jury shall be preserved, and no fact tried by a jury shall be otherwise re-examined in any Court of the United States, than according to the rules of the common law.

Amendment VIII.

Excessive bail shall not be required, nor excessive fines imposed, nor cruel and unusual punishments inflicted.

Amendment IX.

The enumeration in the Constitution of certain rights shall not be construed to deny or disparage others retained by the people.

Amendment X.

The powers not delegated to the United States by the Constitution, nor prohibited by it to the States, are reserved to the States respectively, or to the people.

Amendment XI.[1]

The Judicial power of the United States shall not be construed to extend to any suit in law or equity, commenced or prosecuted against one of the United States by Citizens of another State, or by Citizens or Subjects of any Foreign State.

Amendment XII.[2]

The Electors shall meet in their respective states, and vote by ballot for President and Vice President, one of whom, at least, shall not be an inhabitant of the same state with themselves; they shall name in their ballots the person voted for as President, and in distinct ballots the person voted for as Vice-President, and they shall make distinct lists of all persons voted for as President, and of all persons voted for as Vice-President, and of the number of votes for each, which lists they shall sign and certify, and transmit sealed to the seat of the government of the United States, directed to the President of the Senate;—The President of the Senate shall, in the presence of the Senate and House of Representatives, open all the certificates and the votes shall then be counted;—The person having the greatest number of votes for President, shall be the President, if such number be a majority of the whole number of Electors appointed; and if no person have such majority,

---

[1] The Eleventh Amendment was ratified February 7, 1795.

[2] The Twelfth Amendment as ratified June 15, 1804.

then from the persons having the highest numbers not exceeding three on the list of those voted for as President, the House of Representatives shall choose immediately, by ballot, the President. But in choosing the President, the votes shall be taken by states, the representation from each state having one vote; a quorum for this purpose shall consist of a member or members from two-thirds of the states, and a majority of all the states shall be necessary to a choice. [And if the House of Representatives shall not choose a President whenever the right of choice shall devolve upon them, before the fourth day of March next following, then the Vice President shall act as President, as in the case of the death or other constitutional disability of the President—][1] The person having the greatest number of votes as Vice-President, shall be the Vice-President, if such number be a majority of the whole number of Electors appointed, and if no person have a majority, then from the two highest numbers on the list, the Senate shall choose the Vice-President; a quorum for the purpose shall consist of two-thirds of the whole number of Senators, and a majority of the whole number shall be necessary to a choice. But no person constitutionally ineligible to the office of President shall be eligible to that of Vice-President of the United States.

Amendment XIII.[2]

Section 1. Neither slavery nor involuntary servitude, except as a punishment for crime whereof the party shall have been duly convicted, shall exist within the United States, or any place subject to their jurisdiction.

Section 2. Congress shall have power to enforce this article by appropriate legislation.

Amendment XIV.[3]

Section 1. All persons born or naturalized in the United States and subject to the jurisdiction thereof, are citizens of the United States and

[1] Superseded by section 3 of the Twentieth Amendment.

[2] The Thirteenth Amendment was ratified December 6, 1865.

[3] The Fourteenth Amendment was ratified July 9, 1868.

of the State wherein they reside. No State shall make or enforce any law which shall abridge the privileges or immunities of citizens of the United States, nor shall any State deprive any person of life, liberty, or property, without due process of law; nor deny to any person within its jurisdiction the equal protection of the laws.

Section 2. Representatives shall be apportioned among the several States according to their respective numbers, counting the whole number of persons in each State, excluding Indians not taxed. But when the right to vote at any election for the choice of electors for President and Vice President of the United States, Representatives in Congress, the Executive and Judicial officers of a State, or the members of the Legislature thereof, is denied to any of the male inhabitants of such State, being twenty-one years of age, and citizens of the United States, or in any way abridged, except for participation in rebellion, or other crime, the basis *of* representation therein shall be reduced in the proportion which the number of such male citizens shall bear to the whole number of male citizens twenty-one years of age in such State.

Section 3. No person shall be a Senator or Representative in Congress, or elector of President and Vice President, or hold any office, civil or military, under the United States, or under any State, who, having previously taken an oath, as a member of Congress, or as an officer of the United States, or as a member of any State legislature, or as an executive or judicial officer of any State, to support the Constitution of the United States, shall have engaged in insurrection or rebellion against the same, or given aid or comfort to the enemies thereof. But Congress may by a vote of two-thirds of each House, remove such disability.

Section 4. The validity of the public debt of the United States, authorized by law, including debts incurred for payment of pensions and bounties for services in suppressing insurrection or rebellion, shall not be questioned. But neither the United States nor any State shall assume or pay any debt or obligation incurred in aid of insurrection or rebellion against the United States, or any claim for the loss or emancipation of any slave; but all such debts, obligations and claims shall be held illegal and void.

Section 5. The Congress shall have power to enforce, by appropriate legislation, the provisions of this article.


Amendment XV.[1]

Section 1. The right of citizens of the United States to vote shall not be denied or abridged by the United States or by any State on account of race, color, or previous condition of servitude.

Section 2. The Congress shall have power to enforce this article by appropriate legislation.


Amendment XVI.[2]

The Congress shall have power to lay and collect taxes on incomes, from whatever source derived, without apportionment among the several States, and without regard to any census or enumeration.


Amendment XVII.[3]

The Senate of the United States shall be composed of two Senators from each State, elected by the people thereof, for six years; and each Senator shall have one vote. The electors in each State shall have the qualifications requisite for electors of the most numerous branch of the State legislatures. When vacancies happen in the representation of any State in the Senate, the executive authority of such State shall issue writs of election to fill such vacancies: Provided, That the legislature of any State may empower the executive thereof to make temporary appointments until the people fill the vacancies by election as the legislature may direct. This amendment shall not be so construed as to affect the election or term of any Senator chosen before it becomes valid as part of the Constitution.

[1]The Fifteenth Amendment was ratified February 3,1870.
[2]The Sixteenth Amendment was ratified February 1,1913.
[3]The Seventeenth Amendment was ratified April 8,1913.

Amendment XVIII.[1]

Section 1. After one year from the ratification of this article the manufacture, sale, or transportation of intoxicating liquors within, the importation thereof into, or the exportation thereof from the United States and all territory subject to the jurisdiction thereof for beverage purposes is hereby prohibited.

Section 2. The Congress and the several States shall have concurrent power to enforce this article by appropriate legislation.

Section 3. This article shall be inoperative unless it shall have been ratified as an amendment to the Constitution by the legislatures of the several States, as provided in the Constitution, within seven years from the date of the submission hereof to the States by the Congress.l

Amendment XIX.

The right of citizens of the United States to vote shall not be denied or abridged by the United States or by any State on account of sex. Congress shall have power to enforce this article by appropriate legislation.

Amendment XX.[2]

Section 1. The terms of the President and Vice President shall end at noon on the 20th day of January, and the terms of Senators and Representatives at noon on the 3d day of January, of the years in which such terms would have ended if this article had not been ratified; and the terms of their successors shall then begin.

Section 2. The Congress shall assemble at least once in every year, and such meeting shall begin at noon on the 3d day of January, unless they shall by law appoint a different day.

[1]The Eighteenth Amendment was ratified January 16, 1919. It was repealed by the Twenty-First Amendment, December 5, 1933. The Nineteenth Amendment was ratified August 18, 1920.

[2]The Twentieth Amendment was ratified January 23, 1933.

Section 3. If, at the time fixed for the beginning of the term of the President, the President elect shall have died, the Vice President elect shall become President. If a President shall not have been chosen before the time fixed for the beginning of his term, or if the President elect shall have failed to qualify, then the Vice President elect shall act as President until a President shall have qualified; and the Congress may by law provide for the case wherein neither a President elect nor a Vice President elect shall have qualified, declaring who shall then act as President, or the manner in which one who is to act shall be selected, and such person shall act accordingly until a President or Vice President shall have qualified.

Section 4. The Congress may by law provide for the case of the death of any of the persons from whom the House of Representatives may choose a President whenever the right of choice shall have devolved upon them, and for the case of the death of any of the persons from whom the Senate may choose a Vice President whenever the right of choice shall have devolved upon them.

Section 5: Sections 1 and 2 shall take effect on the 15th day of October following the ratification of this article.

Section 6. This article shall be inoperative unless it shall have been ratified as an amendment to the Constitution by the legislatures of three fourths of the several States within seven years from the date of its submission.

Amendment XXI.[1]

Section 1. The eighteenth article of amendment to the Constitution of the United States is hereby repealed.

Section 2. The transportation or importation into any State Territory, or possession of the United States for delivery or use therein of intoxicating liquors, in violation of the laws thereof, is hereby prohibited.

---

[1] The Twenty-First Amendment was ratified December 5, 1933.

Section 3. This article shall be inoperative unless it shall have been ratified as an amendment to the Constitution by conventions in the several States, as provided in the Constitution, within seven years from the date of the submission hereof to the States by the Congress.

## Amendment XXII[1]

Section 1. No person shall be elected to the office of the President more than twice, and no person who has held the office of President, or acted as President, for more than two years of a term to which some other person was elected President shall be elected to the office of the President more than once. But this Article shall not apply to any person holding the office of President when this Article was proposed by the Congress, and shall not prevent any person who may be holding the office of President, or acting as President, during the term within which this Article becomes operative from holding the office of President or acting as President during the remainder of such term.

Section 2. This article shall be inoperative unless it shall have been ratified as an amendment to the Constitution by the legislatures of three fourths of the several States within seven years from the date of its submission to the States by the Congress.

## Amendment XXIII.[2]

Section 1. The District constituting the seat of Government of the United States shall appoint in such manner as the Congress may direct: A number of electors of President and Vice President equal to the whole number of Senators and Representatives in Congress to which the District would be entitled if it were a State, but in no event more than the least populous State; they shall be in addition to those appointed by the States, but they shall be considered, for the purposes of the election of President and Vice President, to be electors appointed by a State; and they shall meet in the District and perform such duties as provided by the twelfth article of amendment.

---

[1]The Twenty-Second Amendmentt was ratified February 27, 1951.

[2]The Twenty-Third Amendment was ratified March 29, 1961.

Section 2. The Congress shall have power to enforce this article by appropriate legislation.


Amendment XXIV.[1]

Section 1. The right of citizens of the United States to vote in any primary or other election for President or Vice President, for electors for President or Vice President, or for Senator or Representative in Congress, shall not be denied or abridged by the United States or any State by reason of failure to pay any poll tax or other tax.

Section 2. The Congress shall have power to enforce this article by appropriate legislation.


Amendment XXV.[2]

Section 1. In case of the removal of the President from office or of his death or resignation, the Vice President shall become President.

Section 2. Whenever there is a vacancy in the office of the Vice President, the President shall nominate a Vice President who shall take office upon confirmation by a majority vote of both Houses of Congress.

Section 3. Whenever the President transmits to the President pro tempore of the Senate and the Speaker of the House of Representatives his written declaration that he is unable to discharge the powers and duties of his office, and until he transmits to them a written declaration to the contrary, such powers and duties shall be discharged by the Vice President as Acting President.

Section 4 Whenever the Vice President and a majority of either the principal officers of the executive departments or of such other body as Congress may by law provide, transmit to the President pro tempore of the Senate and the Speaker of the House of Representatives their

---

[1]The Twenty-Fourth Amentment was ratified January 23, 1964.

[2]The Twenty-Fifth Amendment was ratified February 10, 1967.

written declaration that the President is unable to discharge the powers and duties of his office, the Vice President shall immediately assume the powers and duties of the office as Acting President. Thereafter, when the President transmits to the President pro tempore of the Senate and the Speaker of the House of Representatives his written declaration that no inability exists, he shall resume the powers and duties of his office unless the Vice President and a majority of either the principal officers of the executive department or of such other body as Congress may by law provide, transmit within four days to the President *pro tempore* of the Senate and the Speaker of the House of Representatives their written declaration that the President is unable to discharge the powers and duties of his office. Thereupon Congress shall decide the issue, assembling within forty-eight hours for that purpose if not in session. If the Congress, within twenty-one days after receipt of the latter written declaration, or, if Congress is not in session, within twenty-one days after Congress is required to assemble, determines by two-thirds vote of both Houses that the President is unable to discharge the powers and duties of his office, the Vice President shall continue to discharge the same as Acting President; otherwise, the President shall resume the powers and duties of his office.

### Amendment XXVI[1]

Section 1. The right of citizens of the United States, who are eighteen years of age or older, to vote shall not be denied or abridged by the United States or by any State on account of age.

Section 2. The Congress shall have power to enforce this article by appropriate legislation.

[1]The Twenty-Sixth Amendmendment was ratified July 1,1971.

# BIBLIOGRAPHY

The works listed below include those of recent or contemporary authors who have addressed the topic of civil and political liberty in either their ideological origins or current constitutional interpretations. In some cases, their works arise out of an interpretation of historical events or of particular cases relevant to the topic of our fundamental rights.

Alderman, Ellen and Caroline Kennedy, *In Our Defense: The Bill of Rights in Action* (William Morrow & Co. Inc, NY, 1991)

Abraham, Henry, *Freedom and the Courts* (Oxford University Press, 1972)

American Bar Foundation, *Sources of Our Liberties* (Quinn & Boden, 1959)

Bailyn, Bernard, *Ideological Origins of the American Revolution* (Harvard University Press, 1967)

_____, *Pamphlets of the American Revolution,* Vol. I (1750-1765) (Harvard, 1965)

_____, *The Origins of American Politics* (Alfred A. Knopf, 1968)

Barlow, Levy and Masagi, *The American Founding: Essays on the Formation of the Constitution* (Greenwood Press, 1988)

Bork, Robert, *The Tempting of America* (The Free Press N.Y., 1990)

Chaffee, Zechariah, *Free Speech in the United States* (Harvard University Press, 1941)

Churchill, Winston, *History of the English Speaking Peoples,* Vol. 2 (The New World, London, 1956)

Conway, M (edit), *The Writings of Thomas Paine*

Corwin, Edward S., *Liberty Against Government: The Rise, Flowering and Decline of a Famous Juridical Concept* (Louisiana State University Press, 1948)

Dershowitz, Alan M., *The Best Defense* (New York: Random House, 1982)

Gunther, Gerald, Co*nstitutional Law,* (llth Edition) (Foundation Press, New York, 1985)

Hall, Kermit, *Comprehensive Bibliography of American Constitutional and Legal History* (Greenwood Press, 1985)

Hand, Learned, *The Bill of Rights* (Harvard University Press, 1962)

Howard, A.E. Dick, *The Road From Runnymede* (University of Virginia Press, 1968)

Jacobsen, Donald L. (edit.) *The English Libertarian Heritage (includes Cato's Letters,* Bobbs-Merrill Company, 1965)

Kurland, Philip B. and Lerner, Ralph (editors), *The Founders' Constitution ,* Vols. 1 and 5 (University of Chicago, 1987)

Levy, Leonard, *Constitutional Opinions: Aspects of the Bill of Riqhts* (Oxford University Press, 1986)

_____, *Origins of the Fifth Amendment* (Oxford, l968)

Locke, John, *Two Treatises of Government,* ed. Peter Laslett (Cambridge University Press, 1960)

Madison, Jay and Hamilton, *The Federalist Papers* (ed. Clinton Rossiter) (New American Library, 1961) There are many other publications and editions available.

Meiklejohn, Alexander, *Political Freedom: The Constitutional Powers of the People* (Harper & Brothers, 1960)

Meyer, Howard N., *The Amendment That Refused to Die* (Beacon Press, Boston, 1973)

Montesquieu, *Spirit of the Laws* (in several publications)

Neely, Mark E., Jr., *The Fate of Liberty: Abraham Lincoln and Civil Liberties* (Oxford University Press, 1990)

Reid, John Phillip, *The Concept of Liberty in the Age of the American Revolution* (University of Chicago Press, 1988)

_____, *Constitutional History of the American Revolution: The Authority of Rights* (University of Wisconsin Press, 1986)

Reeves, Dagobert (edit.), *The Selected Writings of Benjamin Rush* (Philosophical Library, 1947)

Rutland, Robert Alan, *The Birth of the Bill of Rights* (Chapel Hill, University of North Carolina Press, 1983)

_____, *James Madison Encyclopedia* (Forthcoming, from University of Virginia Press)

Schwartz, Bernard, *The Great Rights of Mankind: A History of the American Bill of Rights* (Oxford University Press, 1977)

_____, *A Documentary History of the Bill of Rights*

Syrett, Harold C. (ed.), *The Papers of Alexander Hamilton* (Columbia University Press, 1961)

Tribe, Lawrence, *On Reading the Constitution* (Harvard, 1992)

White, Morton, *The Philosophy of the American Revolution* (Oxford University Press, 1978)

_____, *Philosophy, The Federalist and the Constitution* (Oxford University Press, 1987)